Ecology and Modern Scottish Literature

Ecology and Modern Scottish Literature

Louisa Gairn

Edinburgh University Press

© Louisa Gairn, 2008, 2022

Edinburgh University Press Ltd
22 George Square, Edinburgh

First published in hardback by Edinburgh University Press 2008

Typeset in Sabon and Futura
by Servis Filmsetting Ltd, Manchester

A CIP record for this book is available from the British Library

ISBN 978 0 7486 3311 1 (hardback)
ISBN 978 1 3995 0798 1 (paperback)

The right of Louisa Gairn
to be identified as author of this work
has been asserted in accordance with
the Copyright, Designs and Patents Act 1988.

Contents

Acknowledgements		vii
List of Figures		ix
Introduction: Re-mapping Modern Scottish Literature		1
1	Feelings for Nature in Victorian Scotland	14
2	Strange Lands	46
3	Local and Global Outlooks	77
4	Dear Green Places	110
5	Lines of Defence	156
Index		192

Acknowledgements

Most of the research for this book was carried out during my doctoral studies at the University of St Andrews. Special thanks are due to Robert Crawford who, as my doctoral supervisor, supplied three years' worth of helpful advice and insightful suggestions, and who encouraged me to embark on postgraduate research in the first place. I am also greatly indebted to Douglas Dunn and Alan Riach who read and commented on the text, and who, together with Michael Gardiner, encouraged me to seek publication. I would also like to thank Jackie Jones and her colleagues at Edinburgh University Press for good advice, support and patience. My thinking on philosophical and ecocritical matters and on the history of the Scottish landscape has been enriched through conversations with John Burnside, Tom Bristow, Christopher Smout and Christopher MacLachlan. Thanks also to Fiona Benson, Neil Rhodes, Jill Gamble and colleagues in the School of English at St Andrews University, and Brian Johnstone, Anna Crowe and colleagues associated with the StAnza Poetry Festival. At the University of Edinburgh, I thank Susan Manning and Vicki Bruce. I am also grateful to Debbie Baird, Stacy Boldrick, Sue Coleman, Anne Sofie Laegran, Veronica Kessenich and David Wolfenden for much appreciated moral support.

This book would not have been possible without the generosity of the Carnegie Trust for the Universities of Scotland and the Caledonian Research Foundation, who funded my doctoral studies. The always helpful staff of St Andrews University Library, the University of Edinburgh Library and the National Library of Scotland have greatly aided my research, as have the Scottish Rights of Way Association, and the Scottish Geographical Society, with whose kind permission the remarkable illustrations for Patrick Geddes's 'Draft Plan for a National Institute of Geography' are reproduced. Some of the ideas on Edwin Muir and Edwin Morgan in Chapter 4 and Kathleen Jamie in Chapter 5 are also explored in my essays published in David James and Philip

Tew (eds), *New Versions of Pastoral* (Fairleigh Dickinson, in press) and Berthold Schoene (ed.), *The Edinburgh Companion to Contemporary Scottish Literature* (Edinburgh University Press, 2007).

I would like to put in a special word of thanks to Johan Kildal, whose friendship and affection have helped me through the writing process. Most of all, I thank my parents, James and Margaret Gairn, whose constant support and encouragement have sustained me throughout this project. This book is dedicated to them, with love.

Louisa Gairn
Edinburgh, August 2007

List of Illustrations

Figure 1   Patrick Geddes and M. Galeron, 'Suggested Plan for a National Institute of Geography', *The Scottish Geographical Magazine*, vol. XVIII (1902).
Figure 2   Detail, Patrick Geddes and M. Galeron, 'Suggested Plan for a National Institute of Geography', *The Scottish Geographical Magazine*, vol. XVIII (1902).

Reproduced with permission from the Scottish Geographical Society.

Introduction: Re-Mapping Modern Scottish Literature

Knowing the *how*, and celebrating the *that*, it seems to me, is the basis of meaningful dwelling: what interests me about ecology and poetry is that, together, they make up a science of belonging, a discipline by which we may both describe and celebrate the 'everything that is the case' of the world, and so become worthy participants in a natural history.[1] John Burnside

Biodiversity, whether vegetal, animal, human, geophysical, or astrophysical, is surely the key.[2] Edwin Morgan

Certain gardens are described as retreats when they are really attacks.[3] Ian Hamilton Finlay

This book suggests that the science and philosophy of ecology, which asks questions about being in the world, about 'dwelling' and 'belonging', and most fundamentally, about the relationship between humans and the natural environment, has been a valuable and significant concept in the work of Scottish writers since the mid-nineteenth century. When the Grampian novelist Nan Shepherd wrote that 'Knowledge does not dispel mystery', 'the more one learns of this intricate interplay of soil, altitude, weather, and the living tissues of plant and insect . . . the more the mystery deepens', she picked up on an important idea which has been recognised more recently by John Burnside, whose work speaks of an attempt to fuse ecology and poetry to produce 'a science of belonging'.[4] This book suggests that writing about the natural world is a vital component of a diverse Scottish literature, and demonstrates how successive generations of Scottish writers have both reflected and contributed to the development of international ecological theory and philosophy. In doing so, this is both a book about Scottish literature from the perspective of ecological thought, and a consideration of the development of ecological and ecocritical traditions and discourses since the mid-nineteenth century.

Kenneth White, the poet and theorist of 'geopoetics', has argued for the need to extend the 'referential topography' of Scottish culture through 'a new grounding', the establishment of 'a new relationship' with nature (and specifically with Scottish 'wilderness country'), which is fundamentally distinct from the 'rural bucolics' of the English tradition.[5] The environmental historian T. C. Smout echoes White in suggesting the validity of a 'special Scottish context for the study of ecology', a distinctively Scottish tradition developed by the ecological thinker and cultural protagonist Patrick Geddes in the late nineteenth and early twentieth centuries, 'remarkable as seeing man as a prime actor among other animals, instead of searching for a "natural" world uninvaded by man, which was more characteristic of ecology in the south of Britain'.[6] The recognition that humans are part of the world of nature, affecting and affected by it, is central to modern global environmental consciousness. However, it also has important implications for local environments, highlighting, for example, the danger of viewing rural areas such as the Scottish Highlands as untouched 'wild' landscapes, a playground without a history.[7] The Scottish writers considered in this book are particularly sensitive to such concerns; fascinated, as Robert Louis Stevenson was, by the echoes of the 'primitive wayfarers' of the past.[8] For Sorley Maclean, the resonances of Gaelic community lingered in the wooded landscape of Raasay, while the ancestral 'folk' of the Mearns in Lewis Grassic Gibbon's fiction are a presence 'so tenuous and yet so real'.[9] To ignore the history of human inhabitation in the rural environments of Scotland, Kathleen Jamie suggests, 'seems an affront to those many generations who took their living on that land . . . they left such subtle marks'.[10] While we need to be cautious of an overly anthropocentric outlook on the natural world, for Jamie and Burnside as for previous generations of Scottish writers and theorists from Geddes to George Mackay Brown, we must also acknowledge those 'subtle marks' in order to make sense of our own relationship to the earth; to gain a meaningful sense of ourselves as 'participants in a natural history'.

Recent Scottish criticism has spoken of an 'urgent need to approach Scottish texts from a range of different and complementary perspectives', and to recognise Scottish writers' engagement with and contribution to critical theory.[11] By asserting the importance of ecological concerns in Scottish writing, this book seeks to re-map Scottish literary culture according to a thematic perspective which has often been thought of as marginal to modern society. *Ecology and Modern Scottish Literature* demonstrates that ecologically-aware criticism is a potentially liberating influence on the study of Scottish literature, placing it within a field of enquiry that is of global relevance. At the same time, this ecological viewpoint reveals meaningful interconnections between Scottish writers not always considered together, challenging, for example, the assumption that there is a fundamental division between urban and rural perspectives in modern Scotland. The facile categorisation of Scottish literature into the critical themes of 'tartanry, Kailyard and latterly Clydeside-ism' has been attacked by critics such as Adrienne Scullion, who contends that such restrictive perspectives obscure the subtleties and the complexity of Scottish writing.[12] While those reductive categories are being eroded, the supposed rift between 'rural' and 'urban' literature remains, encouraging a distorted outlook on Scottish literature: either writers are indulging in sub-Romantic escapism or they are exposing brutal realities – a dichotomy which Douglas Dunn has, with tongue in cheek, identified as one of 'Romantic Sleep' versus 'Social Responsibility'.[13] The truth is that the situation is not so black and white – nor so green and red. Jamie states that 'I take my solace in the natural world . . . my local landscape, the energy of the land', although she admits 'Being in the thick of it rather prevents one from wandering lonely as a cloud'.[14] I would like to suggest that writing which considers our relationship to the natural world need not be some sort of avoidance tactic, but can bring both writer and reader back to 'being-in-the-world', understanding what it means to be 'in the thick of it'.

Since the potential range of its subject is vast, *Ecology and Modern Scottish Literature* is not intended to be an exhaustive survey; the writers discussed have been selected for their literary significance and for the interesting and often unexpected ways in which ecological ideas are reflected or examined in their work. This has meant that certain authors have received less attention than might be expected. Naomi Mitchison and Norman MacCaig might seem obvious candidates for an ecologically-minded outlook on Scottish literature, while figures such as Hugh MacDiarmid, Alan Warner and Edwin Morgan, who have received significant attention in the present study, may seem surprising choices. The intention here is to challenge preconceptions about Scottish literature and the natural world, and in doing so, offer some provocative re-readings of writers across the spectrum of Scottish literary culture. This approach demonstrates how 'canonical' writers like Robert Louis Stevenson and Hugh MacDiarmid can continue to be read in new ways, and how urban writers such as Archie Hind have a relevance to debates over rural and environmental issues which is rarely acknowledged. Equally importantly, this ecological viewpoint sets apparently 'marginal' rural writers like Nan Shepherd, Ian Hamilton Finlay and George Mackay Brown firmly at the centre of Scottish literary culture, showing how their work connects with international ecological theories and debates.

Ecology and Modern Scottish Literature quite deliberately begins in the mid-nineteenth century, past the height of the Romantic period, and at a time when the environmental sciences were being formed into distinctive and provocative new discourses about the relationship between humans and the natural world.[15] There are, certainly, distinctive precursors to modern ecological awareness in Scottish literary culture, and it is important to acknowledge the significance of earlier writers, particularly those writers of the late eighteenth and early nineteenth centuries who might broadly be termed 'Romantic' – James Macpherson, Walter Scott, James Hogg and Robert Burns – and, equally importantly, poets from the Gaelic tradition such as Dunan Ban MacIntyre. In his landmark work of British ecocriticism, *The Song of the Earth* (2000), Jonathan Bate suggests that William Wordsworth 'could not have known that one effect of his writing on the consciousness of later readers would have been the establishment of a network of National Parks, first in the United States and then in Britain'.[16] But it was not Wordsworth's, but Burns's poems that John Muir, the Scots-born founder of the National Parks movement in the United States, carried with him on his wilderness walks.[17] Burns's essentially democratic approach appealed to Muir, who valued his sense of sympathy between the human and natural worlds, the acknowledgement of 'the essential oneness of all living beings', the 'kinship of God's creatures . . . [as] earth-born companions and fellow mortals'.[18] Scott has been similarly influential. While, at times, he has been criticised for eclipsing the geopolitical realities of the Highlands in favour of what some critics have termed 'romantic illusions', Scott's centrality to the Romantic tradition alone merits consideration from the perspective of ecology.[19] Shades of Scott's wonder at the 'wild and precipitous . . . heathy and savage' Highland landscapes of *Waverley* (1814), and the Romantic national sentiment of the 'Caledonia! Stern and wild' variety, can be traced in Muir's evocation of the 'stern, immovable majesty' of Yosemite.[20] Muir's National Parks were, like Scott's Highlands, also lands of 'the shaggy wood . . . the mountain and the flood', although Muir, post-Darwin and writing with the knowledge of the new earth sciences, finds a heightened sense of wonder as he pauses to consider how 'the crystal rock[s] were brought to light by glaciers made up of crystal snow', the result of the 'sublime ice-floods of the glacial period'.[21]

While Romanticism undoubtedly continued, and continues, to be influential, realisations of its limitations have provoked varied responses in the formation of modern Scottish writers' models of attentiveness, observation and representation. 'Why did Wordsworth bury his head in an illusory intuition into the message of hills or hedge-rows?' asked

Sorley Maclean in 1938.²² Looking back to traditions in Gaelic poetry, and writers like Duncan Ban MacIntyre, Maclean argued for the importance of descriptive 'realism' suffused with genuine emotion, in contrast to what he saw as escapist Romantic ideologies, whose emotions were fundamentally inauthentic responses, 'mere fancifulness, day-dreaming, wish-fulfilment, or weak sentimentality'. For Maclean, Gaelic poetry's 'realisation of dynamic nature' carries a greater philosophical significance than English Romanticism.²³ While this is a polemic from a writer conscious of the need to assert Gaelic distinctiveness in the face of the dominant English canon, Maclean's approach suggests a new perspective on 'nature writing', a way of relating to the natural world which critiques anthropocentric or unreflective Romantic responses, and accords a greater significance to physical experience, to being 'in the thick of it'. The possibility of a new form of poetry which can 'realise' the natural world – to 'get into this stone world' as MacDiarmid said in 'On a Raised Beach' (1934) – is something which has proved central to post-war Scottish poetics.²⁴ The contemplation of how best to express the 'real', explored in the post-war work of Gunn, MacDiarmid and Iain Crichton Smith, finds varied expression in Ian Hamilton Finlay's concrete poetry, White's way books, and Mackay Brown's lyrics, and more recently in the poetry and prose of Burnside and Jamie, writers who are consciously setting out to explore constructions of 'self' and 'other' in the context of ecological theory. Modern Scottish views of 'ecology' are not simply the appropriation of Romantic discourses but are attempts to find new ways of thinking about, representing and relating to the natural world.

Whilst ecological values and concepts have a history which pre-dates the official formulation of 'ecology' as a science, it makes sense to begin with the 1866 definition of '*öekologie*' as explained by the inventor of the term, the German biologist Ernst Haeckel, as 'the body of knowledge concerning the economy of nature . . . the study of all those complex interrelations referred to by Darwin as the conditions of the struggle for existence'.²⁵ Literally meaning 'house study', ecology started off as a biological science, a new way of looking at 'natural history' which took its cue from Darwinian evolutionary theory and, as the scientific historian Peter Bowler observes, initially it had 'no clear-cut links to the environmental movement'.²⁶ The eco-critic Neil Evernden points out that ecology 'begins as a normal, reductionist science', but 'to its own surprise it winds up denying the subject-object relationship upon which science rests'.²⁷

The concept of interrelations between organism and environment, and indeed the breakdown of the categories of 'self' and 'other' which have followed in the light of that central idea, is what makes ecological thought so attractive to many modern thinkers and writers. The resolution of dualistic categories allows an escape route from the old Cartesian hierarchies which have defined Western thought for so long: self/other, culture/nature, mind/body. Descartes, and the tradition of scientific authority which followed in his wake, is often blamed by eco-theorists as the source of Western civilisation's perceived alienation from the world of nature, where the 'Cartesian distinction between the *res cogitans*, or thinking self, and the *res extensa*, or embodied substance, sets up the terms for the objectivity of science and the abstraction from historicity, location, nature, and culture'.[28]

Scottish thinkers such as Patrick Geddes recognised early on that there was an ecological interrelationship among individual, community and environment, heralding 'the change from the mechanocentric view and treatment of nature and her processes to a more and more fully biocentric one'.[29] Writing in 1898, Geddes suggests that our understanding of the world is enriched by a combination of scientific knowledge with a complementary focus on 'sight, emotion, experience . . . odour, taste and memory'.[30] In similar vein, phenomenological philosophy asserts the importance of 'lived experience' and suggests that 'it is the body, and it alone . . . that can bring us to the things themselves'.[31] Indeed, the rigid categories suggested by Cartesian philosophy are difficult to maintain in the face of new evidence that, for example, human perception occurs at the point of interface with the environment, rather than by the internal processing of external stimuli, or that the human body itself is permeable, part of its environment rather than a discrete entity.[32] The new perspectives afforded by ecological thought suggest a new 'conception of the human being not as a composite entity made up of separable but complementary parts, such as body, mind and culture, but rather as a singular locus of creative growth within a continually unfolding field of relationships'.[33] Ecological discourses thus not only highlight important environmental concerns; they allow for the growth of a new sense of self, and of the relationship between self and other, which radically differs from what has gone before. One might begin to think of this newly configured relationship between humans and the environment as one of osmosis rather than consumption; with this knowledge, the attentive, semi-permeable, 'natural' self might find it difficult to think of its environment as a functional resource, ready to be exploited.

In parallel with such ecocritical and philosophical considerations, modern environmental science has radically changed our way of thinking about both our local environments and the earth as a whole. 'Nature' is no longer viewed as a stable system of useful commodities or as an immutable backdrop to human life, but as a fragile system which human actions can and do modify, pollute or even destroy. The American naturalist Rachel Carson helped to popularise the environmental cause with the publication of *Silent Spring* in 1962, a book about the devastating effects of agricultural pesticides on ecosystems in the USA, whilst James Lovelock's 'Gaia hypothesis' did much to bring holistic ecological concepts to a wider audience, with his book, *Gaia: A New Look at Life on Earth* (1974). Lovelock's hypothesis was that earth is 'a superorganism composed of all life tightly coupled with the air, the oceans, and the surface rocks' – a holistic idea which, as Lovelock acknowledges, was perhaps first voiced by the Scottish 'father of geology', James Hutton, in 1785.[34]

Attitudes to nature within cultural studies have, however, sometimes tended towards the abstract side of post-structuralism, viewing nature as a 'societal category' or a 'linguistic construct' rather than a discrete entity. Jean Baudrillard is perhaps representative of this sort of view; in his travels across the American desert he saw, instead of natural geological features, a landscape of 'signs'; Monument Valley as 'blocks of language . . . destined to become, like all that is cultivated – like all culture – natural parks'.[35] Jonathan Bate says he started 'doing ecological literary criticism' when he 'grew impatient with a tendency among the most advanced readers of William Wordsworth to claim that there is "no such thing as nature" '.[36] An 'ecological criticism', Karl Kroeber suggests, escapes 'from the esoteric abstractness that afflicts current theorising about literature' and 'seizes opportunities offered by recent biological research to make humanistic studies more socially responsible', resisting 'academic overemphasis on the rationalistic at the expense of sensory, emotional, and imaginative aspects of art'.[37] A variety of definitions of these new perspectives have emerged, but Cheryl Glotfelty's summary is perhaps the most straightforward, stating that 'all ecological criticism shares the fundamental premise that human culture is connected to the physical world, affecting it and affected by it . . . as a theoretical discourse, it negotiates between the human and the nonhuman'. While in most postmodern theory, 'the world' denotes the anthropocentric sphere of language and culture, ecological criticism 'expands "the world" to include the entire ecosphere'.[38] Bate takes up this approach by developing his theory of 'ecopoetics', asserting 'the capacity of the writer to restore us to the earth which is our home' through writing which acknowledges that 'although we make sense of things by way of words, we do not live apart from the world. For culture and environment are held together in a complex and delicate web'.[39]

Despite White's call for a 'new grounding', there have been few overtly 'ecocritical' approaches to Scottish literature.[40] Instead, it is Scotland's creative writers who have led the way in developing such perspectives in their own work and on other Scottish writing. In his essays and editorial work, John Burnside has been developing an ecophilosophical approach related to, but distinct from, Bate's *The Song of the Earth* (2000). Perhaps more significantly, Kenneth White's 'geopoetics', a doctrine of 'contact between the human mind and the things, the lines, the rhythms of the earth', having crystallised in the establishment of the International Institute of Geopoetics in 1989, forms its own distinctive critical categories and predates Bate's 'ecopoetics' by more than a decade.[41]

Related questions have, however, been percolating into Scottish cultural studies for some years. In accordance with critical responses provoked by the 1970s and 80s turn to place or 'territory', represented, for example, by Seamus Heaney's poetry and his influential essay, 'The Sense of Place', there has been a growing critical awareness of the importance of location and environment in shaping Scottish writing.[42] Concurrent with this, critics have begun to acknowledge the significance of rural or 'provincial' locations in the personal and artistic development of key Scottish writers such as Hugh MacDiarmid.[43]

Considerations of Scottish novelistic 'regionalism', despite the parochialising connotations that term sometimes evokes, have also been a significant proportion of the output of Scottish literary criticism over the past decades.[44] The late twentieth-century critical 'rediscovery' of certain rural novels, such as George Douglas Brown's *The House with the Green Shutters* (1901), combined with reassessments of the nineteenth-century 'Kailyard' school by Ian Campbell and others, has helped to foster an awareness of questions about the adequacy of certain representations of Scotland's rural environments.[45] Historians of Scotland's environment, such as T. C. Smout and Robert Lambert, have helped to add ecology to a field which has until recently been dominated by questions of nationalist politics, cultural identity and socio-economic factors.[46] Such publications demonstrate how a variety of disciplines are beginning to recognise the importance of ecological thought, that, as Burnside contends, we are all 'participants in a natural history'. They also demonstrate how far traditional divisions between the humanities and sciences are being bridged by new interdisciplinary, ecologically-aware perspectives – a crucial concern running through Scottish literary culture from Geddes and MacDiarmid to White and Burnside: the need for 'completeness of thought | A synthesis of all viewpoints'.[47]

The proliferation of such outlooks also reflects the growing public and political awareness of environmental issues, in Scotland and elsewhere. Whilst at the height of the industrial era, societal attitudes to the environment were of relatively little concern to legislators, in postindustrial Scotland, coverage of ecological matters in the Scottish press has brought questions of land use and ownership, 'sustainability', wildlife protection and conservation to the fore. There is now a widespread recognition that Scotland's natural environment is both valuable and fragile, and can no longer be viewed as an inexhaustible resource for human industry. The current debates over renewable sources of energy, such as wind farming or wave power, demonstrate just how 'mainstream' ecological questions have become in Scotland, and how global issues such as climate change are related in the public and legislative consciousness to specific, local concerns over land use and environmental impact.

Reflecting these broad theoretical and political questions, *Ecology and Modern Scottish Literature* follows a generally historical trajectory, tracing thematic connections within Scottish writing and setting these in relation to international ecological discourses. Chapter 1 considers the writings of Robert Louis Stevenson alongside those of nineteenth-century mountaineering intellectuals John Veitch and John Stuart Blackie, land rights campaigners and the poetry of Gaelic crofters, which, taken together demonstrate a crucial shift towards a more bodily experience of the natural world, a new 'feeling for nature' spurred by developments in biological science which offered fresh perspectives on the relationship between self and world. Taking up the idea of 'exile' in the context of the philosophy of 'dwelling' developed by ecotheorists, Chapter 2 explores the confrontation of modernity and wilderness in Stevenson's fiction and travel writings, relating this to the work of John Muir and to ideas developed by Henry David Thoreau, Walt Whitman and Charles Baudelaire. The development of ecologically-sensitive local and global perspectives in the work of Hugh MacDiarmid, Lewis Grassic Gibbon and others in the inter-war years, was, as Chapter 3 reveals, a reflection of the 'cosmic and regional' perspectives fostered by Patrick Geddes and other early twentieth-century ecological thinkers. Questions of the local and global become ever more significant in the post-war period, considered in the 'dear green places' of Chapter 4, which contends that post-war 'rural' writers including Nan Shepherd, Neil Gunn, Edwin Muir and George Mackay Brown, often viewed as peripheral, are actually central and of international relevance, and questions the supposed division between Scottish rural and urban writing. The search for ways of encountering and expressing the non-human world through poetry is central to the later work of Hugh MacDiarmid and to the geopoetic practice of Kenneth White, while the poetry and prose of Ian Hamilton Finlay, Iain Crichton Smith and George Mackay Brown constitute a crucial element of resistance in the face of environmental and cultural degradation. As we move into the twenty-first century, such 'lines of defence' become more explicit in Scottish writing. Chapter 5 demonstrates that John Burnside, Kathleen Jamie and Alan Warner are not only reviewing human relationships with nature, but also the role writing has to play in exploring and strengthening that relationship, helping to determine the ecological 'value' of poetry and fiction.

If what emerges is not exactly a 'tradition', perhaps it is related to what the anthropologist and ecotheorist Tim Ingold has described as an 'education of attention', something Kathleen Jamie calls the maintenance of 'the web of our noticing, a way of being in the world'.[48]

> What each generation contributes to the next . . . is an *education of attention* . . . Through this fine-tuning of perceptual skills, meanings immanent in the environment – that is in the relational contexts of the perceiver's involvement in the world – are not so much constructed as discovered.[49]

All writing, one might suggest, involves this 'fine-tuning of perceptual skills'. Scottish writers in particular have been sensitive to the perceived erosion of links between language, traditional culture and the natural world; the need to enact gestures of reconnection and reconciliation. As we move into an era ever more preoccupied with mass consumerism and globalisation on the one hand, and the looming threat of environmental degradation, even devastation, on the other, the search for a place where 'function and form, beauty and objective fact, the laws of nature and a sense of mystery can coexist' becomes ever more vital.[50] This book suggests that such a synthesis of viewpoints has in fact been present in Scottish literature all along, characterised by a quality of lyrical attentiveness, which in many ways fulfils Burnside's criteria for a 'science of belonging' or Bate's definition of 'ecopoetics'. From the theories of landscape and writing developed by Robert Louis Stevenson and his mountaineering contemporaries, to Patrick Geddes's biocentrism, Nan Shepherd's *Living Mountain* or the philosophy of dwelling and belonging explored by Edwin Muir, Scottish writers have been engaging with the science and philosophy of ecology since its inception. Modern Scottish literature constitutes a distinctive heritage of ecological thought which is both vitally relevant to international environmentalism and central to Scottish culture.

Notes

1. John Burnside, 'A Science of Belonging: Poetry as Ecology', in Robert Crawford (ed.), *Contemporary Poetry and Contemporary Science* (Oxford: Oxford University Press, 2006), p. 92.
2. Edwin Morgan, 'Roof of Fireflies', in W. N. Herbert and Matthew Hollis (eds), *Strong Words: modern poets on modern poetry* (Tarset, Northumberland: Bloodaxe Books, 2000), p. 192.
3. Ian Hamilton Finlay, 'Unconnected Sentences on Gardening', in Yves Abrioux, *Ian Hamilton Finlay, A Visual Primer* (Edinburgh: Reaktion Books, 1985), p. 40.
4. Nan Shepherd, *The Living Mountain* in Roderick Watson (ed.), *The Grampian Quartet* (Edinburgh: Canongate, 1996), p. 45.
5. Kenneth White, 'The Alban Project', *On Scottish Ground: Selected Essays* (Edinburgh: Polygon, 1998), pp. 13–14.
6. T. C. Smout, 'The Highlands and the Roots of Green Consciousness, 1750–1990', *Proceedings of the British Academy* 76 (1991), pp. 240–1.
7. The concept of the Scottish 'adventure playground' is discussed in Christopher MacLachlan, 'Nature in Scottish Literature', in Patrick D. Murphy (ed.), *Literature of Nature: An International Sourcebook* (Chicago and London: Fitzroy Dearborn Publishers, 1998), pp. 184–90.
8. Robert Louis Stevenson, 'Roads', *Essays of Travel* (London: Chatto & Windus, 1916), p. 216.
9. Stevenson, 'Roads', *Essays of Travel* p. 216; Lewis Grassic Gibbon, 'The Land' in Valentina Bold (ed.), *Smeddum: A Lewis Grassic Gibbon Anthology* (Edinburgh: Canongate Classics, 2001), pp. 90–1.
10. Kathleen Jamie, *Findings* (London: Sort of Books, 2005), p. 126.
11. Christopher Whyte, *Modern Scottish Poetry* (Edinburgh: Edinburgh University Press, 2004), pp. 8–9; Michael Gardiner, *From Trocchi to Trainspotting: Scottish Critical Theory since 1960* (Edinburgh: Edinburgh University Press, 2006).
12. Adrienne Scullion, 'Feminine Pleasures and Masculine Indignities: Gender and Community in Scottish Drama', *Gendering the Nation: Studies in Scottish Literature* (Edinburgh: Edinburgh University Press, 1995), p. 202.
13. Douglas Dunn, quoted in Sean O'Brien, *The Deregulated Muse* (Northumberland: Bloodaxe Books, 1998), p. 65.
14. Kathleen Jamie, quoted in Clare Brown and Don Paterson (eds), *Don't Ask Me What I Mean: Poets in their own words* (London: Picador, 2003), p. 125; 127.
15. Charles Darwin's *On the Origin of Species* was first published in 1859; the Scottish psychologist Alexander Bain's *The Senses and the Intellect* appeared in 1855; the term 'ecology' first appeared in Ernst Haeckel's *Generelle Morphologie* (1866).
16. Jonathan Bate, *The Song of the Earth* (London: Picador, 2000), p. 23.
17. John Muir, A Thousand Mile Walk to the Gulf, in Terry Gifford (ed.), *The Eight Wilderness Discovery Books* (London: Diadem Books, 1992), p. 124.
18. John Muir, 'Thoughts on the Birthday of Robert Burns', cited by Graham White in, *The Wilderness Journeys* (Edinburgh: Canongate, 1996), p. xviii.

19. Cairns Craig, *The Modern Scottish Novel: Narrative and the National Imagination* (Edinburgh: Edinburgh University Press, 1999), p. 117.
20. Walter Scott, *Waverley* (London: Penguin, 1972), pp. 144–5; Walter Scott, 'The Lay of the Last Minstrel', in James Reed (ed.), *Selected Poems*, (London: Routledge, 2003), p. 47; John Muir, 'The Yosemite', in Terry Gifford (ed.), *The Eight Wilderness Discovery Books* (London: Diadem Books, 1992), p. 615.
21. Muir, 'The Yosemite', p. 680.
22. Sorley Maclean, 'Realism in Gaelic Poetry', *Ris a' bhruthaich: criticism and prose writings* (Stornoway: Acair, 1985), p. 19.
23. *Ibid.* pp. 16–17; p. 34
24. Hugh MacDiarmid, 'On a Raised Beach', *Complete Poems*, Vol. I, pp. 422–33; p. 429.
25. Ernst Haeckel, quoted by Jonathan Bate in *Romantic Ecology: Wordsworth and the Environmental Tradition* (London: Routledge, 1991), p. 36
26. Peter J. Bowler, *The Norton History of the Environmental Sciences* (New York: W.W. Norton and Co., 1992), p. 377.
27. Neil Evernden, 'Beyond Ecology: Self, Place, and the Pathetic Fallacy', in Cheryll Glotfelty and Harold Fromm (eds), *The Ecocriticism Reader: Landmarks in Literary Ecology* (Athens, GA: University of Georgia Press, 1996), pp. 92–104; p. 93.
28. Michael Serres, quoted by Jonathan Bate in *The Song of the Earth* (London: Picador, 2000), p. 87.
29. Lewis Mumford, cited in Ramachandra Guha, 'Lewis Mumford, the Forgotten American Environmentalist', in David Macauley (ed.), *Minding Nature: The Philosophers of Ecology* (New York: Guilford Press, 1996), p. 211.
30. Patrick Geddes, 'Notes for an Introductory Course of Geography given at University College Dundee' (Spring 1898), Geddes Papers, National Library of Scotland, MS 10619.
31. Maurice Merleau-Ponty, in Thomas Baldwin (ed.), *Basic Writings* (London: Routledge, 2004), p. 253.
32. Andy Clark, *Being There: Putting Brain, Body, and World Together Again* (Cambridge, MA: MIT Press, 1997), and Tim Ingold, *The Perception of the Environment: Essays in Livelihood, Dwelling and Skill* (London: Routledge, 2000), pp. 1–7.
33. Tim Ingold, *The Perception of the Environment: Essays in Livelihood, Dwelling and Skill* (London: Routledge, 2000), pp. 4–5.
34. Hutton said 'I consider the earth to be a superorganism, and its proper study is by physiology'. Quoted in James Lovelock, *Gaia: A New Look at Life on Earth* (Oxford: Oxford University Press, 1995), p. xvii.
35. Jean Baudrillard, *America*, trans. Chris Turner (London: Verso, 1986), p. 4.
36. Jonathan Bate, 'Out of the twilight', *New Statesman*, 16 July 2001, v.130 i.4546, p. 25
37. Karl Kroeber, *Ecological Literary Criticism: Romantic Imagining and the Biology of Mind* (New York: Columbia University Press, 1994), pp. 1–2.
38. Cheryl Glotfelty, 'Introduction', in Cheryl Glotfelty and Harold Fromm (eds), *The Ecocriticism Reader: Landmarks in Literary Ecology* (Athens, GA: University of Georgia Press, 1996), p. xix.

39. Bate, *The Song of the Earth*, p. ix; p. 23.
40. MacLachlan, 'Nature in Scottish Literature'.
41. Kenneth White, cited in Tony McManus, 'Kenneth White: a Transcendental Scot', in Gavin Bowd, Charles Forsdick and Norman Bissell, *Grounding a World: Essays on the Work of Kenneth White* (Glasgow: Alba, 2005), p. 17. The International Institute of Geopoetics was founded in 1989 at Trébeurden in France.
42. Seamus Heaney, 'The Sense of Place', in *Preoccupations: Selected Prose, 1968–1978* (London: Faber, 1980). Critical studies which consider the relationship between writers and localities include Robert Crawford *Identifying Poets: Self and Territory in Twentieth-Century Poetry* (Edinburgh: Edinburgh University Press, 1993).
43. Robert Crawford, *Devolving English Literature* (Edinburgh: Edinburgh University Press, 2000) and Scott Lyall, *Hugh MacDiarmid's Poetry and Politics of Place: Imagining a Scottish Republic* (Edinburgh: Edinburgh University Press, 2006).
44. Douglas Gifford, *Neil M. Gunn and Lewis Grassic Gibbon* (Edinburgh: Oliver and Boyd, 1983).
45. Ian Campbell, *Kailyard* (Edinburgh: Ramsay Head Press, 1981).
46. Robert A. Lambert, *Species History in Scotland: Introductions and Extinctions Since the Ice Age* (Edinburgh: Scottish Cultural Press, 1998); T. C. Smout, *Nature Contested: Environmental History in Scotland and Northern Ireland since 1600* (Edinburgh: Edinburgh University Press, 2000).
47. Hugh MacDiarmid, 'In Memoriam James Joyce', in *Complete Poems*, vol. I, p. 802.
48. Kathleen Jamie, 'Diary', *London Review of Books*, vol. 24, no. 11 (6th June 2002), p. 39
49. Ingold, *The Perception of the Environment*, p. 22.
50. John Burnside and Maurice Riordan, 'Introduction', in J. Burnside and M. Riordan (eds), *Wild Reckoning: an anthology provoked by Rachel Carson's Silent Spring* (London: Calouste Gulbenkian Foundation, 2004), p. 14.

Chapter 1

Feelings for Nature in Victorian Scotland

> We shall need to reawaken our experience of the world as it appears to us in so far as we are in the world through our body, and in so far as we perceive the world with our body . . . by this remaking contact with the body and the world, we shall also rediscover ourself, since, perceiving as we do with our body, the body is a natural self and, as it were, the subject of perception.[1]
> Maurice Merleau-Ponty

Mind, body, environment – and poetry

The Scottish scientist Alexander Bain described his groundbreaking psychological treatise, *The Senses and the Intellect*, published just four years before Charles Darwin's *On the Origin of Species* (1859), as a 'first attempt to construct a natural history of the feelings'.[2] 'Feeling', in the Romantic period, had come to be associated with the emotions evoked by aesthetic or sentimental subjects, famously characterised by Henry MacKenzie's *The Man of Feeling* (1771), or the contemplation of the picturesque or the sublime in novels such as Walter Scott's *Waverley* (1814) or in the poetry of William Wordsworth. However, Bain's scientific approach to sensation and perception is remarkable in its emphasis on bodily movement, and its novel way of thinking about experiences which had, until then, been largely the preserve of the Romantic poet. Contending that 'action is a more intimate and inseparable property of our constitution than any of our sensations, giving them the character of compounds while itself is a simple and elemental property', his study theorises the aesthetic experience of the 'sublime', or the pleasure to be obtained from touching rocks when mountain climbing.[3] While his scientific approach was criticised by some of his contemporaries such as the literary critic John Campbell Shairp, who claimed that 'the psychologist's error is to attempt to "botanize" the human personality', Bain's move towards a theory of embodiment, the linking of perception and cognition, tends towards more modern debates about human identity and relationship with the natural world, 'explor[ing] connections not just between the contents of consciousness but also between mind and body, and mental organism and environment'.[4] Bain's conception of the 'emotional sensibility of muscle' foreshadows the attitudes expressed by phenomenological philosophers such as Gaston Bachelard, who in the mid-twentieth century wished to understand 'the psychology of each muscle', or Maurice Merleau-Ponty who suggested 'that the body is given in movement, and that bodily movement carries its own immanent intentionality . . . the subject's action is, at one and the same time, a movement of perception'.[5]

The mixed connotations of the term 'feeling' in the post-Romantic period are suggested in the work of many Scottish writers of the mid-late nineteenth century. On travelling across the wilderness landscape of North America by railroad, Robert Louis Stevenson describes what might seem at first sight a Romantic landscape:

> It was a clear, moonlit night; but the valley was too narrow to admit the moonshine direct, and only a diffused glimmer whitened the tall rocks and relieved the blackness of the pines. A hoarse clamour filled the air; it was the continuous plunge of a cascade somewhere near at hand among the mountains. The air struck chill, but tasted good and vigorous in the nostrils – a fine, dry, old mountain atmosphere. I was dead sleepy, but I returned to roost with a grateful mountain feeling at my heart.[6]

This passage, an interlude from Stevenson's travels westwards across North America, evokes what may seem to be a commonplace sentiment about the natural world, the idea of the restorative properties of a natural landscape on a passive beholder – an idea which had been first developed during the Romantic period, with its emphasis on the aesthetic categories of the 'sublime' and the 'beautiful'. The mountain landscape, with its crags, cascades and woodlands, may seem a typical scene for Romantic musings, however Stevenson's writing relishes the animal or birdlike sensation of 'returning to roost', laced with a hint of irony which makes this mountain scene post-Romantic. This self-conscious, ironical 'grateful mountain feeling', together with his emphasis on the olfactory experience of the 'mountain atmosphere' rather than a visual experience of a landscape here only discernible by a 'diffused glimmer' of moonshine, places the physical at the centre of nature experience. Can one discern, in the cultural productions of late nineteenth-century Scotland, a change in attitude to the natural world, distinct from their Romantic forerunners? What is it about the wild landscape that makes Stevenson, and his contemporaries, feel better?

John Veitch, a Scottish philosophy professor, attempted to answer that very question. In *The Feeling for Nature in Scottish Poetry* (1887), published the year after Stevenson's *Kidnapped*, Veitch undertook an ambitious critical survey of Scottish poetry's treatment of 'Nature', as theme, aesthetic category and moral influence. Born in the Scottish Borders in 1829, Veitch held a professorship at the University of St Andrews before being made Professor of Logic and Rhetoric at the University of Glasgow from 1864 until his death in 1894, and was President of the Scottish Mountaineering Club in the early 1890s. While his scholarly publications include an 1850 translation of Descartes' *Method and Meditations* and a volume of philosophical essays entitled *Knowing and Being* (1889), he was also the author of several poetry books and prose works on the culture and landscape of Scotland. Veitch explores the influence of the Borders landscape on its inhabitants in *The History and Poetry of the Scottish Border* (1878) – a volume which was ordered by Stevenson during his residence in the South Seas, along with other books he wanted sent from home.[7]

The description of Veitch's motivations in writing *The Feeling for Nature* suggest a historical and evolutionary tenor to his analysis of Scottish nature appreciation:

> I wished to know how far one's feeling for nature had been shared in by other people before the present time, – how it had grown up possibly from small beginnings or lower forms, and become what it now is, to some men at least. It is a matter of curious speculation to find how the same scenes in the past affected people centuries ago, – whether it was in precisely the same way as now, – if not, how far and in what modes different, – and if there has been growth, accretion of richness, how that has taken place, or in modern though not unobjectionable phraseology, been evolved.[8]

As part of this effort, he attempts to trace the history of aesthetic reactions to the natural landscape in Western culture – a sort of natural history of nature appreciation. Veitch traces a development in 'nature feeling' from the 'organically agreeable' phase, which he describes as a state of 'open-air feeling . . . connecting itself with a consciousness of life and sensuous enjoyment',[9] to the appreciation of cultivated nature, a form of utilitarian aesthetics. Veitch suggests that the delight in man's 'victory over nature', through its 'mingling of material and aesthetic feeling' has proved 'incalculably hurtful and degrading' to humankind, since it denies access to the 'noble and purifying aesthetic feeling' which may be gleaned from an appreciation of wild landscapes.[10]

The highest form of nature feeling, according to Veitch, is 'free [and] pure' where nature is 'the direct, absolute source of gratification':

> The reaching of this stage of feeling marks a great advance in civilisation. And it is only possible, as a general national characteristic, after agriculture and the arts have progressed to such a degree as to make men feel that they

are no longer in daily struggle with earth and elements . . . The war between the wants of man and the forces of nature has ceased, or man is in the daily consciousness of being the master – of having his physical needs supplied; and now he has time, opportunity, and leisure for that free, pure pleasure – to listen to that still small voice that solicited him from the first, but which was lost in the bustle of daily toil . . .[11]

The end product of civilisation, it seems, is gentlemanly 'leisure', albeit a recreation which involves paying heed to the 'still small voice', the presence of God, or the Romantic suggestion of a transcendent morality to be found in the natural world. Although Veitch wants to highlight the numinous properties of nature revealed to the modern enlightened human, his rhetoric of 'gratification', 'physical needs' and 'mastery' run against this latent strain of Romanticism, and suggest instead the needs of the body and the requirements of a society for which Nature has been commodified, by the empire of man over natural resources. Arguing for a Romantically-derived conception of nature appreciation, Veitch identifies the imagination as the main conduit for experience and understanding. The 'Symbolic Imagination' allows:

that power of insight into the world of outward nature, which sees in things the expression of intellectual, moral, and spiritual qualities; fuses, so to speak, the unconscious life of nature and the conscious life of man in the unity of feeling, communion, sympathy. It is not merely a process of impersonation under excited emotion. It is the power under the influence of love and holy passion, of 'seeing into the life of things'. It is this symbolical Power alone which can fuse the dualism of Man and Nature. For speculative thought this opposition must always subsist; for the Symbolical Imagination there is a common life in the two great spheres of Humanity and the World; and finally, even a community of life and thought, with the Power which transcends all, yet lives in all.[12]

Considering Veitch was a translator of Descartes, his approach in *The Feeling for Nature* may appear to confirm the Cartesian dualistic view of the natural world, where rational man is the master of unthinking nature, whose workings were likened by Descartes to that of a mere automaton. But there is hope, Veitch insists, through the 'Symbolical Imagination', exercised in poetry, which allows humans to attain the Wordsworthian ideal of 'see[ing] into the life of things' – an argument taken from Wordsworth's 'Lines Written a Few Miles Above Tintern Abbey'.[13] Veitch's theory of the power of the imagination also recalls Coleridge's idea of the 'Primary Imagination' in his *Biographia Literaria*, which he considered 'the living Power and prime Agent of all human Perception, and as a repetition in the finite of the eternal act of creation in the infinite I AM'.[14] It is worth noting that Coleridge's philosophy also exerted considerable influence on the transcendentalist philosophy of Ralph Waldo Emerson, whose work became popular in the United States with the publication of *Nature* in 1836. However, Veitch's approach appears to be less self-centred than Coleridge's outlook, and arguably less anthropocentric, stressing the possibility of 'community' between humanity and the natural world, a vision of fusing the two spheres which has at least an inkling of ecological sensibility.

While this is similar to Emerson's notion of a 'radical correspondence between visible things and human thoughts', Veitch does not go quite so far as to posit the existence of an 'occult relation between man and the vegetable'.[15] Instead, he appears to be equally interested in the physical properties of natural objects as an end in themselves, with a role in the everyday life of man, whose practicalities do not always allow for musings of a more spiritual character. Positing the existence of a network between mental space and physical nature, Veitch seems to suggest that the viewing eye imaginatively constructs nature through acts of perception, gaining access to a higher truth which binds together the physical and the abstract. This opposition between physical nature and spiritual significance is a point of tension within Veitch's thinking, and one which he repeatedly attempts to negotiate with varying degrees of success. His approach to Scottish nature poetry sets out to reconcile his physical enjoyment of the land with a set of moral and aesthetic theories regarding the natural world, derived from his reading of the Romantic poets, and his philosophical studies. Veitch feels he must acknowledge the validity of science and the study of the physical world as forms of knowledge about nature, and as part of the 'feeling for nature' he identifies in contemporary culture. Although his Darwinian rhetoric is notable, with talk of 'lower forms', 'evolution' and 'heredity', it is clear Veitch, who, like Shairp, was a member of the Free Church of Scotland, remains a little uneasy about employing it, keen to make use of the Christian terminology of 'The Creation' and references to a 'higher power' present through the appreciation of a morally significant, numinous 'Nature'.[16]

Despite such misgivings, however, Veitch admits retaining 'some sort of dim faith' in the theory of heredity, suggesting the possibility of biological inheritance as a determining factor in nature appreciation:

> I can hardly believe otherwise than that somehow those manor and Tweeddale glens have had a gradually educating and moulding effect on the many generations of the men who lived before me there, and from whom I come, and that my present state of feeling is somehow due to the earth and sky visions with which they were familiar.[17]

This notion of the experience of natural landscape being transmitted in the blood of its inhabitants is expressive of the beginnings of environmental psychology, and foreshadows much of early twentieth-century Jungian-influenced writing about the interconnection between land and communities, such as Lewis Grassic Gibbon's *Sunset Song* (1934).

The 'moulding' effect of the natural world upon the Borders people was also explored by Veitch in *The History and Poetry of the Scottish Border*, where he explains this theory with special reference to Borders literature. The environment, he argues, has a direct influence upon the psychology, or 'character' of the people and therefore 'directly or indirectly, give[s] a cast and colouring to those feelings, fancies and imaginings that find outlet in song and ballad'.[18] The 'greywacke heights and haughs' of the Borders country have produced a race of 'hardy, sinewy men',[19] with the ancient Gaels and Cymri appearing as proto-mountaineers, loving the manifestations of 'Stern nature' whose 'might and mass of mountain [was] their natural protection' – rather than the fertile plains which the classical poets privileged in their pastoral verses.[20]

> No doubt a series of tragic incidents may give a prevailing tone to the feeling and the poetry of a district, apart in a great measure from the character of the scenery. But I cannot help thinking that in this case the nature of the scenery has a great deal to do in predisposing the imagination to a melancholy case, and thus fitting the mind for receiving and retaining, if not originating the tragic or pathetic creation. This influence, too, might be wholly an unconscious one for many generations. It would thus affect the singer without his knowing it . . . .[21]

Veitch's version of Darwinism was also employed by his fellow mountaineer and friend, Professor G.G. Ramsay, President of the Scottish Mountaineering Club at its inception in 1889, who argues in his consideration of the roots of Scottish mountaineering published in *The Scottish Mountaineering Club Journal*:

> The fowler and the sportsman in the Highlands – still more the Islesman – have from time immemorial known and practised the art of finding their way up and down the most impracticable cliffs; and our forefathers have thus, I believe, handed down to us a steadiness of hand and eye, of foot and nerve, which are not equally the birthright of the southerner.[22]

Both Veitch and Ramsay (the latter with a touch of bombast) seem convinced of the 'naturalness' of this perceived affinity with the Scottish hills, arguing that the capacity for nature appreciation or mountaineering is somehow embedded in the biology of individuals; a collective biological memory of the Scottish landscape transmissible to the individual psyche.

All this theorising would suggest an emergence of an avowedly physical ideology of nature appreciation, building on the aesthetics of the Romantic 'sublime'. Veitch opens *The Feeling for Nature* with an appeal for a childlike approach to the natural world – an attitude which is rooted in physical sensation. Speaking of the 'unalloyed delight' he took as a boy in the characteristic Borders landscape, Veitch speculates on the importance of naïve feeling, when the child is 'content to live in the world of simple and spontaneous enjoyment'.[23] Although he does not problematise this 'enjoyment' of nature, Veitch's boyhood 'feeling for nature' is ambiguous, partly an aesthetic reaction, partly an emotional connection to the local and, retrospectively, national landscape, partly enjoyment in the (pre-Freudian) bodily experience of exploring that landscape. 'Feelings', in the child, are not sub-divided into emotion and sensation, or the culturally loaded sense of nature aesthetics he goes on to outline later in his study. This attitude bears some resemblance to Emerson's neo-Wordsworthian views on the subject:

> To speak truly, few adult persons can see nature. Most persons do not see the sun. At least they have a very superficial seeing. The sun illuminates only the eye of the man, but shines into the eye and the heart of the child. The lover of nature is he whose inward and outward sense are still truly adjusted to each other; who has retained the spirit of infancy even into the era of manhood.[24]

Veitch does indeed seem to be aware of the division between innocence and experience in understanding human 'feelings for nature', or of 'Idealism' and 'Materialism', as Emerson might phrase it. However, the 'innocent' perception of the child is still one of physical enjoyment. Veitch seems to value the more basic response of the child, a feeling for nature rooted in the here and now, which encourages a form of poetry which is 'simple, outward, direct . . . true to feelings of the human heart'.[25] As a published authority on the literary representations of the Scottish natural landscape, and in his role as President of the Scottish Mountaineering Club whose interest was focused on the active clambering of middle-class Victorians in that Scottish landscape, Veitch seems peculiarly positioned as mediator between the two realms of nature experience – aesthetic and athletic. How can these seemingly oppositional modes of negotiating the natural world be reconciled? And what sort of 'feeling' does this dualistic activity inspire or represent?

A 'delightful and inspiring playground'? Highland mountaineering

The period from the 1850s until the end of the century saw the activity of mountaineering become increasingly popular in the British Isles. At first, practitioners of the sport were few, however eventually a group of

British mountaineers formed themselves into the first association, the Alpine Club, in 1857. Alpine exploits were popularised by the publication of *Peaks, Passes and Glaciers* (1861), a collection of essays written by Alpine Club members cataloguing their experiences on the European mountains. One of the more famous members of the Alpine Club was Sir Leslie Stephen, editor of *The Cornhill Magazine* and future editor of the *Dictionary of National Biography* (and father of Virginia Woolf), who published his account of his Alpine adventures as *The Playground of Europe* in 1871. Other well-received narratives of Alpine conquest include Edward Whymper's *Scrambles Amongst the Alps in the Years 1860–69* (1871), and John Tyndall's *Mountaineering in 1861* (1862). These outdoor clubs were no less high profile in their memberships than the lists of contributors to magazines such as *The Cornhill*. It is notable how many nineteenth-century mountaineers were Classicists; the *mens sana in corpore sano* ethic suggested by the study of classical literature certainly found an outlet in the activities of these outdoors clubs and associations. Despite the accomplishments of this eminent mountaineering fraternity, however, the activity was propelled into the public imagination by Albert Smith, journalist and showman, who made a living out of travelling to exotic destinations and returning to lecture large audiences at home. In 1851 he made an extravagant and well-publicised ascent of Mont Blanc, and in the following year mounted a one-man show in a London theatre, a hugely popular and lucrative enterprise which attracted crowds for several years. The Alps and mountaineering had certainly been brought to public attention, but perhaps without the proper reverence some might have preferred. Mont Blanc, which had been the subject of Byronic musings, was now reduced to what *The Times* described as 'a mere theatrical gimcrack'.[26] But if mountain admirers were concerned about the demystification of the Alps and other mountainous terrain as Romantic landscapes, the practice of mountaineering was itself surely complicit in this changing attitude.

The Scottish Mountaineering Club was founded in 1889 as a result of a correspondence in the letters page of the *Glasgow Herald* between Professor G.G. Ramsay, Professor of Humanity at Glasgow University (1863–1906) and one Mr Naismith, who proposed to set up a 'Scottish Alpine Club' in imitation of the extremely popular Alpine Club based in London. Ramsay had formed the Cobbler Club, which he describes as the first Scottish mountaineering club, with Veitch and another student in their days at Edinburgh University, but there were few broad-based outdoors organisations in Scotland at the time of this correspondence. Naismith described mountaineering as 'one of the most manly as well as healthful and fascinating forms of exercise' and stolidly contended that it was 'almost a disgrace to any Scotsman whose heart and lungs are in proper order if he is not more or less of a mountaineer, seeing that he belongs to one of the most mountainous countries in the world'.[27] Later, in his first presidential address to the newly formed club, Ramsay would speak of the 'love of the hills' as being 'implanted in the heart of every Scot as part of his very birthright', reviving Veitch's inheritance theory by contending that 'our mountains have been the moulders of our national character' (a nice example of the appropriation of 'Highland' qualities as national ones by Lowland Scots).[28] Ramsay is quick to explain the English ascendancy in the sport, claiming that England's 'dull flats drove them in sheer desperation to seek for heights elsewhere' whereas in Scotland, 'every man has his hill or mountain at his door; [therefore] every man is potentially a mountaineer; and a mountaineering club, in its simple sense, must thus have included nothing less than the entire nation'.[29] The Scottish club was formed, Ramsay contends, out of the need to foster a 'love' for the Scottish landscape and at the same time:

> to bring home to the hearts and minds of our fellow countrymen the fact that we have here, in our Highland hills, the most delightful and inspiring playground that is to be found from one end of Europe to the other . . .[30]

Ramsay is writing with Stephen's *The Playground of Europe* in mind here, but to apply that sort of rhetoric to one's native 'national' landscape is perhaps more of a risky business than at first it seems – especially considering the devastating clearances of Highland tenants which made the Highlands into the 'delightful' arena Ramsay describes. By the late nineteenth century, mountaineering had become not only a sport but 'a science of a highly complex character, cultivated by trained experts, with a vocabulary, an artillery, and rigorous methods of its own'.[31] The Highland 'playground' offered the allure of the battlefield, obstacle course and laboratory for the gentleman mountaineer.

Mountaineering had been transformed from amateur pastime (or, in the case of the Highlands, a supposed native talent) into a 'rigorous science' largely through the activities of the Alpine Club, of which Ramsay's brother was a prominent member, making one of the many Alpine Club ascents of Mont Blanc in 1854. It was widely acknowledged that mountaineering in the Alps was inspired by the work of James Forbes, the Scots glaciologist who had been a friend of Veitch's during their university years.[32] Forbes's pioneering study of the Alpine glaciers was published as *Travels through the Alps of Savoy* in 1843. The scientific aspect of the club's activities are evidenced by the dual urge not only to climb mountains, but to gain a greater understanding of their physical properties, encouraging the practice of mapping and photography, as well as geological survey. British mountaineers, like their counterparts in the military and the Christian missions, were performing a dual function, largely in the service of the Royal Geographical Society. The members of Victorian mountaineering clubs were mapping the Alps and the Himalayas while Livingstone was revealing the secrets of the African interior, and the naval explorers of the Arctic were opening up the possibility of new trade routes. This form of scientific research privileged first-hand experience over observation from a distance and had its own set of aesthetics or 'feelings' for the natural world, as Simon Schama argues:

> The premise of the Alpine Club aesthetic was that only traversing the rock face, inching his way up ice steps, enabled the climber, at rest, to see the mountain as it truly was. And once he had experienced all this, it became imprinted on his senses in ways totally inaccessible to the dilettante, low-altitude walker.[33]

Physical activity becomes a way of accessing the 'truth' about the natural world – linking action and perception, as in Bain's psychological theory. But for the mountaineer, this 'truth' was a privileged discourse, open only to those with the expertise, health and wealth necessary to attain it. The ideologies which underlie the practice of mountaineering appear tangled and confused. How far is this fascination with the hills a product of Romanticism, and how far can it be read as a symptom of a new trend in nineteenth century attitudes to the environment? Is mountaineering just another form of Victorian 'recreational colonialism', part of the establishment which cleared out Highland crofters and replaced them with gaudily tartaned deer stalkers?[34] By appropriating a Romanticised and basically apolitical version of the Highlands, certain Scottish lowland and English discourses helped to propagate a form of domestic orientalism; an attitude to the Highlands and their inhabitants which served to generalise and mythologise, subsuming Highland culture into an exotic unreality, containing it within the Romanticised past. The Scottish Mountaineering Club, like the Alpine Club before it, was indeed a kind of exclusive gentlemen's club, which claimed to encourage a nationalistic brotherhood of mountaineers, but whose limited membership revolved to a certain extent around 'hotel holidays and black-tie dinners'.[35] The emergence of organised mountaineering in the middle of the nineteenth century might be read, in part, as the efforts of the bourgeois Victorian gentleman to establish a masculine identity, a sort of middle class imperialism which made up for the fact that many of these professionals were reduced to playing at imperial adventure rather than truly living it.

In pursuit of this, writers in the *Scottish Mountaineering Club Journal* appropriated the sort of rhetoric employed by British military explorers or American frontiersmen. Ramsay notes, in his essay on the formation of the Scottish Mountaineering Club, how:

> district after district has been attacked, route after route projected and made out by our pioneers; how all Scotland has been laid under contribution – all, I believe, without once, on any occasion, interfering with the rights of farmers, or tenants, or proprietors, or giving rise to one unseemly altercation.[36]

The Scottish landscape seems here to have been 'pioneered' with permission from its landowners. This wish to avoid 'unseemly altercations' between members of the Scottish Mountaineering Club and landowners speaks of the Victorian ethos of genteel sportsmanship, and seems to locate the practice of mountaineering within the same spectrum of outdoors activities as deer stalking and grouse shooting. Indeed, other club members seem at times ambivalent or even hostile to the 'much vexed "Rights of Way" question', claiming that 'All of us love sport and recreation too well ourselves to wish to spoil it for anyone else'.[37] Ramsay was similarly unimpressed with the motives of the rights of way campaigners, maintaining that:

> I and my friends had no desire to see the proposed Club mixed up with any attempt to force rights-of-way. We did not desire the Club to become a stravaging or marauding Club, insisting on going everywhere at every season, with or without leave, and indifferent to the rights and the enjoyments of farmers, proprietors, and sportsmen.[38]

'Man is a land animal': Land rights and reform

To *stravag*, or *stravaig*, is 'to wander about aimlessly', and in this respect seems to be the Gaelic equivalent of rambling, to travel or walk 'in a free unrestrained manner and without definite aim or direction' – what one might think of as a rural version of the urban *flâneur*.[39] Both stravaiging and rambling are terms associated with freedom of movement and access, although the first contains a hint of recklessness and illegality (associated by Ramsay with 'marauding') whilst the second, in the nineteenth century at least, suggested a more harmless activity, associated with scientifically-minded excursions or tourism, a notable example being the Scottish naturalist Hugh Miller's *Rambles of a Geologist* (1858) – although rambling botanists and geologists could also be subversive.[40] However, stravaiging carries with it different cultural connotations from its Lowland cousin, and is in some ways a kind of Scottish aboriginal 'walkabout', 'indicative of the traditional (and Gaelic) custom to wander at will in all seasons on open moorland, and uncultivated land'.[41]

Despite the Scottish Mountaineering Club's officially-stated wish to avoid political questions of rights of way, and the militaristic or imperial overtones of some of this mountaineering literature, it is important to acknowledge the often radical cultural background of the mountaineering movement and associated hiking and rambling clubs of Britain and elsewhere, which problematises a straightforward reading of such activity as imperialistic. Robert Lambert has highlighted the Aberdeen-based Cairngorm Club's engagement with radical politics, while, as Rebecca Solnit has noted, hiking and climbing clubs on the continent such as the *Naturfreunde*, or 'Nature Friends', established in 1895, were composed of 'socialists and anti-monarchists', associated with anti-establishment values, seeking to reappropriate the landscape from elitist landowners who prevented the use of the land by the working people.[42] Enacting a campaign they called 'the forbidden path', this Austrian-based group claimed the leisure rights of the upper classes for themselves, transplanting this ethic across the Atlantic to the United States around the turn of the century. Indeed, this reappropriation of 'forbidden' ground had already been embarked upon throughout the British Isles.

This attitude finds its roots in the beginnings of the Rights of Way movement in Scotland by popular appeal to the Lord Provost of Edinburgh and book publisher, Adam Black, in 1845 – just as John Veitch started his studies at the University of Edinburgh. The motion was proposed that:

> The citizens of Edinburgh have cause to complain of various encroachments on their rights of access to many rural localities of traditional interest and picturesque aspect which afforded innocent gratification to them and proved objects of attraction to strangers.[43]

Veitch joined the rights of way cause when popular discontent with the landowners of the Edinburgh area led to the formation of the Association for the Protection of Public Rights of Roadway, later to become The Scottish Rights of Way Society in 1885, with Black as its first President. Student resistance to the Duke of Atholl's attempts to deny public access to a newly enclosed commercial deer forest in the eastern Highlands in 1847 – the so-called 'Battle of Glen Tilt' – was the first active assertion of these rights, organised by John Balfour, Professor of Botany at the University of Edinburgh. Balfour, who is now chiefly remembered for designing the Botanic Gardens in Edinburgh, took up the cause of public access to private land with a certain impish enthusiasm, encouraging his students to trespass on the Duke's lands on a botanical excursion – an outing which saw the Duke himself involved in a scuffle with a couple of the stravaiging undergraduates, who gave him a black eye for his trouble. Atholl, satirised in mock-Ossianic verse as 'the tourist-baffling Duke of the impassable glen', lost the resulting court battle following the testimony of local drovers and other rural workers who confirmed the existence of a traditional right of way through his land.[44]

Professors and students alike appear to be peculiarly susceptible to the allure of stravaiging across forbidden landscapes. Arthur Hugh Clough's *The Bothie of Toper-na-fuosich* (1848), described in its subtitle as a 'long-vacation pastoral', celebrates the rehabilitating effects that a holiday to the Highland landscape has on a reading party of Oxford students, focusing on their friendships, debates, and activities, with special attention to a holiday romance between one of the party and a local Highland 'lassie' whom he later marries. The young men, 'in the joy of their life and glory of shooting jackets . . . read and roamed', seeking to escape the constraints of study:

> Weary of reading am I, and weary of walks prescribed us;
> Weary of Ethic and Logic, of Rhetoric yet more weary,
> Eager to range over heather unfettered of gillie and marquis,
> I will away with the rest . . .[45]

An aversion to 'prescribed' walks is shared by Alpine Club grandee, Leslie Stephen, who expresses an evident glee in his deliberate transgression of official boundaries in his essay 'In Praise of Walking', where he describes his deliberate flouting of the laws of trespass in order to indulge in some 'delicious bits of walking . . . contrived by a judicious combination of a little trespassing with the rights of way happily preserved over so many commons and footpaths'.[46] Stephen calls into question the supposed rationalism of the landlord, who has the supremely rational Law on his side, ridiculing the 'superstitious reverence' for such claims. Reflecting on his early experiences of rambling in the countryside near his school, he recalls the pleasure of going 'out of bounds' as particularly important in the formation of his character, with the freedom of choice over his route, combined with his enjoyment of the natural world around him, allowing for his development as 'an individual being, not a mere automaton set in movement by pedagogic machinery'.[47] 'Prescribed' walking routes serve to constrain independence of both mind and body, the going 'out of bounds' which Stephen so values.

The rights of way question was enlarged by the activities of another Alpine Club president, the Aberdeenshire Liberal politician, James

Bryce, who later became British Ambassador to the United States, and a friend of the environmentalist John Muir. Bryce, the son of a geologist, was himself an acclaimed international mountaineer, who had climbed in most of the major mountainous regions in the world at some time or another. Inspired by his contact with the National Park movement in the United States, between 1884 and 1908 Bryce introduced a series of (unsuccessful) 'Access to the Mountains' Bills, demanding rights of access to 'uncultivated mountain or moorland' for 'purposes of recreation and scientific or artistic study'.[48] Bryce was affiliated with the radical side of the land access campaign, demonstrated by his presidency of the Cairngorm Club in 1889. Recognising the need for public access to the countryside in an era of increasing industrialisation, Bryce called for legislation to ensure 'the opportunity of enjoying nature and places where health may be regained by bracing air and exercise and where the jaded mind can rest in silence and in solitude'.[49]

In England, the question of access to the countryside had been brought to public attention by local groups such as the Association for the Protection of Ancient Footpaths founded in Yorkshire in 1824, in reaction to a parliamentary act allowing the closure of 'unnecessary' paths by landowners – and, no doubt, to the continued enclosure of the common grounds throughout the late eighteenth and early nineteenth centuries. The Commons Preservation Society, which helped to preserve the green spaces around London, was launched in 1865 by a group of intellectuals which included John Stuart Mill – the same group who were involved with the foundation of the National Trust in 1895, and campaigned for public access to the Lake District in the 1880s. Surely the ethos of the mountaineering clubs, with their rhetoric of freedom and exploration, and their emphasis on the opening up of 'new routes' across mountainous terrain – whether in Scotland or in Switzerland – would concur with this exercise of rights?

If one looks at the members' register of the Alpine Club in the thirty years following its formation in 1857, it becomes clear that the club was largely composed of 'professional' men, with the largest proportions taken up by lawyers, businessmen and teachers, and perhaps surprisingly, low numbers of members drawn from the military or the landed gentry. Members of the Alpine Club, like the Scottish Mountaineering Club, tended to be well-educated, mostly university graduates, and generally 'more likely to be Liberal dissenters than Tory Anglicans'.[50] If this is the case, then their outlook might tend to be oriented more towards the popular appropriation of the landscape than the closing off of the land by wealthy owners. Radical liberals, in the later nineteenth century, were associated with emergent forms of Scottish socialism, with the 'common principles' of 'temperance, pacifism, a belief in evangelical religion, land reform, and Home Rule for Scotland'.[51] There were indeed a number of radicals hidden within the ranks of the Scottish mountaineering fraternity.

The landlordism prevalent in the mountainous regions of Scotland in the mid-nineteenth century impinged on the activities of humans and wildlife alike. Enclosure of land for country sports ensured that, as the environmental historian David Evans has pointed out, 'the survival or otherwise of Britain's fauna was determined predominantly by the landed proprietors and their gamekeepers. Britain became the most intensively gamekeepered country in the world'.[52] The activities of the gamekeepers, ghillies and factors on Highland estates constrained the lives of crofters and rural workers no less than the wildlife of these regions. The landlords and their wealthy guests were killing game on a scale unlike anything that had gone before, with literally thousands of grouse, deer and other animals shot each year, while their gamekeepers were exterminating huge numbers of wild animals which posed a threat to the jealously-guarded game – birds of prey, weasels, foxes, wildcats, badgers, otters, and pine martens – all species now protected by law, many driven to the edge of extinction in the Highlands.[53]

It should be noted that there is a Gaelic tradition of ecologically-sound gamekeeping, exemplified best, perhaps, by the eighteenth-century Gaelic poet and gamekeeper, Duncan Ban MacIntyre. However, throughout the nineteenth century, the families who had lived for centuries on these West Highland estates, and depended upon access to the land for their livelihoods, were pushed more and more to the periphery; with much of the inland countryside cleared for sheep farming or deer forests, many tenants were moved onto coastal small-holdings. The typical croft was composed of a narrow strip of land, beginning on the hillside or 'black land' which provided grazing for livestock, and stretching down to the more fertile flat land, the 'coastal machair' or 'dune meadow' where the family grew their crops.[54] Altogether it was a fragile way of life, relying on subsistence farming and seasonal work in nearby towns. The 1880s saw the emergence of a generation of Scottish workers and political reformers in the Highlands and elsewhere who sought to challenge the traditional rights of landlordism, which had been carried out to their fullest and most brutal extent during the Highland Clearances – a process which continued well into the 1850s and in attenuated form into the 1870s by some accounts.[55] The 'Battle of the Braes' and other conflicts in the West of Scotland during the Crofter's War of the 1880s saw a new movement to reclaim the rights of the working people to the land which had been appropriated by landowners for the use of elitist recreation and sheep farming. This land use conflict was perceived as a re-emergence of the Highland threat by many observers in England and lowland Scotland, but gained public support in an era less forgiving of heavy-handed government tactics, as well as the backing of prominent intellectuals amongst the Scottish establishment. These included John Stuart Blackie, Professor of Greek at Edinburgh University. Blackie, who, like Veitch, studied both Scottish and Classical verse, producing his own study of national poetry, *Scottish Song: Its Wealth, Wisdom, and Social Significance* in 1889, held a genuine interest in both Gaelic culture (demonstrated by his campaign for the Chair of Celtic Literature at the University of Edinburgh) and Home Rule.[56]

As T. M. Devine argues, Blackie's writings 'projected a potent message of literary romanticism and political radicalism', a message contingent with the emergent claims for the redistribution of land use – not least through his association with the Free Church of Scotland, which rejected patronage from the landed classes.[57] And the Free Kirk, of course, looked to its roots in the Covenanting movement, whose religious meetings appropriated the use of the natural landscape in defiance of establishment authority. Veitch, like Blackie, was a member of this Church. Originally intending to join the ministry of the Free Church on his graduation, Veitch joined the ranks of the dissenters at the time of the 'Disruption' of the Scottish Kirk in 1843, and was admitted to the New College at Edinburgh University in 1845, which had just been created 'for the benefit of free-church students'.[58] He abandoned this intention, turning instead to the study of theology and ultimately to philosophical theory, 'repelled by the dogmatic tendencies of the day'.[59] It is interesting to speculate upon Veitch's own feelings on the question of land rights, given his early association with liberal evangelical religion, his backing of the controversial Rights of Way movement, his life-long affection for the Scottish landscape, and his passion for mountaineering. It may be possible to view him as the Borders equivalent of these other Highland campaigners: involved later in life with Peebleshire politics, and taking 'an active part in the leading border associations' – an area of the country no less constrained by the conflicting needs of landowner, crofter and hill walker – Veitch can be located at least on the periphery of this tradition.[60]

The American political activist Henry George, the adopted champion of the People's cause in the Highlands, was in no doubt as to the importance of land rights and, tellingly, asserted those rights in quasi-ecological terms as a nexus of biology and economics:

> What is man? In the first place, he is an animal, a land animal who cannot live without land. All that man produces comes from land; all productive labour, in the final analysis, consists in working up land; or materials drawn

> from land, into such forms as fit them for the satisfaction of human wants and desires. Why, man's very body is drawn from the land. Children of the soil, we come from the land, and to the land we must return. Take away from man all that belongs to the land, and what have you but a disembodied spirit? Therefore he who holds the land on which and from which another man must live, is that man's master; and the man is his slave.[61]

Strikingly, this socialist political rhetoric appears to offer a direct critique of Cartesian dualism. For George, human dependence on the environment is the essential fact of life – a fact which was no less applicable in the Scottish Highlands as it was in North America. George proclaimed in 1884 'the grand truth that every human being born in Scotland has an inalienable and equal right to the soil of Scotland – a right that no law can do away with, a right that comes from the Creator who made earth for man and placed him upon the earth'.[62] This declaration of 'rights' borrows some of its rhetoric from North American politics, but it also found a corresponding philosophy in traditional Gaelic culture – the fundamental notion of *duthchas*, the idea of ancestral land rights associated with kinship and clan society.[63] However, the crofters' claim to such rights was by no means secure, with the weight of the law firmly on the side of the landowner. 'Love of the hills' may, as Ramsay trumpeted, have been 'implanted in the heart of every Scot as part of his very birthright', but access to those hills was an entirely different matter when the wishes of the landlord had anything to do with it.

Blackie's critical study of the contemporary Highland situation, *The Scottish Highlanders and the Land Laws: a Historico-Economical Enquiry* (1885), engages with such political debate to voice the key problem of unacknowledged cultural differences between the ways in which Gaelic crofters and the British establishment viewed the natural landscape. The twin sources of Highland discontent, he alleged, were the imposition of 'economic theories alike unhuman and impolitic' and 'aristocratic pleasure-hunting which sowed the seeds of disaffection and stirred up class against class throughout the land'.[64] British law, Blackie argues, did not take into account the idea of *duthchas* – the 'territorial traditions' of the Highland world – with the result that 'the rights of the landowners were held to be "sacred," [whilst] the rights of the tillers of the soil were neither sacred nor secular'.[65] Instead, he contends:

> The whole Highlands are only a very small matter in the imagination of metropolitan legislators, not a few of whom are only too apt to look upon the whole region of trans-Grampian Scotland as only one grand playground and hunting field.[66]

Blackie is hostile to Ramsay's rhetoric of the Highland 'playground' which merely serves to support the vested interests of the landowners.

The sort of 'love' which someone can nurture for a mere 'playground' is difficult to imagine as anything more than trivial and self-interested. Blackie, by contrast, also enjoyed Highland hillwalking, and spent his 'summer holidays among the breezy Bens of dear old Scotland at Braemar' in the Western Highlands – a holiday location which Robert Louis Stevenson was also to visit.[67] However, he combined these activities with an affection for, and sense of respect and obligation towards the ordinary people who inhabited these remote areas, as his 'yearly rambles . . . into remote parts of the Highlands assumed more and more the character of a grave social duty going hand in hand with a healthy summer recreation'.[68]

The latter-day Highland uprising employed different tactics and was characterised by a new 'proactive rather than reactive' political effort to mobilise public opinion and political legislation, which included the formation of the Highland Land Law Reform Association in the 1880s. This association became the Highland Land League in 1886, in imitation of the Irish Land League, whose more violent struggle with landlords on Irish soil resulted in eventual legislative success in 1881, with Gladstone's passing of the Irish Land Act. The Scottish crofters were to achieve their aims eventually, with a Royal Commission headed by Lord Napier in 1883 and the passing of The Crofter's Holdings Act by Gladstone in 1886. The 'Land Question' was high profile, partly due to the events across the Irish Sea, and partly due to the greater publicity available to the cause by the end of the nineteenth century, with Highland Associations springing up in every major Scottish town, and the support of newspapers such as *The Oban Times*, which published political verses in Gaelic expressing the resentment and determination of the local people.[69]

A staunch supporter of Bryce's Access to the Mountains bills, Blackie, too, had been involved in disputes over recreational access to private land. In 1867 he climbed Buachaille Etive Mor near Fort William against the landowner's wishes. On arrival in Fort William he met up with Alpine Club mountaineer Edward Tyndall and the local judge who told him over a glass of port and a 'hearty laugh at the baffled deer-stalkers' that he was to be prosecuted for trespass.[70] The reports of such encounters demonstrate that the interests of frustrated landowners were viewed with amusement by a large section of Scottish society. Blackie's jocular verses in support of Bryce's campaign are expressive of this:

> Bless thee, brave Bryce! all Scotland votes with thee,
> All but the prideful and the pampered few,
> Who in their Scottish home find nought to do
> But keep our grand broad-shouldered Grampians free
> From tread of Scottish foot . . .[71]

The matter was taken up with more seriousness by Gaelic writers, however, as land access and traditional rights of way were just as hotly contested in the Western Highlands. Some Gaelic poets spoke of the supposedly idyllic times when 'Neither water nor moorland | was banned or excluded, | and freedom and goodness | filled the youth of the land'.[72] Others asserted more aggressively their sense of injustice at the obstruction of traditional rights of access. Although 'you deprived us of the rights of way | that the kindreds had from the beginning', the factor is told:

> An reachd a bh' againn cha trèig sinn,
>   'S cha leig sinn eug i dhar deòin,
> Dh'airdeoin bagradh a shèidear
>   No thig 'nar dèidh air ar tòir;
> Siùbhlaidh sinn na cos-cheuman
>   Mar bhios are feum a' toirt oirnn
>
> We will not forsake the law that we had,
>   and we will not let it lapse willingly,
> in spite of whatever threat is breathed against us
>   or comes in our pursuit;
> we will walk in the rights of way,
>   just as our needs require us to do . . .[73]

Embroiled in such geo-political debates, the Gaelic verses of this period, according to Sorley MacLean, are characterised by a 'great decline in full-bloodedness of matter', unlike the poetry of Ban MacIntyre and Alexander MacDonald in the eighteenth century, which although 'splendid', displayed 'a relative unconcern with humanity'.[74] However, as Maclean suggests, nineteenth-century Gaelic poetry, written with the terrible knowledge of the Highland Clearances, explores the vital human relationship to the land, demonstrating that 'the ravages wrought on man are aggravated by ravages even on the face of nature' – something which Blackie had noticed and turned to political use in his 'historico-economical' enquiry into the Highland land question.[75] What the poetry may lose in immediacy to nature and 'full-bloodedness', it certainly gains in a sense of community. With Henry George's rousing speeches and Blackie's campaigning in mind, the verses reveal a certainty that the Highland 'land question' is significant not just for the crofters, but also for the inhabitants of the cities (admittedly many were themselves migrants from the Highlands), in highlighting the essential relationship between the landscape and its inhabitants, as in this poem, 'In Praise of Henry George':

> Mòr-shluagh na cruinne air èirigh,
>   Dh'ionnsaich an èiginn tuigse dhaibh;

> Crìoch air gach cogadh is eucoir,
> Is bràithrean gu lèir mar rugadh sinn.
>
> Cuideachan Ghlaschu 's Dhun Edieann,
> Cuideachdan Eirinn 's hunnainn leinn;
> Duthaich is baile le chèile,
> Muinntir tìr chèin – 's bidh a' bhuil orra.
>
> The population of the world has arisen;
> hardship has taught them understanding;
> there should be an end to every war and injustice,
> because we are all brothers as we were at birth.
>
> The societies of Glasgow and Edinburgh,
> the societies of Ireland and London support us;
> town and country stand together,
> along with the people of foreign lands – and results will follow.[76]

These Gaelic poets, influenced by George's stance on the 'crime of poverty', show an awareness of the internationalism of land rights, a sort of Burnsian 'shall brithers be, for a' that' idea, commenting on the ruthlessness of landlord-businessmen who exploit the worker – whether in China or in rural Scotland. Physical needs and physical experiences, George's idea of humans as 'land animal[s]' with a natural right to the land itself, resonate with the Gaelic sense of brotherhood or community – an essentially socialist view of fraternity which sheds an equivocal light on the concept of 'brotherhood' propagated by Victorian mountaineering clubs.

However, the crofting community's love of the soil, and their wish to remain in their traditional homelands, even in the face of extreme poverty and failing crops, was looked upon as somewhat irrational by many mercantile town-dwellers who could visit the area for a hill walking holiday whenever they pleased. 'Solutions', in the form of a one-way ticket across the Atlantic, or a better-paid occupation in the towns, were often refused, with crofters choosing the subsistence economy of time immemorial over the possibility of higher wages elsewhere. This preference had been remarked upon by Clough in *The Bothie*, where an elderly crofter describes to a young student, 'How on his pittance of soil he lived', '. . . although he could get fine work that would pay, in the city, | Still was fain to abide where his father abode before him'.[77] Heritage, if not heredity, was a decisive factor for many Highland crofting communities.

The logic behind this must have seemed abstruse to the *Self-Help* generation, schooled as it was in the '*ober dicta* of classical political economy', but then, the Lowland idea of mercantile economy propagated by Adam Smith, and the values of the British gentleman expounded by Samuel Smiles were not universally influential.[78] Smiles's writings were not particularly popular with the 'proletarian reader', and, as Smith himself knew, 'Gaelic Highlanders often refused to conform to the model of the Smithian man'.[79] Indeed, this 'land-preference', as Smout calls it, is perhaps not so surprising, when one considers that the actual standard of living for many in the industrial towns of Scotland was little better if not considerably worse than in rural areas.[80] Of course, there were many who did migrate to the towns and cities in search of a better life, including David Livingstone's family, who gave up their croft on the Isle of Ulva and moved to Blantyre. The move certainly provided Livingstone the chance to educate himself – his study time snatched between long hours spent as a cotton spinner in a Lanarkshire mill – but his is an extraordinary story of 'Perseverance' which Smiles himself went on to celebrate as an exemplar of the *Self-Help* doctrine. The reality for many more would have been a cycle of poverty and deprivation without any of the consolations of the clean air and water of a rural location. It was bitterly ironic, for commentators such as Blackie, that the gentleman mountaineer or grouse-shooter's 'love' for the Scottish soil he visited on holiday was lauded as a virtue and praised as a duty fulfilled, whilst the crofting tenant's ancestral sense of connection to the land was regarded as an unsustainable tradition which ought to be discouraged.

Constraints of access, perhaps, constrain the autonomy and independence of the individual, in a psychological as well as a physical sense. Maintaining traditional rights of way helps society to maintain its links with the natural world which, as the Gaelic poets contended (and some modern environmentalists assert) is only artificially divided up according to the concept of mercantile ownership or political allegiance, and which, if the writings of Veitch and others are considered, is necessary to maintain the psychological and spiritual, not to mention the physical, health of the population. Given the complex of allegiances amongst hill-walker, botaniser, crofter and conservationist, it is possible to think of the rural-based land agitation of crofters in the Western Highlands, and the urban-based campaign for rights of way in the East, as essentially two sides of the same coin: a feeling for nature that demanded rights of access to the rural environment for the ordinary people of Scotland, not just the more privileged members of society.

Health and mountains

It is clear that mountaineers and other middle-class wanderers were as much concerned with their own circulatory systems as with the potential ecopolitical significance of establishing hiking routes across the

Scottish landscape. Ramsay speaks of his friendship with Veitch as a 'delightful companionship, of heart and brain and body', a physical, emotional and intellectual bond between them mediated by their feelings for nature.[81] Mountaineering and hill walking had come to be seen as healthy, manly pursuits which, although they did allow for hilltop musings and marvellings at the wonders of the 'creation', nevertheless were all about physical action, the body moving across the landscape, the sensations and the benefits of exercise – for physical, mental and moral health alike. Blackie's characterisation of the typical Highlander draws on this interest in the healthy body, which was allied in the Victorian mind with the values of British imperialism. The Highlanders, he maintains, 'grown strong by the stimulus of a healthy air and the exercise of a hardy life, presented a type of physical manhood equalled only by Roman senators and Venetian doges in their best days'.[82] Blackie attempts to recast Gaelic manhood – and in so doing, the concerns of Gaelic culture – at the centre, rather than at the periphery, of empire. Stressing the physical prowess of the Highlander, particularly in military action, Blackie maintains that this is derived from the traditional 'Celtic' environment:

> As the country in which he dwelt was small, and arable land scanty, the Highlander naturally grew up into the habits of hardihood and healthy energy, with a well-exercised capacity for shifting himself under difficult circumstances. He was a healthy man, a sturdy peasant, a good workman, a natural gymnast, an intrepid fighter, a daring commander, and the best of colonists.[83]

Blackie's 1885 theory of hale and hearty Highland youth supplies a vigorous, politically-inflected rejoinder to the 'Celtic Twilight' view of the sensitive, emotionally unstable Gael suggested by Matthew Arnold, who contended in 1866 that 'the Celtic genius is more airy and unsubstantial, goes less near the ground' than the German or Anglo-Saxon peoples.[84] While recasting the Highlander as a healthy stalwart fit for the service of empire is somewhat problematic, given the history of (sometimes forced) recruitment of Highlanders to military service, Blackie's attempt to rescue Gaeldom from Celtic Twilight stereotyping demonstrates how far the issue of health and its moral associations had become a central concern in Victorian culture.

The Victorians were not healthy, and it worried them. Waves of epidemics had swept over the country in the middle years of the century, then untreatable and devastating for huge sections of the population. Housing and sanitary conditions were poor, even among the middle classes, and diseases such as tuberculosis were endemic. The proportion of the British population living in urban areas rose from twenty-five per cent at the beginning of the century to eighty per cent at the end.[85] The polluted atmosphere of the Victorian industrial city was considered (not unreasonably) as the main culprit. Indeed, the healthy male body was a sort of Victorian imperial fetish, representative of Christian values, hard work and national allegiance. The depressing reality of the unhealthy Victorian was entirely out of kilter with this imperial image the nation wished to project – of manly vitality, strength and industriousness. This, combined with an increasing concern with degeneration (physical, mental and moral) towards the end of the century was a source of considerable anxiety within the culture. The Victorian establishment, represented by worried articles in the medical journal, *The Lancet*, was aware of 'centres of decay' in nineteenth-century British culture, which were to be found at 'points of social tension' – tensions resulting from social deprivation and poor living conditions amongst the slums of the industrial cities of empire.[86] Gradually, an image of the ideal 'healthy man' emerged, based around rhetoric of nature, work, morality and physical sensation:

> When his blood is in harmony with the ceaseless activities of nature; when his body is warm with the soft kiss of air, his muscles vigorous with hearty toil, his brain fertile in wise and generous thoughts, his heart glowing with generous purposes. When a man lives most out of himself, then does he truly live . . . The living body should thrill with every thrill of the wide earth, as the aspen leaf trembles in the tremulous air. Its perfectness lies in continual change.[87]

Physicality had positive as well as negative repercussions – one need only think of the decadent 'sensation novels' popular in the last decades of the nineteenth century which derived much of their popularity from their ability to provoke physical sensations for thrill-seeking readers eager for 'Shocks to the Nervous System'.[88] However, this concern for the physical opened up parallel paths to improvement and rehabilitation. The above quotation from *The Cornhill* in the 1860s encapsulates the sort of physical experience which the Scottish Mountaineering Club and others sought to propagate later in the century. It also glances towards the ethic of 'muscular Christianity' of the likes of Charles Kingsley, author of *Westward Ho!* (1855). Health had become a duty to the empire, and was central to the related idea of self-improvement put forward in the Scots-born Samuel Smiles's treatises, such as the pivotal *Self-Help* (1859). Smiles's writings carried titles which became the buzzwords of Victorian culture – *Character* (1871), followed by *Thrift* (1875), *Duty* (1880) and *Life and Labour* (1887). These volumes and his other works were essentially secular, working- and middle-class histories, which focused on the active lives of everyday people, rather than the grand doings of monarchy and war detailed in more conventional histories. Included with these were biographies of men and women whom he felt exemplified the qualities he was extolling.

Perhaps no single Victorian figure summed up the physical and moral potentialities of empire better than the Scots-born missionary and explorer, David Livingstone. Livingstone's life's work was indeed all about ceaseless duty, industriousness and activity, and his travels strengthened his sense of self-reliance and autonomy – of both mind and body:

> The effect of travel on a man whose heart is in the right place is that the mind is made more self-reliant: it becomes more confident of its own resources – there is greater presence of mind. The body is soon well-knit; the muscles of the limbs grow as hard as a board, and seem to have no fat; the countenance is bronzed, and there is no dyspepsia. Africa is a most wonderful country for an appetite, and it is only when one gloats over marrow bones or elephant's feet that indigestion is possible. No doubt much toil is involved, and fatigue of which travellers in the more temperant climes can form but a faint conception; but the sweat of one's brow is no longer a curse when one works for God: it proves a tonic to the system, and is actually a blessing. No one can truly appreciate the charm of repose unless he has undergone severe exertion.[89]

Stevenson noted the interconnection between health and morality (admittedly a slightly more pagan version than Livingstone's), mediated by man's experience of the natural world, in an essay entitled 'Forest Notes': 'it is not so much for its beauty that the forest makes a claim on men's hearts, as for that subtle something, that quality of the air, that emanation from the old trees, that so wonderfully changes and renews a weary spirit'.[90] This seems to be a romance of the body rather than the mind. But of course the Romanticism of Wordsworth and his contemporaries did entertain a certain fascination and delight with the physical properties of the natural world, although this ultimately tended to act as a conduit for the experience of the more divine properties mediated by nature, a way of 'seeing into the life of things'. What begins to emerge in the later portion of the nineteenth century, however, is a burgeoning interest in the purely physical experience of the natural world in and for itself, with less and less reference to the spiritual aspect. Leslie Stephen writes that his interest in mountain landscapes was first piqued by reading John Ruskin's *Modern Painters* (1843–60). However, Ruskin's aesthetic view of the natural world ('All the best views of hills are at the bottom of them') was somewhat rarefied, removed from experience and antithetical to much of what the Alpine Club and its ilk came to stand for.[91] Stephen rejects the truthfulness or the desirability of this approach, arguing that many 'nature lovers':

have inclined to ignore the true source of their impulses. Even when they speak of the beauties of nature, they would give us to understand that they might have been disembodied spirits, taking aerial flights among mountain solitudes, and independent of the physical machinery of legs and stomachs.[92]

'Legs and stomachs' contrast markedly with 'disembodied spirits' (a phrase also employed by Henry George in his argument for land access), and suggest the musings of aesthetes are vaguely ridiculous in the face of the matter-of-fact business of life. Similarly, Stevenson revels in the physical rehabilitative effects of nature, which is almost a form of decadence:

> The air penetrates through your clothes, and nestles to your living body. You love exercise and slumber, long fasting and full meals. You forget all your scruples and live a while in peace and freedom, and for the moment only . . . Your ideal is not perhaps high, but it is plain and possible. You become enamoured of a life of change and movement and the open air, where the muscles shall be more exercised than the affections.[93]

This concern for the 'open air' is perhaps not entirely surprising in Stevenson, a life-long sufferer of what was thought to be tuberculosis; frequently ill as a child, his dreams of the world beyond the sickroom are explored in *A Child's Garden of Verses* (1885).[94] It is this love of the open air which is most fully expressed in *Kidnapped*, and which he writes of approvingly in 'A Gossip on Romance' as the 'problems of the body and the practical intelligence, in clean, open-air adventure'.[95] Indeed, Stevenson provides a very real sense of such practicalities in *Kidnapped*, where hardships and physical strains form the essence of the adventure. David Balfour and Alan Breck Stewart's 'roughing it' in the wilds of the Scottish landscape seems all very vital and energetic, particularly when compared with the conduct of Scott's youthful Romantic hero, Edward Waverley, who seems to spend most of his time in the Highlands either admiring the prospect or being carried over the rough ground by sturdy 'natives'. Although David and Alan also suffer illness and fatigue in the Highlands, they are nevertheless 'fit' in a way which the Romantic spectator, Waverley, could never hope to be.

'There has come a change in medical opinion,' Stevenson wrote in his essay, 'Health and Mountains', 'and a change has followed in the lives of sick folk'.[96] The possibilities of the curative properties of a fresh atmosphere had come to the fore in the medical (and later, the public) imagination in the years following Stevenson's birth. The first European sanatoria for the treatment of tuberculosis were founded in the Alps in the 1850s, and the first American sanatorium was founded in the Adirondack mountains, on the Saranac River, New York in 1882 – Stevenson stayed at both of these locations as part of his treatment. His frustration with the life of the invalid, who is constrained by his ill health to be 'idle among spiritless idlers; not perhaps dying, yet hardly living either' is based on the definition of the healthy man current in this culture of health and usefulness.[97] He criticises the languid atmosphere of the southern health resorts to which invalids had previously been sent, the 'lack of a manly element; the air was not reactive . . . you did not feel that here was a good spot to repair your tissue or regain your nerve'.[98]

One doesn't tend to think of Stevenson as a mountaineer, but he had travelled extensively in mountainous areas in search of better health, even living on top of one – Mount Helena in California – for a short while, an experience recorded in *The Silverado Squatters*:

> A rough smack of resin was in the air, and a crystal mountain purity. It came pouring over these green slopes by the oceanful. The woods sang aloud, and gave largely of their healthful breath. Gladness seemed to inhabit these upper zones, and we had left indifference behind us in the valley . . . There are days in a life when thus to climb out of the lowlands seems like scaling heaven.[99]

Stevenson corresponded with Leslie Stephen, who had also suffered from lingering ill health as a child; it was Stephen who first encouraged Stevenson to write for *The Cornhill Magazine*, Stephen who introduced Stevenson to W. E. Henley, incapacitated by an amputation and languishing in an Edinburgh hospital – a meeting which was to lead to a life-long, if not always harmonious, friendship and creative partnership. This sort of networking is perhaps typical of the period – 'these are the days of combinations and associations', as Ramsay says – but it is interesting to note how many of these meetings of minds take place around nodes of health, writing, and the natural world.[100]

Adventure writing and the life of the pioneer are associated at this period with this ethic of health and the outdoors, with rhetorical tropes emphasising the 'healthy' aspect of literature. Andrew Lang notes with approval the burgeoning trend for adventure literature in British culture:

> There has, indeed, arisen a taste for exotic literature: people have become alive to the strangeness and fascination of the world beyond the bounds of Europe and the United States. But that is only because men of imagination and literary skill have been the new conquerors . . . have gone out of the streets of the over-populated lands into the open air; have sailed and ridden, walked and hunted; have escaped from the fog and smoke of towns. New strength has come from fresher air into their brains and blood, hence the novelty and buoyancy of the stories which they tell.[101]

Brains and blood and fresh air are the key concerns of these adventure tales, representatives of the Empire itself – and part of the same impulse which moves Mark Twain to glorify the 'stalwart, muscular, dauntless' young men of California in *Roughing It* (1872).[102] Indeed, mountaineering has been read as the physical embodiment of the adventure novel, with the 'British conquest of the natural world . . . [symbolising] British imperial domination of other territory during the nineteenth century'.[103] This rhetoric of the outdoors was also employed by Veitch in his study of Scottish poetry, to commend the 'simple' and 'direct' nature feelings of boyhood and naïve poetry which, he contends, is:

> a form of poetry with which we can at no time dispense, if we are to keep our literature healthy; and it is especially needed in these times. For we have abounding morbid introspection and self-analysis; we have greatly too much of the close hot atmosphere of our own fancies and feelings. We depend for our interest in literature too much on the trick of incident or story, too little on character which embodies primary human emotion. We need, as people did at the commencement of the century, some reminder of the grandeur of a simple life, of the instinctive character of high motives and noble deeds, of the self-satisfying sense of duty done; and the close work-shops of our literary manufactures would be all the better for a good fresh breeze from the hills and the holms of the Teviot and the Yarrow.[104]

Veitch is calling for a modern literary figure to fill the role Wordsworth did at the beginning of the nineteenth century, to cut through the miasma of stagnant writing and rejuvenate Scottish culture. This yearning for 'the grandeur of a simple life' with its fresh air ethic is notably similar to Stevenson's own yearnings for the vigorous life of the frontiersman amongst the mountains of Colorado:

> Anyone who has travelled westward by the great transcontinental railroad of America must remember the joy with which he perceived, after the tedious prairies of Nebraska and across the vast and dismal moorlands of Wyoming, a few snowy mountain summits along the southern sky. It is among these mountains in the new State of Colorado that the sick man may find, not merely an alleviation of his ailments, but the possibility of an active life and an honest livelihood. There, no longer as a lounger in a plaid, but as a working farmer, sweating at his work, he may prolong and begin anew his life. Instead of the bath-chair, the spade; instead of the regulated walk, rough journeys in the forest, and the pure, rare air of the open mountains for the miasma of the sick-room – these are the changes offered him, with what promise of pleasure and of self-respect, with what a revolution in all his hopes and terrors, none but an invalid can know. Resignation, the cowardice that apes a kind of courage and that lives in the very air of health resorts, is cast aside at a breath of such a prospect. The man can open the door; he can be up and doing; he can be a kind of man after all and not merely an invalid.[105]

For Stevenson, health and nature are bound up with a love for adventure – a love which he returns to almost obsessively in his writings, and which is itself in many ways the product of the sickroom. The feeling for nature which Stevenson is concerned with is not so much the abstract experience gained by a contemplation of scenery, as the delight in the moving body, a direct and youthful relationship with the natural world typified by the stravaiging, mountaineering tradition – a tradition which manifests itself in the figure of the rural *flâneur*. Physicality thus comes to be privileged over Romantic spectatorship, signalling a march away from Romantic aesthetics into the different sort of nature feeling suggested by a culture of adventure, health and physical needs. Writing itself can give the reader a sense of physical participation, and so seems itself health-giving. Stevenson's 'grateful mountain feeling' is ultimately not only of the mind, but more fundamentally, of the body.

Notes

1. Maurice Merleau-Ponty, *The Phenomenology of Perception*, trans. Colin Smith (London: Routledge, 2002), p. 239.
2. Alexander Bain, *The Senses and the Intellect* (London: John W. Parker and Son, 1855), p. vi.
3. Ibid., p. 67; 73; 249.
4. Rick Rylance, *Victorian Psychology and British Culture, 1850–1880* (Oxford: Oxford University Press, 2000), p. 154; 170.
5. Bain, p. 107; Gaston Bachelard, *The Poetics of Space*, trans. Maris Jolas (Boston: Beacon Press, 1994), p. 91; Maurice Merleau-Ponty, cited in Tim Ingold, *The Perception of the Environment: Essays in Livelihood, Dwelling and Skill* (London: Routledge, 2000), p. 170.
6. Robert Louis Stevenson, *Across the plains, with other memories and essays*, 12th edn (London: Chatto & Windus, 1905), p. 73.
7. Veitch also published three collections of poetry with a Borders interest: *Hillside Rhymes* (1872), *'The Tweed' and other poems* (1875) and *'Merlin' and other poems* (1889).
8. John Veitch, *The Feeling for Nature in Scottish Poetry*, vol. I (Edinburgh: William Blackwood and Sons, 1887), p. 5.
9. Ibid., p. 11.
10. Ibid., p. 13.
11. Veitch, *The Feeling for Nature in Scottish Poetry*, vol. I, pp. 14–15.
12. Ibid., p. 68.
13. William Wordsworth, 'Lines Written a Few Miles Above Tintern Abbey' (1798), Nicholas Roe (ed.), *Selected Poetry* (London: Penguin Books, 1992), pp. 76–80; p. 77.
14. Quoted in James McKusick, *Green Writing: Romanticism and Ecology* (London: MacMillan Press, 2000), p. 116.
15. Ralph Waldo Emerson, 'Nature', *The Complete Works*, vol. I (New York: The Riverside Press, 1903), p. 29; Veitch, *Feeling for Nature in Scottish Poetry*, p. 10.
16. Veitch, *Feeling for Nature*, pp. 3–5.
17. Ibid., p. 3.
18. John Veitch, *The History and Poetry of the Scottish Border* (Glasgow: James Maclehose, 1878), p. 3.

19. Ibid., pp. 6–7.
20. Ibid., p. 61.
21. Ibid., p. 424.
22. G. G. Ramsay, 'The Formation of the Scottish Mountaineering Club', *The Scottish Mountaineering Club Journal*. IV (1896), pp. 73–91.
23. Veitch, *Feeling for Nature*, p. 3.
24. Emerson, *Nature*, p. 9.
25. Veitch, *Feeling for Nature*, p. 3.
26. Peter H. Hansen, 'Albert Smith, the Alpine Club, and the Invention of Mountaineering in Mid-Victorian Britain,' *Journal of British Studies*, 34 (1995) pp. 300–24; p. 308.
27. Ramsay, 'The Formation of the Scottish Mountaineering Club', p. 82.
28. G. G. Ramsay, 'The President's Address', *The Scottish Mountaineering Club Journal*, Vol. I (1891), pp. 1–11.
29. Ibid., p. 2.
30. Ramsay, 'The Formation of the Scottish Mountaineering Club', p. 81.
31. Ramsay, 'President's Address', p. 3.
32. John Ball (ed.), *Peaks, Passes and Glaciers: A Series of Excursions by Members of the Alpine Club* (London: Longman, Brown, Green, Longmans and Roberts, 1859), p. v.
33. Simon Schama, *Landscape and Memory* (London: Fontana Press, 1996), p. 504.
34. For a discussion of 'recreational colonialism' in the context of the debates over land use in the Scottish Highlands, see Iain Fraser Grigor, *Highland Resistance: The Radical Tradition in the Scottish North* (Edinburgh: Mainstream Publishing, 2000), and Grigor, 'Whose Hills?', *Scottish Left Review* no. 25 (November–December 2004), pp. 20–1.
35. Robert A. Lambert, *Contested Mountains: Nature, Development and Environment in the Cairngorms Region of Scotland* (Cambridge: White Horse Press, 2001), p. 37.
36. Ramsay, 'The Formation of the Scottish Mountaineering Club', p. 81.
37. J. G. Stott, 'Note on Access to the Mountains Bill', *The Scottish Mountaineering Club Journal*, vol. I (1891), p. 328.
38. Ramsay, 'The Formation of the Scottish Mountaineering Club', p. 81.
39. *Oxford English Dictionary*.
40. Such writings include: Hugh Miller's *Rambles of a Geologist* (1858), James Arthur Lees' 'A Ramble in British Columbia' (1888) and John Hill Burton's 'Hints for the Vacation Ramble', serialised in *Blackwood's Magazine* (1881).
41. Lambert, *Contested Mountains*, p. 37.
42. Rebecca Solnit, *Wanderlust: A History of Walking* (London: Penguin Books, 2000), p. 150.
43. ScotWays, unpublished 'Briefing Notes: The Scottish Rights of Way Society 150th Anniversary', p. 1.
44. Quoted in Robert Aitken, 'Stravagers and Marauders', *Scottish Mountaineering Club Journal*, vol. 30 (1972–75), p. 353.
45. Arthur Hugh Clough, in Patrick Scott (ed.), *The Bothie of Toper-na-fuosich* (Queensland: University of Queensland Press, 1976), ll.304–307.

46. Leslie Stephen, 'In Praise of Walking', *Studies of a Biographer*, vol. 3 (London: Smith, Elder and Co., 1907), p. 258.
47. Ibid., p. 241.
48. Quoted in Lambert, p. 61.
49. Ibid., p. 62.
50. Hansen, pp. 310–11.
51. T. M. Devine, *The Scottish Nation 1700–2000* (London: Penguin Books, 2000), p. 305.
52. R. Perry quoted in David Evans, *A History of Nature Conservation in Britain* (London: Routledge, 1992), p. 33.
53. T. C. Smout quotes the following statistical account from Osgood MacKenzie's Game Book in 1868: 'My total for that year was 1,314 grouse, 33 blackgame, 49 partridges, 110 golden plover, 35 wild ducks, 53 snipe, 91 rock-pigeons, 184 hares, without mentioning geese, teal, ptarmigan and roe etc., a total of 1,900 head. In other seasons I got as many as 96 partridges, 106 snipe and 95 woodcock'. *Nature Contested: Environmental History in Scotland and Northern Ireland since 1600* (Edinburgh: Edinburgh University Press, 2000), p. 67.
54. James McCarthy, *An Inhabited Solitude: Scotland, Land and People* (Edinburgh: Luath Press Ltd, 1998), p. 104.
55. Devine, p. 304.
56. John Stuart Blackie's other publications include: *The Gaelic Language: Its Classical Affinities and Distinctive Character* (1864) and *The Union of 1707 and its Results: A Plea for Scottish Home Rule* (1892).
57. Devine, p. 435.
58. *The Dictionary of National Biography.*
59. Ibid.
60. Ibid.
61. Henry George, *The Crime of Poverty: an Address Delivered in the Opera House at Burlington, Iowa, April 1, 1885* (Glasgow: Scottish Land Restoration League, n.d.), p. 7.
62. Quoted in Donald E. Meek (ed.), *Tuath Is Tighearna – Tenants and Landlords: An Anthology of Gaelic Poetry of Social and Political Protest from the Clearances to the Land Agitation (1800–1890)* (Edinburgh: Scottish Academic Press, 1995), p. 129n.
63. David C. Harvey, *Celtic Geographies: Old Culture, New Times* (London: Routledge, 2002), p. 46.
64. John Stuart Blackie, *The Scottish Highlanders and the Land Laws* (London: Chapman and Hall, 1885), p. ix.
65. Ibid., p. 107.
66. Ibid., p. 109.
67. Ibid., p. vii.
68. Ibid., p. ix.
69. Grigor, *Highland Resistance*, chapters 4–7, and Meek, *Tuath Is Tighearna*.
70. Aitken, pp. 351–7; p. 353.
71. Ibid., p. 356.
72. Naill MacLeòid / Neil MacLeod, 'Na Croitearan Sgiathanach' / 'The Skye Crofters', ll.57–60, *Tuath Is Tighearna – Tenants and Landlords*. pp. 102–4; 224–6.

73. Alasdair MacIlleathain / Alasdair MacLean, 'Duanag don Triùir Ghàidheal a thi'a nn am Priosan Dhun Eideann' / 'A Poem to the Three Highlanders who are in the Edinburgh Prison', *Tuath Is Tighearna – Tenants and Landlords*, pp. 119–21; 234–6.
74. Sorley Maclean, 'The Poetry of the Clearances', in William Gillies (ed.), *Ris A' Bhruthaich: Criticism and Prose Writings* (Stornoway: Acair Ltd, 1985), p. 57.
75. Ibid., p. 63.
76. Anonymous, '[Moladh Henry Seoras]' / '[In Praise of Henry George]', ll. 25–32, *Tuath Is Tighearna: Tenants and Landlords*, pp. 128; 240.
77. Clough, *The Bothie*, V, ll.17–25.
78. T. C. Smout, *A Century of the Scottish People* (London: Collins, 1986), p. 65.
79. Ibid., p. 249; p. 67.
80. Ibid., p. 67.
81. Ramsay, 'The Formation of the Scottish Mountaineering Club', p. 83.
82. Blackie, *The Scottish Highlanders and the Land Laws*, p. 6.
83. Ibid., p. 19.
84. Matthew Arnold, *On the Study of Celtic Literature* (London: Smith, Elder and Co., 1891), p. 85.
85. Bruce Haley, *The Healthy Body and Victorian Culture* (Cambridge, MA: Harvard University Press, 1978).
86. Daniel Pick, *Faces of Degeneration: A European Disorder, c.1848–1918* (Cambridge: Cambridge University Press, 1989).
87. Cited in Haley, pp. 20–1.
88. Lyn Pykett, *The Sensation Novel: from The Woman in White to The Moonstone* (Plymouth: Northcote House in association with The British Council, 1994).
89. David Livingstone, Horace Waller (ed.), *The Last Journals of David Livingstone 1856 until his Death*, 2 vols (London: John Murray, 1874), p. 14.
90. Robert Louis Stevenson, 'Forest Notes', *Essays of Travel* (London: Chatto and Windus, 1916), pp. 158–9.
91. Fergus Fleming, *Killing Dragons: the Conquest of the Alps* (London: Granta Books, 2001), p. 142.
92. Stephen, p. 250.
93. Stevenson, 'Forest Notes', pp. 159–60.
94. Stevenson's ill health is now thought to be the result of the respiratory condition, bronchiectasis, rather than tuberculosis. See Richard Woodhead, *The Strange Case of R.L. Stevenson* (Edinburgh: Luath Press, 2001).
95. Robert Louis Stevenson, 'A Gossip on Romance', *Memories and Portraits* (London: Chatto and Windus, 1917), p. 153.
96. Robert Louis Stevenson, 'Health and Moutains', *Essays of Travel* (London: Chatto and Windus, 1916), p. 197.
97. Ibid.
98. Ibid.
99. Robert Louis Stevenson, 'The Silverado Squatters', *The Works of Robert Louis Stevenson*, vol. II (London: Chatto and Windus, 1911), p. 206.

100. Ramsay, 'President's Address', p. 3.
101. Cited in Andrea White, *Joseph Conrad and the Adventure Tradition: Constructing and Deconstructing the Imperial Subject* (Cambridge: Cambridge University Press, 1993), p. 8.
102. Mark Twain, *Roughing It* (Hartford, CT: American Publishing Company, 1872), p. 415.
103. Hansen, p. 323.
104. Veitch, *History and Poetry of the Scottish Border*, pp. 555–6.
105. Stevenson, 'Health and Mountains', p. 198.

Chapter 2

Strange Lands

It is not only when we cross the seas that we go abroad.[1]
Robert Louis Stevenson

Contemplating exile

Born in the Scottish east coast town of Dunbar in 1838, the environmentalist John Muir emigrated with his family to Wisconsin at the age of eleven. Very much a 'lad o' pairts' in the Scottish tradition, Muir embarked on independent study in the rare hours he was spared from labouring on his father's farm, and following some years of botanising and stravaiging across the American continent, was to become the founder of the North American national parks movement. Writing of his thousand mile walk from Indiana to the Gulf of New Mexico in 1867–8, Muir relates his experience of a 'long, complex series of changes' in the environments he encounters on the journey. Finding himself amongst the semi-tropical plant life of Florida, he has a sense of being a 'stranger in a strange land', as the palms and atmosphere of that unfamiliar place 'severed the last strands of the cord that united me with home . . . the winds made strange music, and at the coming-on of night had overwhelming power to present the distance from friends and home, and the completeness of isolation from all things familiar'.[2] In relating his travels, Muir's reference points are typically not the boundaries of ownership or political territory marked on his pocket map, but the features of the natural environment around him; the scents carried on the wind, the particular species of flowers and shrubs, or the quality of the earth trod underfoot. Fully immersed in the environments he encounters – deliberately following the 'wildest, leafiest and least trodden way' on his journey south – Muir relies upon his senses as well as his botanical and zoological knowledge to find his way.[3] Such sensory information can be misleading however, as he discovered on reaching the Florida coast:

> I caught the scent of the salt sea breeze which, although I had so many years lived far from sea breezes, suddenly conjured up Dunbar, its rocky coast, winds and waves; and my whole childhood, that seemed to have utterly vanished in the New World, was now restored amid the Florida woods by that one breath from the sea. Forgotten were the palms and magnolias and the thousand flowers that enclosed me. I could see only dulse and tangle, long-winged gulls, the Bass Rock in the Firth of Forth, and the old castle, schools, churches, and long country rambles in search of birds' nests.[4]

This flux of memory, emotion and physical sensation, momentarily linking together Florida and Dunbar, also feeds into Muir's telling of his early life and emigration to the New World in *The Story of My Boyhood and Youth* (1913), which traces his 'first excursions' along South East Scotland's rocky coastline as 'the beginnings of lifelong wanderings'.[5] Muir's experience in Florida almost exactly parallels Robert Louis Stevenson's contemplations in the South Seas, in which exile is, above all, a visceral experience:

> I was standing out on the little verandah in front of my room this morning, and there went through me or over me a heave of extraordinary and apparently baseless emotion. I literally staggered. And then the explanation came, and I knew I had found a frame of mind and body that belonged to Scotland, and particularly to the neighbourhood of Callander. Very odd these identities of sensation, and the world of connotations implied; Highland huts, and peat smoke, and the brown swirling rivers, and wet clothes, and whisky, and the romance of the past, and that indescribable bite of the whole thing at a man's heart, which is – or rather lies at the bottom of – a story.[6]

This passage, drawn from one of Stevenson's South Seas letters to his friend Sidney Colvin, draws together mind and body in a complex of memory, imagination and physical sensation – that 'indescribable bite' – all centred on a specific remembered environment, in this case an area of the Highlands which he had visited in his youth. Stevenson had recently begun work on what was to become his last (and unfinished) novel, *Weir of Hermiston* (1896). At the same time, he was reading stories by Barbey d'Aurevilly, the Parisian dandy and journalist, and found in them the 'reek of the soil and the past', 'an identity of sensation; one of those conjunctions in life that had filled . . . [him] to the brim, and permanently bent his memory'.[7] A sensitive observer of his own and other people's reactions to displacement, Stevenson's travels led him to theorise not only the condition of exile but also the experience and value of travel in making sense of place and homeland. Elsewhere he remarks that 'the strangest thing in all man's travelling, [is] that he should carry about with him incongruous memories. There is no foreign land; it is the traveller only that is foreign, and now and again, by a flash of recollection, lights up the contrasts of the earth'.[8] The experience of these 'identities of sensation' underscores the difficult position of the traveller in establishing or retaining a sense of place or belonging – and, for Stevenson, also calls attention to the human need to come to terms with the experience through memory and narrative, to populate the ground with stories. Even 'unpleasant places', Stevenson suggests, may be subject to this process: 'if we only stay long enough we become at home in the neighbourhood. Reminiscences spring up, like flowers, about uninteresting corners'.[9]

The idea of 'home', and its opposite, what Heidegger identified as 'the strange, the *unheimlich* . . . that which casts us out of the "homely" ', particularly in the context of technology, is linked with the question of dwelling, the possibility of making an authentic home on the earth.[10] Stevenson's generation experienced an unprecedented acceleration of 'progress', where rapid developments in technology and urbanisation disrupted the idea of home and homeland (a process which, as the ecocritic Jonathan Bate has shown, is explored in Victorian fiction such as Thomas Hardy's *The Woodlanders*).[11] Progress, for Stevenson and other Scots such as the poet James Thomson, brought with it the possibility for international travel, and exposure to exotic lands and wilderness areas which appeared, to the Old World observer, as somehow ahistorical, a confusing mix of primordial nature and the markers of nineteenth-century modernity. While on his South Seas travels, Stevenson writes that 'the Pacific is a strange place; the nineteenth-century only exists there in spots; all round, it is a no man's land of the ages, a stir-about of epochs and races, barbarisms and civilisations, virtues and crimes'.[12] Colonisation of such places posed a distinct threat to local culture and environment alike – a threat which was recognised, commented on and campaigned about by Muir. Stevenson was also to write about this, as witness to and critic of the disruption of traditional ways of life in both the United States and later, the South Seas islands – the latter riddled with social problems resulting from the disruption of traditional ways of life by the émigrés and exiles who drifted to these places, the 'scattered men of many European races' Stevenson wrote of in *The Ebb-Tide* (1894).[13]

As a young man, Stevenson seems optimistic about the ability to make a home anywhere. However, the transition from Scotland, a landscape richly underscored with history at every step, to North America or the South Seas, places which could hold few cultural or historical associations for the exile, creates a sense of dislocation which may amount at times to alienation – reactions explored in Stevenson's later fiction, such as *The Master of Ballantrae* (1889), where the wilderness is almost actively obstructive to the characters' progress through the landscape: 'stumbling, falling . . . hewing our way, our eyes almost put out with twigs and branches, our clothes plucked from our bodies'.[14] Drawing on Heidegger's notion of 'dwelling', Jonathan Bate suggests that the basis for human connection with the earth is ultimately rooted in 'local knowledge', Hardy's term, which signifies the understanding of a locality and one's own position in it, a sense of 'old association – an almost exhaustive biographical or historical acquaintance with every object, animate and inanimate, within the observer's horizon'.[15] For Hardy, and by extension, Bate, memory and personal connection with the landscape appear to be at the core of true inhabitation:

> To become 'dwellers in the land' . . . to come to know the earth, fully and honestly, the crucial and perhaps only and all-encompassing task is to understand the place, the immediate, specific place, where we live . . . We must somehow live as close to it as possible, be in touch with its particular soils, its waters, its winds; we must learn its ways, its capacities, its limits; we must make its rhythms our patterns, its laws our guide, its fruit our bounty. That, in essence, is bioregionalism.[16]

In contrast to such rootedness, Stevenson once remarked that 'I travel not to go anywhere, but to go. I travel for travel's sake. The great affair is to move; to feel the needs and hitches of our life more nearly'.[17] Stevenson admired William Hazlitt, and his writings on travel and walking frequently refer back to Hazlitt's essay, 'On Going a Journey', which asserts that the 'soul of a journey is liberty, perfect liberty, to think, feel and do just as one pleases'.[18] This impulse to travel appears to privilege the journey over the destination, not quite the same sense of home and travel which Bate theorises. If close association with a particular location is fundamental to the development of an authentic, 'dwelling perspective' which fosters a respect for the earth, one might ask how far can this sense of place extend? To the bottom of the garden? A county, country or continent? Stevenson's life and imagination moved between all of these, while demonstrating a lasting albeit equivocal relationship with his homeland, revisiting Scottish scenes in his imagination even while his globetrotting life was leading him to the South Seas. It was a life characterised above all by change and travel, a curious mix of familiar places and far-off destinations, of alternating sick-room confinements and health-seeking holidays. His travelling brought him new homes; temporary residences at Davos in the Alps and Saranac Lake in the Adirondacks, the abandoned miner's cabin in California, the wished-for houses in the south of France, and ultimately Vailima and his 'martin's nest' study in Samoa. Despite retaining what he called 'a strong

Scottish accent of the mind', it is perhaps difficult to pin Stevenson down to a defining locale.[19] Kenneth White, the Scottish writer and theorist of 'geopoetics' who has also chosen to live abroad, has noted the difficulty of this duality, asking instead: 'Might it be possible to conceive of a 'great residence' that would reconcile movements and things, removing and remaining, stravaiging and staying?'[20] Stevenson himself seems to suggest that travel is an essential characteristic of the writer or poet, who 'must study his fellow-countrymen and himself somewhat like a traveller on the hunt for his book of travels'.[21]

'Living deliberately': Stevenson and North American thought

Stevenson read widely, and among his catalogue of early influences, he lists Walt Whitman and Henry David Thoreau, devoting separate essays to each writer in *Familiar Studies of Men and Books*.[22] Stevenson's essays make it possible to read these Americans as it were 'over his shoulder', and they reveal his burgeoning interest in the culture and landscape of the United States, before he had the opportunity to experience the country at first hand – and when he finally did, as Wendy Katz notes, his view of the place and its people was tinged with that early reading.[23] Thoreau, whose *Walden, or Life in the Woods* (1854), explored the aesthetics and economies of a life lived close to nature, has since been hailed as one of the founding fathers of modern environmentalism, and much has been written on his ecological and political significance in modern thought from his day onwards.[24] Thoreau and Whitman are in many ways representative of nineteenth-century America's sense of potential, of the ideal nation that could be about to unfold; their works linking together ideals of democracy, liberty and landscape.

Thoreau's *Walden* is both a partial biography and a write-up of his extended experiment in natural living – a life somewhat self-consciously stripped of possessions and complexities, focused on the day-to-day experience of a particular place, a local environment. Thoreau explained that he 'went to the woods because . . . [he] wished to live deliberately, to front only the essential facts of life' – an objective which emphasises simplicity, certainly, but also ideals of personal and political independence – the sort of political and societal ideals which led him to publish *On the Duty of Civil Disobedience* in 1849.[25] Choosing to live on the edge of society, sustaining himself on home-grown crops, and living in a shelter of his own making, Thoreau's *Walden* project is a peculiar example of 'domestic individualism', an experiment in practical living which parallels other North American experiments of the time. From the mid-nineteenth century onwards, a number of experimental 'utopian' communities sprang up, allied with the transcendentalist movement and putting the theory of 'Communitarian Socialism' into practice. Robert Owen, George Ripley, Bronson Alcott and others began their ideal communities, which attracted devotees from the Old World as well as the New.[26]

Thoreau's solitary existence in the woods might be seen as his own version of this movement for political and social independence. Setting up house in this manner would seem to be the ideal of the 'dwelling' perspective, emphasising the organic connection between the individual and the patch of earth he or she inhabits, with this natural link being in some way expressed in the construction of the house itself. Thoreau argues that 'there is some of the same fitness in a man's building his own house that there is in a bird's building its nest', contending that the human 'poetic faculty' is bound up with such honest and 'natural' craftsmanship.[27] The house in many ways grows out of the landscape, suggested by the environment, called into being by the man's organic connection with his chosen place. Thoreau's theory of the simple house anticipates Gaston Bachelard's phenomenological image of the hut containing the essence of primordial dwelling, where 'a dreamer of refuges dreams of a hut, of a nest . . . the taproot of the function of inhabiting'.[28] Thoreau remarked that the only previous habitations he had owned were a boat and a tent, and wrote of houses as the 'shells' of their inhabitants, his own shelter forming 'a sort of crystallization around me'.[29] Contrasting the artifice of planned architecture with the spontaneous growth of home-building, he develops a theory of organic architecture as having 'gradually grown from within outward, out of the necessities and character of the indweller, who is the only builder, – out of some unconscious truthfulness, and nobleness'.[30]

Stevenson, too, wrote about the organic links between the landscape and human constructions – an interest which seems related to his family's heritage of lighthouse engineering, the creation of buildings which mediate the relationship between man and the elements in an equivocal way, as a dwelling place for the lighthouse keeper and also a technological apparatus, built in challenging, even dangerous environmental conditions. His grandfather, Robert Stevenson, the famed constructor of the Bell Rock lighthouse off the east coast of Scotland was, he suggests:

> above all things a projector of works in the face of nature, and a modifier of nature itself. A road to be made, a tower to be built, a harbour to be constructed, a river to be trained and guided in its channel – these were the

problems with which his mind was continually occupied; and for these and similar ends he travelled the world for more than half a century, like an artist, note-book in hand.[31]

Despite having given up on the study of engineering himself, Stevenson undoubtedly admires his grandfather's expertise – there is a certain craftsmanship in these calculations, and that touch of intellectual or romantic kinship in the description of his grandfather's wanderings, artist-like, across the globe. However, the engineer's 'intimate study of the ways of nature', involving construction, projection and modification, differs from Stevenson's own interest, which tends more towards the spontaneous, bodily and fundamentally ecological relationship between people and place.

In his essay on 'Roads', Stevenson theorises the 'natural growth' of roads and paths in contrast to the deliberately planned and engineered highway – perhaps an unconscious echoing of his sense of contrast in the structure of Edinburgh, with its organic jumble of medieval roads in the Old Town and its carefully planned Enlightenment streets in the New.

> We might reflect that the present road had been developed out of a tract spontaneously followed by generations of primitive wayfarers; and might see in its expression a testimony that those generations had been affected at the same ground, one after another, in the same manner as we are affected to-day.[32]

This notion of a spontaneous, intuitive and organic connection between place and human behaviour is a striking idea, perhaps all the more interesting because here it is applied to a place of travel, rather than of habitation. Stevenson's idea of the road seems somehow related to Heidegger's example of the bridge in 'Building, Dwelling, Thinking', which, by spanning the river, 'assembles' various elements of the surrounding countryside into a unity, creating a 'lodging' or dwelling place as meaningful and valuable as a temple or a home.[33] Stevenson's road, however, is not consciously 'built', but unconsciously, intuitively, 'grown'; it reveals an ongoing relationship between humans and environment, a history of human wayfinding, and suggests a narrative, a way of 'reading' the landscape. The footpath's 'human waywardness and unaccountability', he suggests, 'will always be more to us than a railroad well engineered through a difficult country'. In the contemplation of the meandering path, Stevenson playfully suggests, 'we seem to have slipped for one lawless little moment out of the iron rule of cause and effect'.[34] From an ecotheoretical perspective, an 'understanding of the landscape as a course to be followed' stands in opposition to the Western (Cartesian) 'understanding of the natural environment as a resistance to be overcome, a physically given, material substrate that has first to be 'humanised' by imposing upon it forms whose origins lie in the imagination, before it can be inhabited'.[35] The distinction between the railroad and the path also connects with Heidegger's distinction between modern technology (as a 'challenging' or 'enframing' of nature) and craft or *techne*, which does not reduce nature to utility, but 'reveals' or 'brings forth' its essence, and as such is a form of *poiesis*.[36] Significantly, in Stevenson's view, the human imagination is not typified by the reductive, 'enframing' approach, but often stifled by it: the railroad's unerring straight line through the landscape neglects the 'saving imperfection' of the country path or road, which forms a conceptual dwelling place, an object of poetic contemplation and the source of a story.

In pursuit of such phenomenological and imaginative stimulation, Thoreau's practical and poetic experiments in 'living deliberately' must have seemed refreshing to Stevenson, who was attracted first by the romantic and then the physical possibilities of outdoor life in the New World – and indeed experienced these at first hand in his own makeshift shelter in California, described in *The Silverado Squatters* (1883). Thoreau's earnestness was, in Stevenson's eyes, admirable although it was also a source of tension, the sense of a writer straining to connect the practical and romantic sides of his nature:

> The seeming significance of nature's appearances, their unchanging strangeness to the senses, and the thrilling response which they waken in the mind of man, continued to surprise and stimulate his spirits. It appeared to him, I think, that if we could only write near enough to the facts, and yet with no pedestrian calm, but ardently, we might transfer the glamour of reality direct upon our pages, and that, if it were once thus captured and expressed, a new and instructive relation might appear between men's thoughts and the phenomena of nature.[37]

What Stevenson finds in Thoreau is an attempt to let the process of writing itself embody the relationship between humans and the natural world. Thoreau's technique is not one of objective detachment but requires a different kind of dedication and attentiveness which aims to evoke an encounter with the real. While it seems that Stevenson remained unconvinced by Thoreau's philosophy, he adopts values associated with 'living deliberately' in his own work, contrasting, in *The Silverado Squatters*, two different ways of rural life encountered during his residence in California:

> the hunter living really in nature; the clodhopper living merely out of society; the one bent up in every corporeal agent to capacity in one pursuit, doing at least one thing keenly and thoughtfully, and thoroughly alive to all that

touches it; the other in the inert and bestial state, walking in a faint dream, and taking so dim an impression of the myriad sides of life that he is truly conscious of nothing but himself.[38]

This distinction is significant, and appears to draw upon his reading of both the prose writings of Thoreau and the poetry of Walt Whitman – it is also a viewpoint shared by John Muir, who contended that 'Most people are on the world, not in it – have no conscious sympathy, or relationship to anything about them – undiffused, separate, and rigidly alone like marbles of polished stone, touching but separate'.[39] Stevenson's study of Whitman remarks upon the American poet's attempts to 'shake people out of their indifference, and force them to make some election in this world, instead of sliding dully forward in a dream'.[40] Similarly, Stevenson remarks of Thoreau (even while criticising the severity of his denial of the customs of civilisation) that he was 'alive . . . in every fibre' and speaks with a certain admiration for the man who preferred 'an easy, calm, unfettered, active life among green trees to dull toiling at the counter of a bank'.[41] For Stevenson, both Whitman and Thoreau seek to encourage humanity to escape from the 'faint dream' which is the lot of many, to embrace a 'thoroughly alive' existence he identifies in *The Silverado Squatters*, which means tapping into an innate vein of 'woodland poetry'.[42] Despite this potential for revelation, however, Stevenson is wary of what he perceives as the 'cold, distant personality' of Thoreau, a certain humourlessness, combined with his position as a societal outsider which affords him the status of an observer, rather than an active participant in human life. Stevenson says he is more interested in 'a man rather than a manner of elm-tree' and as such is closer to Whitman's absorption in the life of the people. Comparing the two writers, he argues that Thoreau's self-improving is merely theoretical, focused inwards on the self, thus becoming 'arid, abstract, and claustral', whilst Whitman's interpretation of the 'same doctrine' appears 'buxom, blythe and debonair' – and is so precisely because it includes others in its self-celebration.[43]

One senses that what appealed most to Stevenson about Whitman, as it did to his other admirers, was that startlingly frank approach to life. 'Voluptuous, inhabitive, combative, conscientious, alimentive, intuitive, of copious friendship, sublimity, firmness, self-esteem, comparison, individuality, form, locality, eventuality': Whitman chants the list of his attitudes and attributes, revealing the fullness of his multitudinous character.[44] The poet's self-portrait in *Leaves of Grass* (1855) reveals himself as 'Walt Whitman, a kosmos, of Manhattan the son, | Turbulent, fleshy, sensual, eating, drinking and breeding, | No sentimentalist'.[45] The sensuality and directness of Whitman's poetry were all the more remarkable since it was produced in an age where Victorian tender sentiment was sanitising the human experience in its poetic representations. It is not for nothing that Whitman contrasts himself, as self-proclaimed poetic voice (or 'Barbaric yawp') of America, with Britain's contemporary poet laureate, Alfred, Lord Tennyson.[46] Whitman admits in an essay on Tennyson that he admires the English poet, but states that he does not share his point of view or aesthetics. Despite the sensuality of poems like 'Now sleeps the crimson petal', for Whitman, Tennyson represented the decadence of Old World poetry, and provided yet more grist for his rough-hewn American mill.[47] Stevenson picked up on this stance towards English writers, quoting Whitman's wish for American and democratic 'hymns of the praise of things . . . a brave delight fit for freedom's athletes' in contrast to the English 'literature of woe' (in this respect, one might reflect that Whitman's aesthetic intersects with Highland cultural traditions, the 'praise poems' of the Gaelic poets).[48]

Whitman's influence was a liberating one for Stevenson – linked, in his imagination, with the freedom and revelation of travel (definitely not tourism, but something more akin to 'roughing it'). Stevenson writes that his first reading of *Leaves of Grass* 'tumbled the world upside down for me, blew into space a thousand cobwebs of genteel and ethical illusion, and . . . set me back upon a strong foundation of all the original and manly virtues' – a response which seems to kindle a desire to 'come down off this feather-bed of civilization'.[49] Whitman's democratic stance seems to have fed into Stevenson's journey to North America in the 1880s, related in *The Amateur Emigrant* and *Across the Plains* – travel books marked by what Katz calls a 'Whitmanesque sense of acceptance, tolerance and, very often, affection' which, as Frank McLynn notes, left Stevenson's more conservative friends perturbed by 'the ease with which he slipped through class barriers'.[50] The notion of Old World artifice and decadence was the favoured conceit of American cultural propagandists such as Whitman, who were seeking to forge a new art which was to reinforce culturally America's political independence from Europe – and to engage in a little cheerful iconoclasm along the way. This new method of representation must reflect a new aesthetic of 'roughs and beards and space and ruggedness and nonchalance'.[51] The experience of the 'common people' is paramount, and within this diversity Whitman detects vast scores of 'unrhymed poetry' which 'awaits the gigantic and generous treatment worthy of it'. Stevenson was sensitive to, and attracted by, the epic scale of this American poetic impulse, recognising in Whitman the desire both to theorise and to facilitate the emergence of a specifically American voice, celebrating diversity whilst emphasising unity. As such, democracy and human interrelationship form the core of Whitman's poetic vision – and these are certainly important values for Stevenson's own work and travels, perhaps particularly in the South Seas. Such observational wanderings, though, are also related to a co-emergent poetic practice Whitman helped to influence and develop: the observational walks and wanderings of the *flâneur*, the figure who, as Walter Benjamin suggests, enjoys 'botanising on the asphalt'.[52]

Rural *flâneurs*

The *flâneur*, largely through the work of Benjamin and his landmark study on Charles Baudelaire, has come to be seen as an archetypal figure of the nineteenth century city.[53] An urban stroller and observer, he remains detached, leisurely, fascinated by the bustle of the crowd and the life of the city streets; by turns a dandy, detective, poet or philosopher, the perspective he embodies is typically one of urban modernity and bohemian sensibility. In his student days, Stevenson cultivated this sort of persona, as the idling truant who explores the city for purposes of poetic inspiration and private reflection. Valuing the knowledge gleaned through his youthful wanderings, he celebrated this necessary capacity for idleness in 'An Apology for Idlers', contrasting the worth of knowledge gained through school room (or lecture room) study and the superior value of 'certain other odds and ends that I came by in the open street while I was playing truant' (a stance which links him to other nineteenth-century ramblers and mountaineers).[54] It was at this time that he began to experiment with prose poetry and *vers libre*, forms which reflected the leisure and unfettered wanderings of the *flâneur*, and which enjoyed a limited vogue amongst European writers at the time. Baudelaire had also experimented with the form, most notably in his *Petits poemes en prose* (1869), as did Whitman, whose lyrical flashes and epic listings are framed in stanzas of sprawling prose.

Stevenson read the work of both Baudelaire and Whitman, and the mixed influence of both writers is visible in his poetry and essay writing of this period. The poem, 'My brain swims empty and light', shows the student *flâneur* speaking of his city spectatorship as one 'stand[ing] apart from living . . . In my new-gained growth of idleness'. His detached gaze takes on a secular sacredness; 'Apart and holy', he wanders the streets with an ambiguous purpose.

> I love cool pale morning,
> In the empty by-streets,
> With only here and there a female figure,

> A slavey with lifted dress and the key in her hand,
> A girl or two at play in a corner of waste-land
> Tumbling and showing their legs and crying out to me loosely.⁵⁵

Perhaps this is not Stevenson's best poetry, but it does give some insights into the theory and practice of his city walking. The poem hints at ideals of acceptance and tolerance, but far more marked is the male voyeuristic glance – the spectacles of the 'shop-girl', the prostitutes and streetgirls which populate this version of Edinburgh. The emphasis on the spectatorship of female sexuality is a typical stance of the *flâneur*, whose scopophilia objectifies and commodifies the people and the sights of the city – a form of cynical detachment which would seem to be at odds with the ideals of social inclusion which Stevenson finds attractive in Whitman's walking and way finding. However, the idea of the *flâneur* intersects with anxieties about communal belonging in the modern city, the loss of the sense of place.

Baudelaire had proposed that for the archetypal *flâneur*, 'it is an immense joy to set up house in the heart of the multitude, amid the ebb and flow', and that part of the *flâneur*'s experience is:

> To be away from home, yet to feel oneself everywhere at home; to see the world, to be at the centre of the world, yet to remain hidden from the world . . . The lover of universal life enters into the crowd as though it were an immense reservoir of electric energy. We might also liken him to a mirror as vast as the crowd itself; or to a kaleidoscope endowed with consciousness, which, with each one of its movements, represents the multiplicity of life and the flickering grace of all the elements of life.⁵⁶

Baudelaire's writings suggest that the street is the dwelling place for the crowd and the *flâneur* alike, even while it is simultaneously the site of disorientation and alienation. The wanderings of the urban *flâneur* involved an odd mixture of domesticity and adventure, in an urban environment which 'splits' for the *flâneur* 'into its dialectical poles. It opens up to him as a landscape, even as it closes around him as a room'.⁵⁷ Something of this dualistic sense can be gleaned from a passage in 'Edinburgh: Picturesque Notes', a sort of quirky tourist guide to Stevenson's native city of crowded streets and 'draughty parallelograms', in which the night-time appearance of the tenements produces an uneasy feeling.

> One night I went along the Cowgate after every one was a-bed but the policeman, and stopped by hazard before a tall land. The moon touched upon its chimneys, and shone blankly on the upper windows; there was no light anywhere in the great bulk of building; but as I stood there it seemed to me that I could hear quite a body of quiet sounds from the interior; doubtless there were many clocks ticking, and people snoring on their backs. And thus, as

I fancied, the dense life within made itself faintly audible in my ears, family after family contributing its quote to the general hum, and the whole pile beating in tune to its time-pieces, like a great disordered heart.[58]

The city is 'othered' under his gaze, the individual building both a 'land' (a traditional Edinburgh expression for a tenement building) and a collection of rooms, disclosing the life within them but also concealing it. This sensation is perhaps rooted in his troubled childhood experiences of the urban night from his nursery window, and was later to be most fully reflected in *The Strange Case of Dr Jekyll and Mr Hyde* (1886), where 'labyrinths of lamplighted city' produce a nightmarish, disorientating effect on the imagination.[59] The dialectic of expanding landscape and confining room finds its parallel in the structure of Stevenson's own life, a perpetual cycle of sickroom confinements and adventurous travel. Something of this duality is reflected in his own family history, as Stevenson notes the 'sharply defined' contrast 'between the lives of the men and women of this family: the one so chambered, so centred in the affections and the sensibilities; the other so active, healthy and expeditious'.[60] The contrast between the chamber and the expedition could be taken to characterise Stevenson's own life and, as Benjamin has suggested, the experience of the *flâneur* in general. The *flâneur*'s experience of his environment is one of half-familiarity, half-strangeness, a sort of psychological dislocation which precludes the sense of the uncanny which was to influence so much of later Modernist thought.

Surely this sort of social and environmental dislocation is at odds with the very notion of 'dwelling', with the solitary wanderings of the *flâneur* precluding any kind of ecological sensibility. The image of the kaleidoscope (a Scottish invention) was also used by Whitman and later, by Stevenson, in their portrayal of North American life. Stevenson picks up on this sense of kaleidoscopic multiplicity, writing with fascination of the evolving modernity of American culture and landscape in *The Amateur Emigrant*:

> Vast cities that grow up as if by enchantment; the birds, that have gone south in autumn, returning with the spring to find thousands camped upon their marshes, and the lamps burning far and near along populous streets; forests that disappear like snow; countries larger than Britain that are cleared and settled, one man running forth with his household gods before another, while the bear and the Indian are yet scarce aware of their approach; oil that gushes from the earth; gold that is washed or quarried in the brooks or glens of the Sierras; and all that bustle, courage, action, and constant kaleidoscopic change that Walt Whitman has seized and set forth in his vigorous, cheerful, and loquacious verses.[61]

Stevenson's sense of restless change echoes Whitman's poem, 'Starting from Paumanok', where the reader is invited to 'See, vast trackless spaces | As in a dream they change, they swiftly fill, | Countless masses debouch upon them, | They are now cover'd with the foremost people, arts, institutions known'.[62] This celebration of progress is part of Whitman's optimism, but Stevenson's Scottish sense of spatial history provides him with an awareness of the obliterating effects of this 'progress' on the wilderness, even while the possibilities of American pioneering attracts his romantic sensibility. The pace of New World change is here measured by its disruption of the ancient cyclical rhythms of the natural world, with the incongruous coexistence of 'telephones and telegraphs, and newspapers, and advertisements' alongside the 'Indians and the grizzly bears'.[63]

Stevenson was certainly fascinated with this juxtaposition of modernity and wilderness in the New World (and in the South Seas), but he might have been familiar with the odd sensations provoked by such contrasts from his reading of Victor Hugo and other French writers, for whom the Old World city could be expressed in similar terminology as the American forests. Benjamin notes that in some of these novels the 'poetry of terror' of the 'American woods' was translated onto the Parisian streets, creating a genre of fiction in which pedestrians, buildings and coaches are of 'the same burning interest . . . as a tree stump, a beaver's den, a rock, a buffalo skin'.[64] In the modernist imagination, aspects of the metropolis can fuse with wilderness landscape to create a liminal space: 'The natural-supernatural . . . presents itself in the forest; in the animal kingdom, and by the surging sea; in any of those places the physiognomy of a big city can flash for a few moments'.[65] While this idea is related to the trope of the 'urban jungle' suggested by Darwinian (and, later, Freudian) anxieties – and explored in Stevenson's *Jekyll and Hyde* – it is also to do with making sense of the experience of modernity, and the possibility of establishing a 'dwelling' place.

Benjamin suggests that the genesis of the *flâneur* is rooted in the rural rather than the urban, contrasting the 'dandy' with another, more ecological trait:

> Yet also in the *flâneur* a long-extinct creature opens a dreamy eye, casts a look that goes to the heart of the poet. It is the 'son of the wilderness' – the man who, once upon a time, was betrothed, by a generous nature, to leisure. Dandyism is the last glimmer of the heroic in times of decadence. Baudelaire is delighted to find in Chateaubriand a reference to American Indian dandies – testimony to the former golden age of these tribes.[66]

The idea of the *flâneur* as a 'son of the wilderness' (an Idle Savage as well as a Noble one) might appear incongruous, but it has a surprising resonance of accuracy, given the experience of Whitman, Thomson and Stevenson – linked as it is with a faculty for romance and leisure.

Stevenson noted with some delight and amusement (commingled at times with a little impatience) the dandies of the South Seas, with their 'invincible inertia' and 'dandy nonchalance'.[67] A sort of attentive idleness becomes a method for living deliberately – a stance perhaps not so far removed from Thoreau's rejection of the principle of labour, and one which anticipates Hugh MacDiarmid's claim in 'On a Raised Beach' that 'culture demands leisure and leisure presupposes | A self-determined rhythm of life; the capacity for solitude'.[68] For Stevenson, a 'faculty for idleness implies a catholic appetite and a strong sense of personal identity' in contrast to the lives of conventionally industrious men, who appear as 'a sort of dead-alive, hackneyed people . . . scarcely conscious of living except in the exercise of some conventional occupation . . . They have no curiosity; they cannot give themselves over to random provocations . . . It is no good speaking to such folk'.[69] Stevenson's attitude to these 'dead-alive' people foreshadows the existentialist's disdain for those who keep 'bad faith', who live an inauthentic, unaware existence.[70] By contrast, the activity of cheerful idleness permits a fuller and truer education which is at the heart of Stevenson's version of authentic living:

> As a matter of fact, an intelligent person, looking out of his eyes and hearkening in his ears, with a smile on his face all the time, will get more true education than many another in a life of heroic vigils. There is certainly some chill and arid knowledge to be found upon the summits of formal and laborious science; but it is all round about you, and for the trouble of looking, that you will acquire the warm and palpitating facts of life.[71]

Dwelling and adventure

The kaleidoscopic properties of the modern city fascinate the *flâneur*, but are ultimately abstracted and fragmented, enjoyed for the passing moment, but never allowed to condense into any kind of unity. Hierarchies and fragmentation are not conducive to the acknowledgement of the ecosystem or the bioregion, and emphasise divisions and discontinuities where an ecological way of looking might seek for networks and relationships.

> An intoxication comes over the man who walks long and aimlessly through the streets. With each step, the walk takes on greater momentum; ever weaker grow the temptations of shops, of bistros, of smiling women, ever more irresistible the magnetism of the next street corner, of a distant mass of foliage, of a street name. Then comes hunger. Our man wants nothing to do with the myriad possibilities offered to sate his appetite. Like an ascetic animal, he flits through unknown districts – until, utterly exhausted, he stumbles into his room, which receives him coldly and wears a strange air.[72]

The 'magnetism' of which Baudelaire speaks is suggestive of a wandering compulsion, something which Stevenson sensed within himself and revisited in his essays and fictions.

> Travel is brought home to us, and we visit in spirit every grove and hamlet that tempts us in the distance. *Sehnsucht* – the passion for what is ever beyond – is livingly expressed in that white riband of possible travel that severs the uneven country . . .[73]

This idea of '*sehnsucht*' corresponds to the 'magnetism' experienced by the urban *flâneur*. A 'yearning' or 'wistful longing', which may signify lust or wanderlust, *sehnsucht* is a certain instinctive, bodily impulse which propels the individual to seek adventure. In this respect, it provides a unified term for the disparate activities of the *flâneur*, and all his suppressed desire and restlessness.

This very bodily urge for travel and change is expressed in Stevenson's short story, 'Will o' the Mill' (1887), where Will's longing for adventure affects him in very physical terms:

> He could see the cities, and the woods and fields, and the bright curves of the river, and far away to where the rim of the plain trenched along the shining heavens. An overmastering emotion seized upon the boy, soul and body . . . Something kept tugging at his heart strings; the running water carried his desires along with it as he dreamed over its fleeting surface; the wind, as it ran over innumerable tree-tops, hailed him with encouraging words; branches beckoned downward; the open road, as it shouldered round the angles and went turning and vanishing faster and faster down the valley, tortured him with its solicitations.[74]

Will's desires are based on his sense of fragmentation and his wish for sensory unity. Living on the mountainside, he can only piece 'together broken notions of the world below'; 'lusting with the eyes' he desires to be a part of the 'many-coloured, many-sounding life' which exists below on the plains.

> If he could only go far enough out there, he felt as if his eyesight would be purged and clarified, his hearing would grow more delicate, and his very breath would come and go with luxury. He was transplanted and withering where he was; he lay in a strange country and was sick for home.[75]

This wish for the sharpening of the senses is part of the *flâneur*'s experience, who shares similar psychological traits to the age-old human desire for adventure. Stevenson's first-person adventure fictions such as *Treasure Island*, *Kidnapped* and *Catriona* (although the latter is perhaps more occupied with political manoeuvrings than the fast-paced practicalities of active adventuring) barely pause to consider the forces which drive the adventurers themselves; reader and author are caught up in flurry of action, of happenings, 'the problems of the body and the practical intelligence' – including the frequently unpleasant sensations of cold, hunger and hardship associated with 'roughing it' in the open air.[76] The exteriority of adventure would later be balanced by the development of a psychological interiority in Stevenson's writings, which serves as a counterpoint to the more traditional elements of romance in *The Master of Ballantrae*. 'Will o' the Mill' is an adventure story characterised precisely by a *lack* of adventure. Here, Stevenson allows himself authorial space to ponder the motivations of explorers, and to evoke the frustrated longings for change and travel which he had himself experienced. Adventure appears not only as a shimmering dream of boyhood but as a central motivating force in the history of mankind. Half-practical, half-spiritual, the adventure impulse is, Stevenson suggests, endemic in human society; it is a 'divine unrest' which characterises mankind itself – 'that old stinging trouble of humanity'.[77] The history of exploration and emigration, 'all that counter-marching of tribes and races' cannot be boiled down to 'the laws of supply and demand':

> To anyone thinking deeply, this will seem a dull and pitiful explanation. The tribes that came swarming out of the North and East, if they were indeed pressed onward from behind by others, were drawn at the same time by the magnetic influence of the South and West. The fame of other lands had reached them . . . they were not colonists, but pilgrims . . .[78]

The nobility of adventure goes hand in hand with its more distasteful, practical consequences. However, Will is to reject adventure in this story, by coming to realise that contentment and fulfilment are to be found at his own door and not by adventure for adventure's sake. In this respect one might think of 'Will o' the Mill' as the embodiment of Benjamin's theory of 'The Storyteller', whose craft combines 'the lore of faraway places, such as a much-travelled man brings home, with the lore of the past, as it best reveals itself to natives of a place'.[79]

However, Stevenson recognises that adventure, motivated partly by curiosity and romance, is also provoked by desires to do with mastery and possession, a sort of Cartesian imperialism which ecocritics argue is the underlying basis for much of Western thought's hierarchical view of the relationship between man and nature:

> Mastery and possession: these are the master words launched by Descartes at the dawn of the scientific and technological age, when our Western reason went off to conquer the universe. We dominate and appropriate it: such is the shared philosophy underlying industrial enterprise as well as so-called disinterested science, which are indistinguishable in this respect. Cartesian mastery brings science's objective violence into line, making it a well-controlled strategy. Our fundamental relationship with objects comes down to war and property.[80]

The imperial impulse is revealed as pointless to Will; issues of mastery and possession lose their hold on him through a series of self-revelations. His youthful encounter with the 'wise young man' whose parables demonstrate to Will the limitations of the human condition allow him to forego the desire for adventure, whilst his conversation with his fiancée Marjory, who is compelled to pick flowers to satisfy her desire to possess them makes Will realise the pointlessness of marriage as a contract of possession, compared to the free giving of companionship, and the acceptance of things as they are.

Perhaps Stevenson's most profound and unsettling treatment of this theme is to be found in the novel whose very title speaks of mastery and locality: *The Master of Ballantrae*. Inspired during Stevenson's stay at Saranac Lake in the Adirondack mountains – an area which was to become one of America's first protected wildernesses in 1885 – it is in his own words 'a tale of many lands', of 'savagery and civilisation'. Stevenson relates how the different components of the story were borne of specific localities; the sections in the American wilderness infused with the winter air of the Adirondack mountains, 'clear and cold and sweet with the purity of forests', while the relationship between the Durrisdeer brothers was 'conceived long before on the moors between Pitlochry and Strathardle . . . in Highland rain, in the blend of the smell of heather and bog-plants'.[81]

Told from the outset that the tale 'extends over many years and travels into many countries', the reader approaches *The Master of Ballantrae* with a ready-made sense of alienation, twice-distanced from the world of the novel, both spatially and temporally dislocated, as the exile of both author and editor provides a narrative framework for what is to come.[82] The supposed 'editor' of MacKellar's century-old revelations introduces himself as 'an old, consistent exile' whose time spent revisiting his native city is 'strange' and 'painful':

> Outside, in foreign spots, he comes by surprise and awakens more attention than he had expected; in his own city, the relation is reversed, and he stands amazed to be so little recollected. Elsewhere he is refreshed to see attractive faces, to remark possible friends; there he scouts the long streets, with a pang at his heart, for the faces and friends that are no more. Elsewhere he is delighted with the presence of what is new, there tormented by the absence of what is old. Elsewhere he is content to be his present self; there he is smitten with an equal regret for what he once was and for what he hoped to be.[83]

The editor had heard something of the history of the Durrisdeers through the whisperings of local knowledge and tradition, and indeed MacKellar's narrative begins with a glance at the countryside reputation of the family – a similar device to that employed in another Scottish novel of duality and doppelgängers, James Hogg's *The Private Memoirs and Confessions of a Justified Sinner* (1824). Indeed, local knowledge shows itself to be central to *The Master of Ballantrae*'s twisting plot. The guides and trackers employed by Henry Durrisdeer are 'well acquainted with the secret paths of the wilderness' while the Master's Indian comrade Secundra Dass fails to resuscitate the Master because his tropical knowledge does not apply to the frozen wastes of the winter Adirondacks.[84]

Places and people, in *The Master of Ballantrae*, are riddled with a profound duality; the experience of the American wilderness's 'thickets, swamps, precipitous rocks' seems as alien to the bewildered Chevalier and Master as the night-time city appeared to James Thomson in *The City of Dreadful Night* (1880) with its 'wild paths' and 'soundless solitudes'.[85] Muir's 'wildest, leafiest and least-trodden way' is here a source of terror and disorientation, as the Irish Chevalier's narrative attests:

> Some parts of the forest were perfectly dense down to the ground . . . In some the bottom was full of deep swamp, and the whole wood entirely rotten. I have leaped on a great fallen log and sunk to the knees in touchwood; I have sought to stay myself, in falling, against what looked to be a solid trunk, and the whole thing has whiffed at my touch like a sheet of paper.[86]

This alienating experience of the wilderness as somehow artificial, uncanny and certainly unhomely (*unheimlich*, in both Heidegger and Freud's senses of the term) stands in contrast to John Muir's assertion that 'going to the woods is going home; for I suppose we came from the woods originally'.[87] This sense of the uncanny extends to The Master himself, who appears as 'something partly spectral', or 'a man of pasteboard' – a sense of 'vacuity' which, one might argue, prefigures T. S. Eliot's 'hollow men' in the twentieth century.[88] However, perhaps this sense of alienation is related, in Stevenson's imagination, to the possibilities of humanity's primitive ancestry. As Julia Reid suggests, Stevenson's writings frequently 'portray the persistence and irruption of precivilized states of consciousness in the modern world'.[89] Specifically, *The Master of Ballantrae* 'disrupts anthropology's progressive narrative by questioning whether superstition succumbs to rationalism, savagery to civilisation', presenting, as Douglas Gifford contends, an image of 'traditional Scottish Conservatism locked in misunderstanding with rootless Disbelief'.[90]

A clever and at times disturbing analysis of psychological motives, *The Master of Ballantrae* is, above all, an extended study of the duality of dwelling and adventure; of who goes off to seek his fortune and who stays behind at home. It might well be expected that adventure, with all its associations with fortune-seeking, exploration and exploitation, is defined by Cartesian mastery and possession, and that the Master, as his title suggests, engages unashamedly with this self-centred way of life. Indeed, that is the way the character is presented for the first half of the novel; a rapacious, ruthless man who sets his own independence and life above everything else. By this analysis, the brother that stays at home is the less guilty of the two; long-suffering, taking care of his lands and family. But it is difficult to see how the house of Durrisdeer is a dwelling place, its bulk and grandeur failing to reflect the schismed family living under its roof; a 'conjoint abstraction of the family itself', an 'airy nothing' which symbolises familial unity whilst masking fratricidal division and deceit.[91] The family's emigration to North America is the final judgement on dwelling at Durrisdeer, 'their faces [set] towards a barbarous country'. For MacKellar, 'It seemed that we who remained at home were the true exiles . . . all that made my country native, its air good to me, and its language welcome, had gone forth and was far over the sea with my old masters'.[92] The locality and its associations are disrupted, the familiar memories stimulating the opposite of the *flâneur*'s pleasure in the unfamiliar resonances of place. The dwelling, deserted by its inhabitants, is a ghostly, equivocal place, appealing to a certain melancholic romance and nothing more.

The ultimate destination or 'home', in *The Master of Ballantrae*, is the wilderness and the only act of 'dwelling' possible in that environment is to die there; all paths lead to the metaphorical fall of the house, and brotherly unity is only possible in the grave. Henry Durie's plot to kill his brother leads his imagination to wander after the Master through the Adirondack forests; his mind 'dwelled almost wholly in the Wilderness, following that party with whose deeds he had so much concern. He continually conjured up their camps and progresses, the fashion of the country . . . And it is the less wonder if the scene of his meditations began to draw him bodily'.[93] Neither dwelling nor travelling can offer any solace in this novel; human community is again and again denied, and any sense of connection with the natural world is rooted in the past of childhood, not in the tragic business of adult life. The obsession with control, with 'mastery' – the business of 'war and property' – is revealed as destructive, a negation of life, and its pursuit leads to tragic ends.

While Stevenson's own adventures in North America were not quite the alienating vision portrayed in *The Master of Ballantrae*, nevertheless at times they evoked a very powerful sense of duality. For the good of his health, following his marriage to Fanny Osbourne in 1880, and unable to afford a stay at a proper hilltop sanatorium, Stevenson and his new family (Fanny, her son Lloyd and their pet dog) took up temporary residence in an abandoned cabin in a derelict silver mine high up in the Californian mountains. The life he encountered at the 'frontier' he believed Mount Helena to represent seemed almost unreal, 'a land of stage-drivers and highwaymen; a land, in that sense, like England a hundred years ago'.[94] Despite the somewhat surreal juxtaposition of telegraph poles and newspapers alongside the sequoia and grizzly bears, Stevenson's North American travels evoke a parallel sense of the ancient, trackless nature of the landscape, an antediluvian landscape where 'the silence of nature reigns in a great measure unbroken'.[95] His feeling that the human is somehow out of place in this wilderness extends to the peculiar honeymoon habitation of the newly-wed Stevensons. Their temporary home was certainly not the picturesque idyll 'humming with bees and nested in by songbirds' which Stevenson had let himself imagine, and was instead a 'glimpse of devastation', with 'mountain and house and all the old tools of industry . . . all alike, rusty and downfalling'.[96] Only part of the cabin was habitable; the rest was in ruins, and in the process of being reclaimed by the mountain's vigorous plant life and crumbling geology. Stevenson finds himself amused but also little discomforted by the cabin's schismed identity:

> Within, it had the look of habitation, the human look. You had only to go into the third room, which we did not use, and see its stones, its sifting earth, its tumbled litter; and then return to our lodging, with the beds made, the plates on the rack, the pail of bright water behind the door, the stove crackling in a corner, and perhaps the table roughly laid against a meal, – and man's order, the little clean spots that he creates to dwell in, were at once contrasted with the rich passivity of nature. And yet our house was everywhere so wrecked and shattered, the air came and went so freely, the sun found so many portholes, the golden outdoor glow shone in so many open chinks, that we enjoyed, at the same time, some of the comforts of a roof and much of the gaiety and brightness of al fresco life.[97]

The literally shattered house calls into question the possibility of making a home in this wilderness; the ridiculous image of the clean dinner plates poised on the edge of the mountain chasm touches Stevenson with a little whimsical humour and a sense of almost childlike freedom, but there remains the impression of the Silverado mine's violation of a somehow sacred, inhospitable and unknowable world. Deserted by fortune-seekers, the industrial ruins were just another example of human intrusion in the ancient wilderness – 'this stir of change and these perpetual echoes of the moving footfall'.[98] Notably, the Stevensons did not last long in their new home; the six days' experiment in Silverado was a 'miserable time' which left Stevenson 'homesick for Europe' and Fanny and Lloyd with a case of diphtheria.[99]

John Muir also recognised the environmental impact of human settlement, writing of the Sierra's natural meadows 'ploughed and pastured out of existence' and forests 'hacked and trampled' in his campaign for wilderness protection.[100] However, Muir's description of human settlers, figured in strikingly organic imagery, reinforces his fundamental belief that 'going to the mountains is going home', blurring the distinction between the human and the non-human worlds:

> Yankee families from adjacent states, who had come drifting indefinitely westward in covered wagons, seeking their fortunes like winged seeds; all alike striking root and gripping the glacial drift soil as naturally as oak and hickory trees; happy and hopeful, establishing homes . . .[101]

Muir's work might be seen as a sort of eco-romance, in contrast to Stevenson's ironic observation of North American settlers, as if in a desperate, almost comical race, 'running forth' into the wilderness with their 'household gods'. Like Muir, Stevenson acknowledges the often ruinous effects of this race for land and resources on the native residents of the supposedly 'untouched' wilderness territory, where 'redwoods and redskins, the two noblest indigenous living things, alike condemned'.[102] This anxiety extends to the South Seas, where Stevenson fears the 'extinction of the Polynesian Islanders by our shabby civilisation'.[103] For Stevenson, Jenni Calder suggests, this is a particularly Scottish sensitivity: 'his sensibility towards this loss was a direct result of his engagement with his own cultural origins'.[104]

Muir's optimistic view of North American settlement relates to his sense of attunement between mind, body and nature, an antidote to the questions of mastery and possession. Out in the wild landscape, 'you lose consciousness of your own separate existence: you blend with the landscape, and become part and parcel of nature'.[105] Elsewhere he relates this, with a little humour, to his Scottish ancestry, an imaginative identification of the body and personal psychology with elements drawn from the natural world:

> Some of my grandfathers . . . must have been born on a muirland, for there is heather in me, and tinctures of bog juices, that . . . oozing through all my veins, impel me unhaltingly through endless glacier meadows, seemingly the deeper and danker the better.[106]

In similar vein, Whitman's democratic inclusiveness extends to a charmingly grotesque resolution of self and other, where 'I find I incorporate gneiss, coal, long-threaded moss, fruits, grains, esculent roots, | And am stucco'd with quadrupeds and birds all over'.[107] Whitman's aesthetic is most assuredly not one of Cartesian dualism, and indeed his efforts on behalf of a democratic art seek to dismantle such hierarchies, to foster a sense of inclusiveness, even hybridity – but never mastery.

Muir's sense of integration with the landscape derives in part from North American transcendental philosophy, which 'gave forceful expression to older ideas about the presence of divinity in the natural world'.[108] But this resolution of Cartesian duality also has a distinctively Scottish tinge. Muir travelled self-consciously light on his nature walks; his knapsack contained nothing more than 'a comb, brush, towel, soap, a change of under-clothing, a copy of Burns's poems, Milton's *Paradise Lost*, and a small New Testament'.[109] Burns, it seems, was an important influence, and there are shades of his 'To a Mouse' sense of universality in most of Muir's work. Muir repeatedly refers to the creatures he encounters on his travels as 'fellow mortals'; no doubt the concept of 'nature's social union' appealed to the environmentalist's sense of interconnection and interdependence.[110] Indeed, his recollection of discovering a mouse's nest in *The Story of My Boyhood and Youth* is reminiscent of Burns's similar poetic encounter. The parallels between the lives of humans and animals, which Burns highlights with his own form of imaginative sympathy, appeals to Muir, just as Burns's democratic sensibility appealed to Whitman, who remarked that Burns's 'concrete, human points of view' made him 'very close to the earth', producing poetry remarkable for its 'boldness' and 'rawness'.[111] Stevenson, too, values Burns's 'easy, racy, graphic, and forcible' Scots verses, in comparison to the 'ultra-academical timidity' employed by English language writers.[112] Seeking to dismantle the hierarchical mode of thinking that places 'Lord Man' at the top of the tree, apart from and superior to the natural world, Muir instead posits an ecological view, a model of interdependence in which humans appear as a part of the whole, no more necessary or unnecessary than a bear or a bacterium.

> Why should man value himself as more than a small part of the one great unit of creation? And what creature of all that the Lord has taken the pains to make is not essential to the completeness of that unit – the cosmos? The universe would be incomplete without man; but it would also be incomplete without the smallest transmicroscopic creature that dwells beyond our conceitful eyes and knowledge.[113]

This is closer to the inclusiveness celebrated by Whitman, who highlights the interconnection of all things, and hints at the properties of 'lower' life-forms which humans share through their evolutionary heritage: 'I believe a leaf of grass is no less than the journey-work of the stars, | And the pismire is equally perfect, and a grain of sand, and the egg | of the wren'.[114] For Whitman as for Stevenson, such acceptance is made possible by a particular kind of philosophy – not unrelated to the adventure impulse – where, through curiosity, attentiveness and acceptance, one can become attuned to 'the warm and palpitating facts of life'.

Open roads

There is something of this philosophy of acceptance which runs throughout Stevenson's work, and is theorised in his essay on 'Walking Tours':

> We are in such a haste to be doing, to be writing, to be gathering gear, to make our voice audible a moment in the derisive silence of eternity, that we forget that one thing, of which these are but the part – namely, to live . . . To sit still and contemplate, – to remember the faces of women without desire, to be pleased by the great deeds of men without envy, to be everything and everywhere in sympathy, and yet content to remain where and what you are – is not this to know both wisdom and virtue, and to dwell with happiness?[115]

Certainly, for Stevenson, walking, and rural walks in particular, seem to bring out the best in people. The pleasant sensations at the end of the walker's day bring him into a sense of community with the people he meets. Stevenson's travels in France and North America can be read as a sort of rural *flânerie*, although he was never quite the 'contemptive' city spectator that Benjamin theorises; instead, his irony and objectivity were infused with a good dose of sympathetic humour, and an inclusiveness which parallels Whitman's approach, whose 'Song of the Open Road' is a poem of spectatorship as well as of inclusion. Optimistic, as one might expect, Whitman sets out on his journey 'Afoot and light-hearted . . . Healthy, free, the world before me', keen to emphasise the democratic possibilities of the road: 'You road I enter upon and look around, I believe you are not all that is here, | I believe that much unseen is also here | Here the profound lesson of reception, nor preference nor denial'.[116] Stevenson liked this poem, and quoted it in his own essay on 'Roads', speaking of the friendliness and cheerfulness of roadside travel, 'the great network of ways that binds all life together from the hill-farm to the city'.[117] This is an image which features in 'Will o' the Mill', but it also anticipates the Scottish ecological thinker Patrick Geddes's 1909 'Valley Section', a geographical model, which, albeit tracing the path of a river rather than a road, affirms the organic interconnection of city and countryside, from 'pastoral hillsides . . . scattered arable crofts and sparsely dotted hamlets' to the larger market towns and finally, the 'great manufacturing city'.[118]

This awareness of roads as the ties that 'bind' together the disparate elements of life is certainly attuned to the ecological perspective, with its emphasis on networks and interrelationships. As Rebecca Solnit argues:

> Walking focuses not on the boundary lines of ownership that break the land into pieces but on the paths that function as a kind of circulatory system connecting the whole organism. Walking is, in this way, the antithesis of owning. It postulates a mobile, empty-handed, shareable experience of the land.[119]

A similar sense is given by Mikhail Bakhtin's discussion of the chronotopic significance of the road:

> The road is a particularly good place for random encounters. On the road . . . the spatial and temporal paths of the most varied people – representatives of all social classes, estates, religions, nationalities, ages – intersect at one spatial and temporal point. People who are normally kept separate by social and spatial distance can accidentally meet; any contrast may crop up, the most various fates may collide and interweave with one another. On the road the spatial and temporal series defining human fates and lives combine with one another in distinctive ways, even as they become more complex and more concrete by the collapse of social distances.[120]

This idea is vital, if we are to imagine a valid mobile counterpart to the rooted 'dwelling' posited by the likes of Thoreau and Heidegger. Both Stevenson and Whitman seem to skirt around the possibilities of the road-as-chronotope:

> You paths worn in the irregular hollows by the roadsides!
> I believe you are latent with unseen existences, you are so dear to me
> . . .
>
> From all that has touch'd you I believe you have imparted to
>   yourselves, and would impart the same secretly to me,
> From the living and the dead you have peopled your impassive
>   surfaces, and the spirits thereof would be evident and
>   amicable with me.[121]

The country road, 'latent with unseen existences', retains a romantic allure, a sort of magnetism which is similar to that experienced by the *flâneur*, for whom 'every street is precipitous', a 'double ground' leading 'downward . . . into a past that can be all the more spellbinding because it is not his own, not private'.[122] The communal past of the beaten path underlies the pleasure of the *flâneur*'s wanderings. There is, for Stevenson's strolling countryside observer and Benjamin's obsessive city-walker, a sort of romance available in the road beneath one's feet. This duality may seem to be the product of urban modernity, but it is ultimately a form of sensation related to the acknowledgement of 'those invisible ones of the days gone by' whose memory is embedded in the landscape. Part of the attraction the *flâneur* feels for the streets is the opportunity to contemplate the lives which intersect chronotopically with his own. The impossibility of attaining that knowledge in an unfamiliar place does not necessarily suggest alienation, but can facilitate an imagined community of person, place and memory. Whitman is convinced that the 'unseen existences' of the road are interconnected with his own existence, the road serving as a chronotopic conduit for his imagination. By contrast, Thoreau entertains a certain revulsion at this idea, noting 'how little does the memory of these human inhabitants enhance the beauty of the landscape . . . Deliver me from a city built on the site of a more ancient city, whose materials are ruins, whose gardens cemeteries. The soil is blanched and accursed there'.[123]

One might recall here Stevenson's interest in the spontaneous making of paths by generations of wayfinders through a particular landscape. Ecological thought suggests that, through wayfinding, 'places enfold the passage of time: they are neither of the past, present or future but all three rolled into one':

> Endlessly generated through the comings and goings of their inhabitants, they figure not as locations in space but as specific vortices in a current of movement, of innumerable journeys actually made . . . wayfinding might be understood not as following a course from one spatial location to another, but as a movement in time, more akin to playing music or storytelling than reading a map.[124]

Rejecting novels like *The Master of Ballantrae* as 'box[es] of tricks', Kenneth White finds in Stevenson's work a 'yearning for something other and greater than just spinning a yarn', and contends that it is only in non-fiction works such as *Travels with a Donkey in the Cevennes* (1879), where he takes the 'high line', an 'intellectual way' in which 'history, culture, religion . . . [are] finally transcended'.[125] While recognising the evident affinities between White's intellectual nomadism and Stevenson's walking theories, I would suggest that storytelling is, for Stevenson, part of that 'something other and greater', a way of being-in-the-world.[126] As Calder and others have noted, Stevenson 'never doubted the value of story-telling', using the telling of tales as a means of creating a bond of friendship, even kinship, between the familiar and the foreign, Scotland and the South Seas.[127] In this sense, Walter Benjamin is right to assert Stevenson's kinship with his figure of the Storyteller, and this inherent duality of rootedness and roaming, 'embodied in the resident tiller of the soil' and in 'the trading seaman'.[128] One might suggest that travel is, for Stevenson and Muir alike, the unfolding of a story, an outlook which offers the possibility of 'stravaiging and staying'. Through essay and story, relating his globe-trotting life and continual meditations on home and homeland, Stevenson suggested the possibility of a sensitive, responsible global consciousness, just as Muir's travel books asserted 'the possibility of [Nature] actually including urbanised 'denatured' readers who lived in cities'.[129] Such ideas are also central to the mode of Scottish ecological thought developed by Patrick Geddes, discussed in the next chapter, which focused on the synthesis of the 'cosmic and regional', together with the inter-war writings of Hugh MacDiarmid, Lewis Grassic Gibbon and other regionally-distinct writers seeking to reconcile the local and the global, the human with the natural world.[130]

Notes

1. Robert Louis Stevenson, 'The Foreigner at Home', *Memories and Portraits* (London: Chatto and Windus, 1904), p. 2.
2. John Muir, *A Thousand Mile Walk to the Gulf*, in Terry Gifford (ed.), *The Eight Wilderness Discovery Books* (London: Diadem Books, 1992), pp. 171–2.
3. Ibid., p. 119.
4. Muir, *A Thousand Mile Walk to the Gulf*, p. 156.
5. John Muir, *The Story of my Boyhood and Youth*, in *The Eight Wilderness Discovery Books*, p. 41.
6. Robert Louis Stevenson, 'Letter 2577 To Sidney Colvin' (Vailima, May 1893), Bradford A. Booth and Ernest Mehew (eds), in *The Letters of Robert Louis Stevenson*, vol. 8, 8 vols (New Haven, CT: Yale University Press, 1995), p. 91.
7. Stevenson, 'Letter 2577 to Sidney Colvin' (Vailima, May 1893), pp. 91–2.
8. Robert Louis Stevenson, *The Silverado Squatters*, in *The Works of Robert Louis Stevenson*, vol. 18, Tusitala Edition (London: William Heinemann Ltd, 1924), p. 190.
9. Robert Louis Stevenson, 'On the Enjoyment of Unpleasant Places', *Essays of Travel* (London: Chatto and Windus, 1912), p. 240.
10. Martin Heidegger, *An Introduction to Metaphysics*, trans. Ralph Manheim (New Haven, CT: Yale University Press, 1959), pp. 150–1.
11. Jonathan Bate, *The Song of the Earth* (London: Picador, 2001), pp. 14–20.
12. Robert Louis Stevenson, Letter to Sidney Colvin (Honolulu, June 1889), *Selected Letters of Robert Louis Stevenson*, p. 404.
13. Robert Louis Stevenson, *The Ebb-Tide*, in *Tales of the South Seas* (Edinburgh: Canongate, 1996), p. 7.
14. Robert Louis Stevenson, *The Master of Ballantrae*, in *The Scottish Novels* (Edinburgh: Canongate, 1999), p. 52.
15. Bate, *The Song of the Earth*, p. 18.
16. Jonathan Bate, 'Poetry and Biodiversity', in Richard Kerridge and Neil Sammells (eds), *Writing the Environment: Ecocriticism and Literature* (London: Zed Books, 1998), p. 57.
17. Robert Louis Stevenson, *Travels with a Donkey in the Cevennes*, in *The Works of Robert Louis Stevenson*, vol. I (Chatto and Windus: London, 1911), p. 179.
18. William Hazlitt, 'On Going A Journey', in George Goodchild (ed.), *The Lore of the Wanderer: An Open-Air Anthology* (London: J. M. Dent and Sons, 1914), p. 49.
19. Stevenson, 'The Foreigner at Home', p. 23.
20. Kenneth White, *The Wanderer and His Charts* (Edinburgh: Polygon, 2004), p. 165.
21. Robert Louis Stevenson, 'Walt Whitman', *Familiar Studies of Men and Books* (London: Chatto and Windus, 1920), pp. 63–88; p. 69.
22. Robert Louis Stevenson, 'Henry David Thoreau', pp. 89–117.
23. Wendy R. Katz, 'Whitman and Thoreau as Literary Stowaways in

Stevenson's American Writings', in Richard Ambrosini and Richard Dury (eds), *Robert Louis Stevenson: Writer of Boundaries* (Madison, WI: University of Wisconsin Press, 2006), pp. 327–37.
24. Daniel G. Payne, *Voices in the Wilderness: American Nature Writing and Environmental Politics* (Hanover, NH: University Press of New England, 1996), pp. 29–54.
25. Henry David Thoreau, *Walden or, Life in the Woods and 'On the Duty of Civil Disobedience'* (New York: The New American Library, 1960), p. 66.
26. Gillian Brown, *Domestic Individualism: Imagining Self in Nineteenth Century America* (Berkeley: University of California Press, 1992), p. 105.
27. Thoreau, *Walden*, p. 36.
28. Gaston Bachelard, *The Poetics of Space*, trans. Maria Jolas (Boston: Beacon Press, 1994), pp. 30–1.
29. Thoreau, *Walden*, p. 62.
30. Ibid. pp. 36–7.
31. Robert Louis Stevenson, *Records of a Family of Engineers*, in *The Works of Robert Louis Stevenson*, vol. 19, Tusitala Edition (London: William Heinemann Ltd, 1924), p. 211.
32. Robert Louis Stevenson, 'Roads', *Essays of Travel* (London: Chatto and Windus, 1916), p. 216.
33. Martin Heidegger, 'Building, Dwelling, Thinking' in *Poetry, Language Thought*, Trans. Albert Hofstadter (New York: Harper Colophon Books, 1971), and Vincent Vycinas, *Earth and Gods: An Introduction to the Philosophy of Martin Heidegger* (The Hague: Martinus Nijhoff, 1969), p. 16.
34. Stevenson, 'Roads', p. 216.
35. Tim Ingold, *The Perception of the Environment: Essays in Livelihood, Dwelling and Skill* (London: Routledge, 2000), p. 58.
36. See George Pattison, *The Later Heidegger* (London: Routledge, 2000), p. 51.
37. Robert Louis Stevenson, 'Henry David Thoreau: Character and Opinions', *Familiar Studies of Men and Books* (London: Chatto and Windus, 1920), p. 105.
38. Stevenson, *The Silverado Squatters*, pp. 210–11.
39. John Muir, *The Wilderness World of John Muir: A Selection from his Collected Works*, ed. Edwin Way Teale (Boston: Houghton Mifflin Books, 2001), p. 313.
40. Robert Louis Stevenson, 'Walt Whitman', *Familiar Studies of Men and Books* (London: Chatto and Windus, 1920), p. 66.
41. Stevenson, 'Henry David Thoreau', p. 96.
42. Stevenson, *The Silverado Squatters*, p. 210.
43. Stevenson, 'Henry David Thoreau', p. 115.
44. Walt Whitman, in Sculley Bradley and Harold W. Blodgett (eds), *Leaves of Grass* (New York: W.W. Norton and Co., 1973), pp. 184–95.
45. Whitman, *Leaves of Grass*, pp. 28–89; p. 52.
46. Walt Whitman, 'Anonymous Self-Review', in Milton Hindu (ed.), *Walt Whitman: The Critical Heritage* (London: Routledge and Kegan Paul, 1971), p. 43.
47. Walt Whitman, 'A Word about Tennyson', in Floyd Stovall (ed.), *Prose Works 1892. Collected and Other Prose*, vol. II, 2 vols (New York: New York University Press, 1964), pp. 568–72; p. 568.

48. Stevenson, 'Walt Whitman', pp. 69–70.
49. Stevenson, *Travels with a Donkey*, p. 179.
50. Katz, p. 331; Frank McLynn, *Robert Louis Stevenson: A Biography* (London: Pimlico, 1995), p. 165.
51. Whitman, *Leaves of Grass*, p. 711.
52. Walter Benjamin, *Charles Baudelaire: A Lyric Poet in an Era of High Capitalism*, Trans. Harry Zohn (London: Verso Publications, 1983), p. 36.
53. Walter Benjamin, *Charles Baudelaire: A Lyric Poet in an Era of High Capitalism*, Trans. Harry Zohn (London: Verso Editions, 1983), p. 61.
54. Robert Louis Stevenson, 'An Apology for Idlers', *Virginibus Puerisque, and other papers* (London: Chatto and Windus, 1920), pp. 71–82; p. 73.
55. Robert Louis Stevenson, 'My Brain Swims Empty and Light', in Roger C. Lewis (ed.), *The Collected Poems* (Edinburgh: Edinburgh University Press, 2003), p. 260.
56. Charles Baudelaire, quoted in Walter Benjamin and Rolf Tiedemann (ed.), *The Arcades Project*, Trans. Howard Eiland and Kevin McLaughlin (Cambridge, MA: The Belknap Press of Harvard University Press, 2002), p. 443.
57. Benjamin, *The Arcades Project*, p. 417.
58. Robert Louis Stevenson, 'Edinburgh: Picturesque Notes', *The Works of Robert Louis Stevenson*, vol. 1, Swanston Edition, 25 vols (London: Chatto and Windus, 1911), p. 283.
59. Robert Louis Stevenson, *The Strange Case of Dr Jekyll and Mr Hyde* and *Weir of Hermiston* (Oxford: Oxford University Press, 2003), p. 16.
60. Stevenson, *Records of a Family of Engineers*, p. 187.
61. Robert Louis Stevenson, 'The Amateur Emigrant', *The Works of Robert Louis Stevenson*, vol. 2, Swanston Edition, 25 vols (London: Chatto and Windus, 1911), p. 81.
62. Whitman, *Leaves of Grass*, pp. 15–28; p. 16.
63. Stevenson, *The Silverado Squatters*, p. 161.
64. Benjamin, *Charles Baudelaire*, p. 42.
65. Ibid., p. 61.
66. Benjamin, *The Arcades Project*, p. 806.
67. Robert Louis Stevenson, *In the South Seas* (London: Penguin, 1998), p. 220; p. 232.
68. Hugh MacDiarmid, 'On a Raised Beach', in Michael Grieve and W.R. Aitken (eds), *Complete Poems*, Vol. I (London: Martin, Brian and O'Keefe, 1993–1994), pp. 422–33.
69. Stevenson, 'An Apology for Idlers', p. 77.
70. Jean-Paul Sartre, *Basic Writings*, in Stephen Priest (ed.) (London: Routledge, 2001), p. 208.
71. Stevenson, 'An Apology for Idlers', p. 75.
72. Benjamin, *The Arcades Project*, p. 417.
73. Stevenson, 'Roads', p. 219.
74. Robert Louis Stevenson, 'Will o' the Mill', in Roderick Watson (ed.), *Tales of Adventure* (Edinburgh: Canongate Books, 1997), pp. 13–14.
75. Ibid., p. 44.
76. Robert Louis Stevenson, 'A Gossip on Romance', *Memories and Portraits* (London: Chatto and Windus, 1917), p. 153.

77. Stevenson, 'Will o' the Mill', p. 14.
78. Ibid., p. 14.
79. Walter Benjamin, 'The Storyteller: Reflections on the Works of Nikolai Leskov', *Illuminations* (London: Pimlico, 1999), p. 85.
80. Michel Serres, cited in Bate, *The Song of the Earth*, p. 99.
81. Robert Louis Stevenson, 'The Genesis of The Master of Ballantrae', *Essays in the Art of Writing* (London: Chatto and Windus, 1905), pp. 135–9.
82. Stevenson, *The Master of Ballantrae*, p. xv.
83. Ibid., p. xv.
84. Ibid., p. 51.
85. Ibid., p. 50; James Thomson, *The City of Dreadful Night* (Edinburgh: Canongate Books, 1993), pp. 28–30.
86. Stevenson, *The Master of Ballantrae*, p. 52.
87. John Muir, cited in Roderick Frazier Nash, *Wilderness and the American Mind*, 4th edn (New Haven, CT: Yale University Press, 2001), p. 128.
88. Stevenson, *The Master of Ballantrae*, p. 154.
89. Julia Reid, *Robert Louis Stevenson, Science and the Fin de Siecle* (London: Palgrave Macmillan, 2006), p. 11.
90. Ibid., p. 132; Douglas Gifford, 'Stevenson and Scottish Fiction: The Importance of The Master of Ballantrae', in Jenni Calder (ed.), *Stevenson and Victorian Scotland* (Edinburgh: Edinburgh University Press, 1981), p. 84.
91. Stevenson, *The Master of Ballantrae*, p. 102.
92. Ibid., p. 144.
93. Ibid., p. 191.
94. Stevenson, *The Silverado Squatters*, p. 159.
95. Ibid., p. 156.
96. Ibid., p. 187.
97. Ibid., p. 236.
98. Ibid., p. 171.
99. Stevenson, quoted in McLynn, p. 177.
100. John Muir, 'Our National Parks', *The Eight Wilderness Discovery Books*, pp. 460–1.
101. John Muir, 'The Story of My Boyhood and Youth', p. 89.
102. Stevenson, *The Silverado Squatters*, p. 144.
103. Quoted in A. Grove Day, 'Introduction' to Robert Louis Stevenson, *Travels in Hawaii* (Honolulu: University of Hawaii Press, 1991), p. xxxiv.
104. Jenni Calder, 'Introduction' to Robert Louis Stevenson, *Tales of the South Seas*, p. xv.
105. Muir, *A Thousand Mile Walk to the Gulf*, p. 183.
106. John Muir, cited in William Frederic Bade in *The Life and Letters of John Muir*, in Terry Gifford (ed.), *John Muir: His Life and Letters and Other Writings* (Seattle: Mountaineers Books, and London: Baton Wicks, 1996), p. 20.
107. Whitman, 'Song of Myself', *Leaves of Grass*, p. 59.
108. Nash, p. 86.
109. Muir, *A Thousand Mile Walk to the Gulf*, p. 124.
110. See Robert Burns, 'To A Mouse', in Robert Crawford and Mick Imlah (eds), *The New Penguin Book of Scottish Verse* (London: Allen Lane / The Penguin Press, 2000), p. 281.

111. Walt Whitman, 'Robert Burns as Poet and Person', in Floyd Stovall (ed.), *Prose Works 1892: Collected and Other Prose*, vol. 2 (New York: New York University Press, 1964), pp. 558–68.
112. Robert Louis Stevenson, 'Some Aspects of Robert Burns', *Familiar Studies of Men and Books*, p. 56.
113. Muir, *A Thousand Mile Walk to the Gulf*, p. 160.
114. Whitman, *Leaves of Grass*, p. 59.
115. Robert Louis Stevenson, 'Walking Tours', *Virginibus Puerisque* (London: Chatto and Windus, 1901), pp. 259–60.
116. Whitman, *Leaves of Grass*, pp. 149–50.
117. Stevenson, 'Roads', p. 216.
118. Patrick Geddes, quoted in Volker M. Welter, *Biopolis: Patrick Geddes and the City of Life* (Cambridge, MA: MIT Press, 2002), p. 60.
119. Rebecca Solnit, *Wanderlust: A History of Walking* (London: Penguin Books, 2000), p. 162.
120. Mikhail Bakhtin, 'Forms of Time and of the Chronotope in the Novel', in Michael Holquist (ed.), *The Dialogic Imagination*, trans. Caryl Emerson and Michael Holquist (Austin: University of Texas Press, 1981), p. 243.
121. Whitman, *Leaves of Grass*, p. 150.
122. Benjamin, *The Arcades Project*, p. 416.
123. Thoreau, *Walden*, p. 177.
124. Ingold, p. 238.
125. White, p. 84; p. 91.
126. Ibid., p. 84.
127. Jenni Calder, 'Introduction', *Stevenson and Victorian Scotland* (Edinburgh: Edinburgh University Press, 1981), p. 9.
128. Benjamin, 'The Storyteller', p. 84.
129. Terry Gifford, 'Introduction' to John Muir, *The Eight Wilderness Discovery Books*, p. 18.
130. Patrick Geddes, 'Nature Study and Geographical Education', *Scottish Geographical Magazine*, vol. XIX (1903), pp. 525–36; p. 526.

Chapter 3

Local and Global Outlooks

Hugh MacDiarmid's earth lyrics

Hugh MacDiarmid argued in the 1920s that the Scots vocabulary he had unearthed by reading Jamieson's *Etymological Dictionary of the Scottish Language* constituted a valuable 'unutilized mass of observation' which was a 'vast storehouse of just the very peculiar and subtle effects which modern European literature in general is assiduously seeking'.[1] The crucial features of this vocabulary, for MacDiarmid, were precisely what had consigned it to obscurity: its roots in the Scottish rural environment, and its ability to describe and facilitate the relationships of rural people to that environment. MacDiarmid writes that the observational power implicit in the Scottish vernacular was 'made by minds whose attitudes to experience and whose speculative and imaginative tendencies were quite different from any possible to Englishmen and Anglicized Scots today'.[2] The implication here is that it is possible to get back to the psychological 'roots' of what MacDiarmid views as authentically Scottish communities through linguistic revival. His early lyrics, such as 'The Watergaw', which parallels an image of a shivery, luminous rainbow with the 'last wild look' of a dying man, demonstrate the potential of rural Scots vocabulary for both precise description and enigmatic complexity.[3] The closing lines of 'The Watergaw' are ambiguous – we do not, as W. N. Herbert notes, entirely understand the connection made between the dying look and the rainbow's 'chitterin' licht' – yet the image itself is very precise; the rainbow appears at a specific point in the season and a particular environmental condition, 'Ae weet forenicht i' the yow-trummle' – which MacDiarmid translates as 'One wet afternoon (or early evening) in the cold weather in July after the sheep-shearing'.[4] The often minutely specific meanings of these Scots words are matched by their difficulty of translation, since some of the vernacular vocabulary employed in the lyrics had developed to represent a rural environment and a way of life which was, by the time MacDiarmid was writing, largely obsolete, or at least unknown to the urban majority.

By the 1920s, traditional rural communities and industries had been dissolving for some time, largely in response to economic circumstances, combined with the growth of machine-age solutions for agricultural processes, such as tractors and later, combine-harvesters, in place of ploughing with horses or 'stooking' (bundling the harvest into sheaves) by hand. By the turn of the twentieth century, out of a total population of approximately 4.4 million, 'just under two hundred thousand people [were left] on the farms of Scotland'.[5] While novelists such as Lewis Grassic Gibbon, Neil Gunn and Nan Shepherd were to portray these dramatic changes in their regional fiction of the 1930s, MacDiarmid hoped to capitalise on the discrepancy between rural language and urban experience in his own writing from the 1920s onwards, as part of a project explicitly aligned with the work of Modernists like James Joyce, and utilising the latest cultural theories to emerge from continental thought. In attempting to revive a vivid, if often lapsed, vocabulary of rural Scots, MacDiarmid was bringing some aspects of contemporary psychological and linguistic theory into play, arguing in 1923 that 'old words, now obsolete or obsolescent, often retain an unexhausted evolutionary momentum'.[6]

The idea that the folk-memory of a people rooted to the land could persist in the words and phrases resurrected from Jamieson's dictionary, in order to express the modern experience of their descendents, is surely of a distinctively Jungian cast. Such ideological strategies had been experimented with in Ireland by Yeats's 'Celtic Twilight', which fed into Scottish culture through writers associated with the work of the polymathic environmental thinker, Patrick Geddes, in his 'Celtic renascence' periodical, *The Evergreen*. Such ideas also converged with some of the new models of 'human ecology' being promoted by Geddes and his circle. A major influence for MacDiarmid, Geddes's suggestion of the need for a revival of Scottish culture at the turn of the century formed part of the inspiration for MacDiarmid's efforts towards a 'Scottish Renaissance' in the 1920s.[7] However, MacDiarmid's cultural movement aimed to do away with the limitations of backward-looking provincialism and rural sentimentality which he and his contemporaries believed both the 'Celtic Twilight' and the 'Kailyard' writers had perpetuated in previous decades. MacDiarmid's project was to 'adapt an essentially rustic tongue to the very much more complex requirements of our urban civilisation'.[8]

The success of this scheme is questionable, if the value of MacDiarmid's 'Synthetic Scots' is to be measured by its ability to represent the experience of 'urban civilisation'. It is true that aspects of the city are evoked at times in MacDiarmid's early poetry, as in the crowds of workers released from factories in 'The Dead Liebknecht' from *Penny Wheep* (1926), while the virtuosic *A Drunk Man Looks At The Thistle* (1926) grapples with questions of Scottish national identity which encompass both rural and urban Scotland – although the poem's narrator, the drunk man himself, is sprawled on a hillside covered in bracken and heather, gazing at a thistle and the moon. Judging from the lyrics of *Sangschaw* (1925) and *Penny Wheep*, it seems MacDiarmid's definition of the 'complex requirements of our urban civilization' extends beyond the party political sphere, or the call for representations of machine age Scotland which MacDiarmid himself demanded of the Scottish Renaissance movement. The 'keckle and bouk' of MacDiarmid's hens in poems like 'Country Life' or 'Farmer's Death' might appear to have little in common with the modern European (and largely metropolitan) intellectual thought he engaged with in avant-garde periodicals such *The Modern Scot*. Many of these early lyrics are built around scenes of rural life and the phenomena of the natural world, incorporating material derived from the Scottish ballad tradition, or vivid sketches of countryside scenes. Attempting to tease out this puzzle, Herbert has suggested that some of these lyrics might be read as 'Kailyard-expressionist pieces' and that MacDiarmid's treatment of rural scenes can be attributed to '[his] desire to reconcile the Scotland of the Kailyardist with the Europe of the *New Age*'.[9]

The details of MacDiarmid's life might themselves help to clarify the motivations behind this choice of rural setting and imagery. Scott Lyall notes that MacDiarmid's move to Shetland in the 1930s saw him 'sailing against the tide of urbanised modernity'.[10] As Robert Crawford has observed, MacDiarmid tended to avoid metropolitan centres, opting instead to live in provincial towns like Langholm and Montrose, or remote rural locales, such as Whalsay in the Shetland Isles. Crawford contends that, far from preventing MacDiarmid from engaging with international politics or Modernism, these provincial locations actually energised his work; through his 'interaction with the minutely local', he 'fused the immediate and vernacular with the transnational and synthetic practices of modernist writing'.[11] Equally, I would argue, MacDiarmid's fascination with Scottish rural life and the natural world is not merely latent Romanticism, but neither is it significant solely as a feature of his nationalist project. In his autobiography, *Lucky Poet* (1943), MacDiarmid explained that he found it 'necessary' to draw on the Scottish landscape in his work and thought because of the new insights to be gleaned from ecological thought:

> Modern ecology has destroyed the delusion which encouraged people to jeer at any suggestion of geographic 'control' and human 'response' to such control . . . today physiology and psychology are agreed that there is a relation, a functional relation, between an organism and its environment.[12]

MacDiarmid is remarkable in that he is one of the very first British literary figures to use the term 'ecology', and probably the earliest Scottish creative writer to consciously and explicitly apply ecological thought to his own work. His familiarity with the concept is likely to have been the result of contact with the Scottish geographer, biologist and town-planner Patrick Geddes, now recognised as a key figure in the development of European ecological thought – being both a student of the Darwinian biologist T. H. Huxley and a collaborator of Ernst Haeckel, the pioneering German botanist who coined the term 'Oekologie' in the 1860s. If it was the case, as MacDiarmid claimed, that in the 1920s and 30s there was 'an extraordinary dearth', in Scottish writing, 'of first-hand observation, intimate knowledge and loving particularity' which 'show[s] a real knowledge of nature', it seems he intended his poetry would fulfil part of that important role – a role which he saw as necessary not only for the reinvigoration of Scottish cultural life but also to fulfil the needs of 'urban civilisation' by offering new outlooks on the relationship amongst individuals, communities and their environments.[13] In this respect, MacDiarmid's project is not unrelated to Kenneth White's call for a 'new grounding', bringing Scottish culture into contact with its physical environment.[14]

A striking characteristic of MacDiarmid's initial poetic output is the frequent appearance of the planet Earth viewed from outer space. We are shown the globe from a variety of viewpoints in these poems; lively yet all too vulnerable in 'The Bonnie Broukit Bairn', the poem which opens MacDiarmid's first collection of lyrics; as a distant point of light in 'The Innumerable Christ'; or cold and eerie in 'The Eemis Stane'. Perhaps MacDiarmid found inspiration for these earth-lyrics through his reading of Charles Murray's 'Gin I Was God', which features a lively description of the 'braw birlin' earth', or the partial visualisations of the globe in some of Thomas Hardy's poetry, such as 'At a Lunar Eclipse' or 'In Vision I Roamed'.[15] Kenneth Buthlay notes that similar cosmological viewpoints are in earlier Russian and German poetry, of which MacDiarmid was no doubt aware.[16] However, this startling outlook on the earth appears to have few direct correspondences with his contemporaries.

In 'Au Clair de la Lune' MacDiarmid offers a glimpse of a fossilised Earth glimmering in space:

> The moonbeams kelter i' the lift,
> An' Earth, the bare auld stane,
> Glitters beneath the seas o' Space
> White as a mammoth's bane.[17]

The chilly Scots vocabulary transmits the eeriness of this transfigured vantage point, an altered perspective in both space and time. This God's-eye view of the world is an outlook which is at once deliberately alienating, eccentric, and yet strikingly complete. The 'kelter' of moonbeams suggests movement, confusion, obscurity – 'kelter' may mean 'to tumble headlong', 'to wriggle, undulate, struggle' or, as a noun, denotes 'a covering, disguise, garment' – whilst 'keethin sicht' indicates either miraculous revelation or the flickering movement of a fish underwater.[18] Making use of the onomatopoeic suggestiveness of the vocabulary itself (as he did later with geological terminology in 'On a Raised Beach'), MacDiarmid's lyric gives the impression of a world of shadows and distortions; however, the solid, stony Earth remains at the core of the poem, providing a focus to this metaphysical scene.[19] In this and other respects it bears a close resemblance to another of MacDiarmid's eerie lyrics, 'The Eemis Stane', itself an evocation of a stony Planet Earth rocking unsteadily on its axis, the 'yowdendrift' of 'eerie memories' distorting the cosmic viewer's sight. MacDiarmid's imagination vaults from scenes of Scottish rural life to other-worldly vistas, swinging into orbit to gain a view of the earth from space, whilst retaining a sense of specific individual experience, embedded in local environments. This swoop from the universal to the particular and *vice-versa* indicates a recognition of what Geddes identified in early twentieth-century geography as a central axis of world-knowledge, with 'two poles of thought, cosmic and regional'.[20] MacDiarmid's poetry speaks of his attempts to integrate these apparently oppositional ways of seeing into his own world-view.

By the end of the 1930s, MacDiarmid was moving on from the lyric to the more 'epic' scale of his 'Mature Art', contending, in a commentary on his poem, 'In Memoriam James Joyce' that:

> Our consciousness is beginning to be planetary. A new tension has been set up between the individual and the universe. It is not new because poets and entire literatures have been lacking in the sense of the vastness of Creation, but new in the response provoked in the writer in relation to his own language and his own environment.[21]

This 'planetary consciousness', MacDiarmid ultimately felt, could only be expressed by an 'epic' poetry, a poetry which celebrates 'diversity in unity' (a favourite MacDiarmid catchphrase) and which can encompass both the universal and the particular.[22] MacDiarmid's ultimate rejection of the lyric form was based on his argument that the short lyric 'cannot reflect the complexities of modern life . . . [and] ignores . . . the enormous new perspective of the sciences'.[23] The lyric form, then, might seem too stylistically constricting, and too anthropocentric for a 'global' poetry, unable to synthesise the 'new perspectives' offered by science, ecology among them. However, in the twenties and early thirties MacDiarmid argued equally strongly for the ability of the lyric to supply such 'new perspectives', a variety of modernist discourse with the potential to facilitate 'Seeing the universe with entirely different eyes'.[24] Paralleling his investigations into the 'potentialities of the Doric . . . in accord with the newest and truest tendencies of human thought', MacDiarmid's adaptive use of the lyric in his early Scots poetry is as crucial to the development of his unique outlook on nature-human relationships as his later 'scientific' poetry.[25] The lyric form, MacDiarmid suggests, can provide the modern poet with 'a new synthesis of consciousness . . . which harmonises with the great discoveries of modern science and modern nescience'.[26]

Indeed, despite limitations of structure and scale, MacDiarmid's Scots lyrics retain a sense of unity and completeness which his 'epic' poetry, often breathless and ragged, does not so easily achieve. MacDiarmid's form of lyrical modernism brought together human psychology and the natural world in new ways. Just as, in the 1920s, 'Synthetic Scots' was the only idiom MacDiarmid felt was capable of representing the complex entanglements of man and environment in the modern world, the compact musicality of the lyric could be harnessed to express the reality of a cairn or the cosmos, as the poet saw fit. MacDiarmid recognised a link between scientific and poetic inquiry early in his career. His short 1922 poem, 'Science and Poetry' reveals the Earth as a planet, this time not the post-apocalyptic vision of 'Au Clair de la Lune' but as a living, yet fragile, world. We see 'All-conscious Earth' swinging in its lonely orbit, an image of unity but also of isolation:

> And all that men are and have
> Is one green-gleaming point of light
> In infinite night.[27]

The lyrics collected in *Sangschaw* and *Penny Wheep* reveal networks of thought, feeling and natural phenomena which convey a sense of synthesis, of 'diversity in unity'. The Scots words allow for complexity, contradiction and ambiguity, enclosed within the formal harmony of the lyric. As Buthlay notes, MacDiarmid's imagery 'combines an eye for the cosmic with the countrified, blunt-spoken quality . . . traditionally associated with Scots speech'.[28] Deploying carefully-selected Scots words for their sound qualities as well as for their condensed meaning, MacDiarmid attempts to achieve an 'othered' perspective – strange words with homely, 'countrified' cadences make for enigmatic and often uncanny poetic effects. In this way, bringing together the homely and the unhomely, the local and the global, within the space of a single lyric, MacDiarmid questions our relationship with the non-human world. Reflecting the beginnings of a 'planetary' consciousness, the knowledge that the Earth is literally 'home', these lyrics contrast this sometimes unsettling global view by drawing on a vivid and intimate sense of the local, a shared heritage of memories, traditions and meanings embedded in the Scottish landscape and mediated by a rediscovered and re-energised Scots vocabulary.

Both 'The Bonnie Broukit Bairn' and 'Empty Vessel', published in *Penny Wheep*, reflect such uncertainties through a continual shifting of emphasis from global to local and vice-versa. These particular lyrics have been interpreted in the past as evidence of MacDiarmid's rejection of metaphysical transcendence, finding in favour of the individual human life against the impassive forces of the universe. Catherine Kerrigan argues that the contrast between the individual human and the cosmos in 'Empty Vessel', a poem which relates an encounter with a girl maddened with grief at the death of her child, is representative of 'the expansiveness of human emotion in the face of a vast and timeless universe'.[29] Indeed, the girl's very earthly sorrow in 'Empty Vessel' is given priority over cosmic forces, the action of the poem taking place beside a cairn – a specifically Scottish, local marker of human existence within the natural environment, a point at which human culture and natural landscape, memory and place, merge. The young mother's song is contrasted with 'wunds wi' worlds tae swing' and her motherly care and attention with the inter-stellar 'licht' enveloping the universe. However, MacDiarmid's evocation of these cosmic elements is also somehow suggestive of motherly care; a baby swung in its mother's arms, a mother bending over an infant in its crib.[30] Equally, as Nancy Gish notes in her commentary on 'The Bonnie Broukit Bairn', the image of the crying earth 'says simply that when it rains you cannot see the stars', but that it also ensures that 'earth becomes suddenly the one solid, defined, and acknowledged reality, carrying with it an undissipated significance' – and a specifically human significance at that.[31] The components of MacDiarmid's Scots lyrics are both specific and non-specific, the elements transcendent yet bound to a kind of locality which can only be made sense of when linked to human experience; the personified Earth brings the cosmos down to an understandable, distinctively local – and colloquial – level.

Patrick Geddes and global ecology

A consciousness of interrelationships between individuals, societies and their environments is at the heart of modern ecology, with the developing idea that the land itself, as the American environmental writer, Aldo Leopold, suggests, 'is a community to which we belong'.[32] Such a sense of networks and interconnection was emerging in the early years of the twentieth century through the efforts of the redefined discipline of geography promoted by MacDiarmid's friend Patrick Geddes in his educational projects and on the pages of the *Scottish Geographical Magazine*. Indeed, it was thanks largely to the efforts of Geddes and his circle that geography had been included in the Scottish school curriculum by the turn of the century, just as he had helped to introduce biology as a school subject in the 1890s. Geography, in Scotland and France in particular, was beginning to move away from its association with exploration and map-making. This movement to redefine geographical practice was reflected not only in scientific debate but also in literary circles. James Leslie Mitchell/Lewis Grassic Gibbon's geographically-themed studies, including his first book, *Hanno, or The Future of Exploration* (1928) and *Nine Against the Unknown* (1934) reflect this changing emphasis, the first pointing towards the future exploration of the cosmic environment (a theme which would be taken up by Edwin Morgan in later decades of the twentieth century), and the second a more jaded view of the adventure impulse, in which the boyish optimism of nineteenth-century writers such as Robert Louis Stevenson is substituted for the post-First World War knowledge that the realities of human endeavour tend to fall short of romance.[33]

Indeed, the perceived affinities between geographic exploration and imperial conquest promoted by the activities of mountaineers, explorers and missionaries in the nineteenth century were, by the early years of the twentieth century, being questioned by environmental scientists. The Scottish geographer A. J. Herbertson remarked that 'imperial patriotism is a middle nineteenth century conception which is too small for this intimately related world of the twentieth century', whilst Geddes commented on the limitations of traditional geographical representation, the 'familiar map of the world' in which a 'shrunken landscape . . . [is] kept in order by its abstract and imaginary lines'.[34] Such views are echoed by modern ecological thinkers such as anthropologist Tim Ingold, who highlights a paradox in modern cartography, such that 'the more it aims to furnish a precise and comprehensive representation of reality, the less true to life this representation appears'.[35] For Ingold as for Geddes, cartography's stance of scientific objectivity elides the significance of lived experience and ecological relationship as ways of comprehending the world. Geddes's frustration with the abstraction of nineteenth-century geography – as well as the sometimes morbid, destructive force of conventional biological science, which he had experienced as a student of T. H. Huxley at the Royal School of Mines in the late 1870s – led him to seek for alternative means of observation and representation. His radically new conception of what the 'science' of geography entailed can be seen from his manuscript notes in preparation for an 'Introductory Course of Geography given at University College Dundee' in 1895, in which he jots down an 'emphasis on sight, emotion, experience', an 'awareness of locality' and a method of observation which incorporates 'odour, taste and memory'.[36]

The new form of geographical study was rapidly recognised as an 'essentially synthetic' discipline, the point at which the various strands of scientific thought met and could be transformed into a more comprehensive view of the world.[37] Such study relied upon acute powers of observation, an aptitude which the ideal geographer shared with the poet or artist. Writing in 1904, Geddes offered a dramatic redefinition of the geographer as a sort of global ecologist, suggesting the sort of 'planetary consciousness' MacDiarmid hoped his poetry could express.

> The geographer's is thus the comprehensive concrete mind, answering to, and supplementing with the needed facts, the philosopher's upon its abstract level. He takes all the various results of the different sciences and reunites them into a series of living and characteristic world-scenes, in which latitude, configuration and relief, rocks and soils, climate and rainfall, flora and fauna, nature races and civilised races, industries and institutions . . . even ideas and ideals – are all expressed as the elements of an intelligible and interacting whole – the dramatic unity of the World and man – say, also of Man in his world.[38]

Geddes is perhaps best known for his pioneering role in town planning and civic studies, with his contribution to civic planning in Israel and India, his theoretical writings on the planning of urban environments, and his plans and proposals for civic improvements at locations throughout the United Kingdom. It is, however, his unique combination of geographical and civic studies, together with his abiding research interests in biology, sociology and culture, which make Geddes such a crucial figure in the development of environmental thought in Scotland and beyond.[39] His diverse array of interests and scholarly friends testify to the synthetic potential of geographic study in early twentieth-century Scotland, while his involvement in the development of environmental science is demonstrated by his engagement with the discourses of 'universal geography' of the late nineteenth and early twentieth centuries. This new geography emphasised ecological relationships, studying how natural landscapes influence human society and settlement, and how human activities in turn modify the environment. Geddes's Edinburgh Summer School, which, had 'By the mid 1890s . . . become a major international cultural event' attracted European intellectuals including Ernst Haeckel, the geographer Elisée Reclus, and the anarchist philosopher Pytor Kropotkin.[40] Reclus, a prominent anarchist thinker and the foremost 'universal' geographer of his time, was the author of *Geographie Universelle*, which first appeared as a series of pamphlets in 1875, preceded by *La Terre* (1868) subtitled, in its English translation, as 'a descriptive history of the phenomena of the life of the globe'. Geddes was thus situated at the hub of a network of thinkers who were exploring new ways of conceptualising human existence in its relationship to the natural world. He stressed the importance of integrating different viewpoints in *The Evergreen*, writing of the essential unity of the arts and the environmental sciences. The naturalist, Geddes claims, does not begin with the study of 'dead anatomy', but 'by wandering deep into the forest and high upon hill; in seeing, in feeling, with hunter and savage, with husbandman and gypsy, with the poet and with the child' – sentiments which seem to echo John Veitch's views in *The Feeling for Nature in Scottish Poetry*.[41]

MacDiarmid and Geddes became friends towards the end of Geddes's life in the late twenties and early thirties, but MacDiarmid had been interested in some aspects of the new environmental sciences even before then. In 1918, under the auspices of the Army Education Scheme, he gave a series of lectures on 'Political and Commercial Geography' and 'Civic and Town Planning' while convalescing in the south of France.[42] In the years before the Great War he had also been involved in research into the 'rural problem' for the Fabian Research Committee on agriculture, claiming to have 'surveyed the whole Scottish aspect of the matter'.[43] He would later comment on his admiration for Geddes's strivings towards synthesis, his blurring of disciplinary boundaries in an attempt to achieve comprehension and insight. In *The Company I've Kept* (1966), MacDiarmid relates Geddes's sometimes meandering trajectory to patterns within his own work, citing Lewis Mumford's observation that Geddes 'practiced synthesis in an age of specialism', and claiming that this was 'the very practice that has been the theme of all my later poetry and work as a teacher and publicist'.[44] He declares his shared interests with Geddes as:

> Form, pattern, configuration, organism, historical filiation, ecological relationship and concepts that work up and down the ladder of the sciences; the aesthetic structure and the social relations are as real as the primary physical qualities that the sciences were once content to isolate.[45]

MacDiarmid's interest in Geddes's version of geography is evident from his article on The Outlook Tower, Geddes's first experimental educational museum in Edinburgh. It was, as MacDiarmid notes:

> designed to aid both citizen and visitor towards a better understanding of Edinburgh, not only as a city with world-wide connections or as primarily capital of Scotland, but as, today not less than in the past, a Burgh central in, and intimately connected with, the life of its Region.[46]

Not only that, it juxtaposed images of the globe itself with this detailed survey of Edinburgh and its region. Geddes's efforts towards new visualisations of the human organism within its environment are in keeping with the experimentation in representations and viewpoints which Modernist poets and writers like MacDiarmid or Joyce were attempting.[47] However, the Outlook Tower is directly representative of Geddes's engagement with the new perspectives fostered by the environmental sciences of biology and geography, combined with perspectives from sociology, philosophy and psychology. The tower, which charts the progression from 'world' (globe) to region (Edinburgh and its environs), reflects Geddesian geography's basic premise of relating the local to the global, where the concept of the region is based on ecological principles. Informed by his reading of Frederic Le Play's sociological writings, Geddes transforms the interconnective model of *Lieulle/Travaille/Famille* to the more locally-appropriate trinity of Place/Work/Folk to indicate the interdependence of geography, economics and culture.[48] This sense of interconnectedness was developed, as Volker Welter has shown, by Geddes's adaptation of ecological principles of plant association developed by botanist Charles Flahault, to the study of human society, enabling him to 'get away from the popular social Darwinist notion of society as a permanent struggle for existence, instead foregrounding cooperation as more important for the evolution of all forms of life'.[49]

Viewing the region as a discrete geographical and a temporal entity, Geddes's outlook offered a remarkably prescient counter-argument to the seemingly 'inevitable' process of metropolitan centralisation and resultant homogenisation of culture. 'The increasing complexity of human affairs,' he writes, 'has enabled the great centres to increase and retain their control; yet their continued advance is also rendering decentralisation, with government of all kinds, increasingly possible'.[50] The roots of regional identities, for Geddes, extend beyond geopolitics; they are instead steeped in a history of ecological relationships between humans and the regional environment – relationships which, significantly, form the basis of urban as well as rural society. Any section of a region, he proposed, represented a specific way in which human beings had related to and lived off the land since the dawn of civilisation, in a series of livelihoods, or 'natural occupations', which related to specific primordial environments, evolving over time into increasingly sophisticated occupations.[51] In this model, primordial hunter transforms, over time, into modern soldier, peasant evolves into banker, and in each modern occupation lies the germ of a primitive 'functional relation' between the human organism and its environment.[52] Similar concepts appear in the work of regional novelists such as Neil Gunn, for whom 'A person's true personality is the archetypal primitive – that of hunter or fisher, maker, searcher, or gazer on bright water'.[53]

Indeed, Geddes's view of the region as locus of both history and geography seems in tune with certain literary manifestations of Jung's theories about archetypes and the collective unconsciousness, or the idea that folk memory is somehow retained by the land itself – viewpoints which, as Douglas Gifford has shown, are important features in the work of both Gunn and Gibbon.[54] Thus, questions of regional survey, mediated through Geddes's environmental schema, were indeed related to some of the currents within Scottish Modernist cultural thought and practice. A regional survey sought to gain a comprehensive view of these interconnecting factors, looking at all the characteristics of the region in synthesis, rather than tackling them separately. The Outlook Tower provided both the opportunity to survey the landscape from a height, but to relate this general view to the particular details of geology, botany, zoology, and the sociological and economic factors which drew town and countryside, individual and community, into a complex web of interrelations – a swoop from the universal to the particular which is also a fundamental characteristic of MacDiarmid's poetry, from the early lyrics to the later 'poetry of facts'.

Perhaps the best example of Geddes's efforts towards a synthesis of these viewpoints is his unrealised plan for a National Institute of Geography (see Figure 1). First outlined in 1902 in the *Scottish Geographical Magazine*, the plan was an audacious one backed by a number of prominent geographers and intellectuals including Elisée Reclus, James Bryce (the mountaineering Liberal MP who campaigned for Scottish national parks) and the geographer A.J. Herbertson. In many ways this plan encapsulates Geddes's way of thinking about the world. Its logically arranged yet puzzlingly diverse layout of themes and ideas, and its provoking juxtaposition of materials and perspectives, could have made the institute into a large-scale version of one of his 'thinking machines', the diagrams which Geddes created in order to condense his socio-geographical methods of thinking and observation into a readily accessible form.[55]

Local and Global Outlooks   89

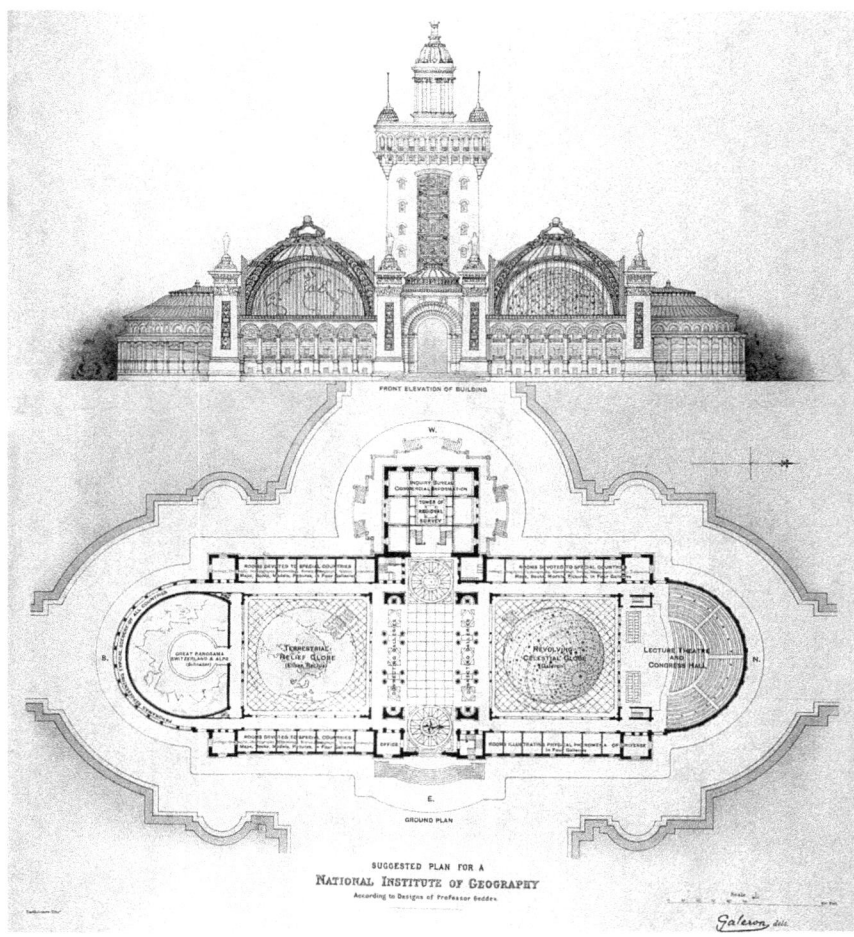

Figure 1   Patrick Geddes and M. Galeron, 'Suggested Plan for a National Institute of Geography', *The Scottish Geographical Magazine*, vol. XVIII (1902).

The Institute was to be a much more ambitious project than the Outlook Tower, comprising a more complex 'Tower of Regional Survey'. But what is perhaps most striking about this proposal are the plans for the inclusion of Reclus's great Terrestrial Globe, a huge relief model of the Earth itself, eighty feet in diameter (see Figure 2).[56] The considerable scale and meticulous detail of this representation of the planet suggests an entirely new perspective on the world and humanity's place in it. Globes had, of course, long been in use as the tool of the cartographer, the navigator, and the commercial geographer, however the sheer scale of this globe, together with its emphasis on natural terrain rather than geopolitical territory, surely marks it out as something more radical than a

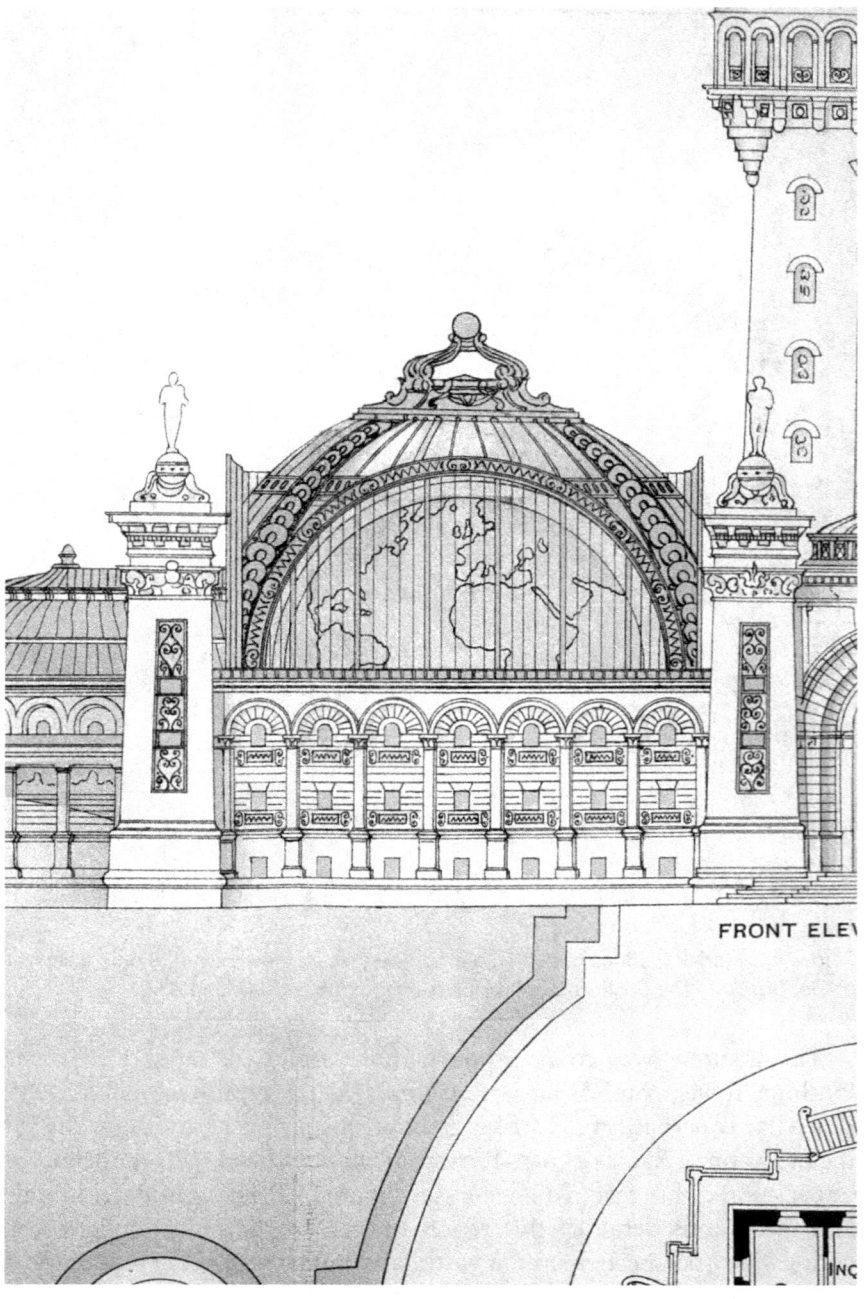

Figure 2 Detail, Patrick Geddes and M. Galeron, 'Suggested Plan for a National Institute of Geography', *The Scottish Geographical Magazine*, vol. XVIII (1902).

mere atlas. Planned to complement Paul Louis Galeron's equally massive Celestial Globe, together with panoramas of various landscapes, map-rooms and libraries, and the regional survey method represented in the tower, Reclus's Terrestrial Globe might have seemed both in and out of context. The scheme had a dual potential; offering an holistic, totalising view of the earth, but at the same time a giddily bizarre perspective, accurate yet unreal. Today the Earth viewed from space has become a commonplace image, but early on in the century the Earth as a planet was still largely known in theory, mapped in segments and only just beginning to be surveyed in glimpses from gas balloons and aeroplanes. 'Universal Geography' must have been an impressive and challenging concept, an attempt to gain concrete views of a hitherto abstracted Earth. One can only speculate whether MacDiarmid, during one of his many long discussions with Geddes, was exposed to these fascinating plans, and if so, whether these influenced his own representations of the planet Earth.

While Geddes considered the globe as 'the image, and shrine, and temple of the Earth-Mother', more recent theorists have suggested that representing the earth as a globe might actually run counter to the development of an authentic ecological sensibility, as the earth-as-globe may appear as 'an object of contemplation, detached from the domain of lived experience'.[57] If we make sense of the world on a local level, the idea of the planet as a whole may seem almost meaningless. However, I would argue that both Geddes and MacDiarmid were attempting to fuse contemplation and lived experience through representations which take account of both the global and the local: the abstract and immense cosmological viewpoint reconciled with the human-scale, intimate, earthy and sensuous way we approach the world in everyday life.

Surveying Scotland

Whilst views of the physical earth were beginning to be developed in geography and education, the events and technological advances of the early twentieth century had brought home the significance of international contexts. Political, cultural and economic global outlooks were beginning to be recognised, with the experience of international conflict, the inception of international peace treaties, the formation of the League of Nations in 1920, even the formation of cultural organisations such as the PEN club, 'that remarkable international literary organisation' which MacDiarmid helped to set up.[58]

This proliferation of international outlooks, of course, had as its corollary the development of nationalist allegiances. The dual nature of this new political scene had implications for geographer and cultural protagonist alike. Geddes's colleague A. J. Herbertson argued in 1902 for the unique status of geographical study:

> The geographer . . . shows forth the dignity of Man in his achievements as a co-operator with Nature, and at the same time the humility of Man controlled by his environment. . . . A geographer is at once a patriot and an internationalist, keenly alive to the necessity of stimulating the full development of local activity and resources, yet worldwide in his outlook and sympathies.[59]

The significance of regional factors within the global environment was being recognised in geographical study, however, regional perspectives were sometimes viewed with suspicion by early twentieth century writers aspiring to operate on an international stage. Jonathan Bate suggests in *The Song of the Earth* that Modernism is antithetical to ecological authenticity, the concept of 'dwelling' which has to involve groundedness, local knowledge – what he calls 'the essence of bioregionalism'.[60] Modernism, Bate suggests, is 'wedded indissolubly to twentieth-century multinational capitalism', while the Modernist poet is 'notoriously deracinated', and is 'the very antithesis of the bioregionally grounded poet'.[61] Bate sets up a division between what he calls literary 'bioregionalism' and 'multinationalism' or 'cosmopolitanism' – in other words, the local and the global. This seems quite an orthodox, unchallenging view of Modernism, and it is one which has now been questioned by critics such as Crawford, who point to the importance of provincial, regional identities in the intellectual development of many writers in the Modernist canon.[62] Certainly, regional identities were important to MacDiarmid, although he is sometimes keen to avoid the label of 'regionalist', fearing its negative associations with petty provincialism.[63]

Questions of regionalism and locality, perhaps more than anything else, dominated Hugh MacDiarmid and Lewis Grassic Gibbon's collaborative book, *Scottish Scene* (1934). The poem 'Scotland', Hugh MacDiarmid's opening contribution, sets about satirising the ignorance and apathy of the average Scot when it comes to knowledge of Scottish geography.

> The names of all the Shetland Isles
> We rattle off like lightning thus,
> The Orkneys then, the Hebrides,
> Like coloured balls in an abacus.
>
> And Cunningham and Lennox
> And all our ancient provinces
> –No fool among us but in his mind
> Better than an ordnance survey sees![64]

The synoptic vision MacDiarmid would like to see instilled into every Scottish school child was perhaps more accessible to the multiple selves (and viewpoints) of C. M. Grieve than it was to the average person. He returns to this theme at the close of *Scottish Scene*, in his essay 'The Future', noting that the perpetuation of distorted representations of the various regions of Scotland – the Highlands and Islands, the Lowlands and the Borders – have served to obscure the true, diverse nature of the country to its inhabitants. MacDiarmid bemoans the obliteration of 'intranational elements', as 'the very regional names – Lennox, Cunningham, Rough Bounds, Angus and the Mearns, the Lammermuirs and the Merse – are not known and mean nothing even to the majority of the Scottish people'.[65]

The situation is compounded, for MacDiarmid, by a lack of adequate surveys of Scotland or its regions by Scottish writers, whether literary, scientific or sociological. 'Germs of promising novelistic regionalism have appeared', he says, alluding to his co-author Gibbon's fictionalisation of the Mearns in *Sunset Song* (1932) and *Cloud Howe* (1933) – *Grey Granite* (1934) the final book of the *Scots Quair* trilogy, had not yet been published – however, 'of descriptive essays and nature study scarcely a beginning has been made'.[66] For MacDiarmid, this dearth is partly due to the problem of language, which in *The Islands of Scotland* (1939) he attempts to relate to human biology itself, quoting from Trigant Burrow, an American psychoanalyst who described the spread of 'a dissociative process that substitutes words for the physiological experience presumed to underlie them' with the result that 'man has lost touch with the hard and fast milieu of actual objects and correspondingly with the biological solidarity of his own organism'.[67] MacDiarmid seeks to apply this scientific perspective to the Scottish situation, demanding that:

> Visitors to the Hebrides should realise that for the same reason, as a spokesman of *An Comunn Gaidhealach* recently showed, there is nothing surprising in the fact that the healthiest parts of Scottish Gaeldom – physically, psychologically, economically and otherwise – are precisely those in which Gaelic is still purest and most generally used, and English intrudes least.[68]

MacDiarmid asserts that the problem of dissociation extends to the survey and travel books themselves. The writers of these books, unable to access the native languages (and hence the psychology) of the places they describe are unable to convey the 'truth' of place: 'the "intellectual climate" in which these books were written made the expression, or (almost wholly) the perception, of the true impossible'.[69] Taking the example of the Shetland Islands, MacDiarmid suggests that the expression and perception of 'the true' is made possible by an 'observant, vigorous, sympathetic and knowledgeable' outlook – characteristics which he identifies in his own writing.[70]

The need for such qualities of attention was reflected in later academic surveys such as the ecologist Frank Fraser Darling's *West Highland Survey*, a project spanning a number of years, which was eventually published in 1955. Neil Gunn, reviewing the *Survey*, suggested that it was successful due to Fraser Darling's 'inner knowledge' and 'long personal experience' stemming from direct involvement with the regional environment 'as a naturalist, [who] studied wild life on Rona . . . [and] as a crofter, [who] dug his own croft'.[71] Books like MacDiarmid's *The Islands of Scotland* and Gunn's *Highland Pack* (1939) can both be read as contributions to this survey literature. In the poem, 'Scotland', published in *Lucky Poet* (1943), MacDiarmid argues for the dedication and careful attention needed to perform the sort of survey he has in mind, the 'great love' required to 'read | The configuration of a land':

> So I have gathered unto myself
> All the loose ends of Scotland,
> And by naming them and accepting them,
> Loving them and identifying myself with them,
> Attempt to express the whole.[72]

There is a certain elitism in this; an assertion that one has to go beyond the limits of convention, of ordinary knowledge and of human society in order to attain a perception of 'the true' – a dedication not unrelated to the 'inconceivable discipline, courage, and endurance, | Self-purification and anti-humanity' MacDiarmid asserts in his elemental Shetlandic work, 'On a Raised Beach'.[73] Of Scotland's 'eight hundred islands' and 'innumerable skerries', he claims, 'Few men can have visited as many of them as I have done . . . with a friend working on H.M. Geological Survey, I landed three or four years ago on several of these in the Shetlands which are not yet marked on the Admiralty Charts'.[74] The Shetland Islands offer a rigorous training ground for the writer, where any attempt at representation requires 'a calm regard for fact and an intimate knowledge of the subject', fused with the poet's 'true creative spirit':

> Anything pettier would be sadly out of place in these little-known and lonely regions, encompassed about with the strange beauty of the North, the fluctuation of unearthly colour at different levels of the sun, the luminous air, the gleam of distant ice, and the awful stillness of Northern fog.[75]

The meaning of such dedication is explored in 'Tam o' the Wilds', another of MacDiarmid's *Scottish Scene* poems. Tam, 'a common workin' man', has an all-consuming interest in natural history which alienates him from his peers; his efforts to observe and understand the interconnected lives of the plants and animals which surround him are an example of the sort of 'ordnance survey' vision MacDiarmid talks about in 'Scotland'. Tam's 'passion for nature and science', a motivation which few understand, leads to an acuteness of attention and observation which few share:

> He had the seein' eye frae which naething could hide
> And nocht that cam' under his een was forgotten.
> Fluently and vividly he could aye efter describe
> The forms, and habits o' a' the immense
> Maingie o' animals he saw . . .[76]

In contrast to the majority of his peers, bogged down in 'a solid basis o' dull conventions', Tam's lifestyle achieves synthesis and meaning by opting out of societal expectations, 'gi'en average routines the bye' in order to spend 'Night after night up a tree wi' the birds'.[77] Certainly, MacDiarmid's portrayal of this ideal self-taught man is not without a little humour, but he is also drawing a parallel between the self-sacrifice and dedication of the ideal poet (himself) and the ideal naturalist (Tam). In doing so, MacDiarmid reveals his own interest in (and parades his knowledge of) zoology, botany and geography, chanting the diversity of the Scottish wildlife and landscape, the names of moths, birds, fish and mountains, and suggesting that this sort of complex regional knowledge is of more value than that transmitted by the Scottish educational system. Tam is possibly based on Thomas Edwards, a Scottish self-taught naturalist who, MacDiarmid claims, 'had no higher educational training at all, but had spent most of his time observing birds and other phenomena of natural history on the Banffshire coast'.[78] According to MacDiarmid, Ford Madox Ford said Edwards had influenced 'the formation of his prose style', and that 'the patient observation of natural history' was one of the crucial ingredients in the formation of the 'literary style of some of our best writers in English'.[79] For MacDiarmid, the dedication and observational skill of the naturalist are necessary for good poetry as well as a healthy culture.

In *Lucky Poet* MacDiarmid felt able to comment with pride on his achievements in fostering this sort of awareness, contending that one of the successes of the Scottish Renaissance was to facilitate 'a steadily increasing flow of better writing on Scottish topography and natural history'.[80] In his 'Direadh' poems, we witness MacDiarmid in the act of performing such a survey, a 'synoptic' view of Scotland which bears some resemblances to the outlooks which Patrick Geddes was promoting earlier in the century. 'Direadh', MacDiarmid notes, is 'a Gaelic word meaning "the act of surmounting" ', suggesting that 'these poems attempt to give birds'-eye views – or rather, eagles'-eye views – of the whole of Scotland, each from a different vantage point'.[81] 'Direadh I' seems to form part of a closed circuit with the aspirations MacDiarmid outlined in *Scottish Scene* and *Lucky Poet*. His claim that 'All the destinies of my land are set before me . . . Like the lines on the palm of my hand' echoes the impossibly hyper-aware Scot in *Scottish Scene*, for whom a litany of Scottish place names appear 'Like the lines on his hands', with the whole country, its history, its landscape and its regional identities 'seen . . . as a unity'.[82]

This vision of unity was not without its critics, however. Edwin Muir's *Scottish Journey* (1936) provides an illuminating contrast to MacDiarmid's views, denying from first to last the possibility of an integrated vision of Scotland.

> Scotland itself could only be known by someone who had the power to live simultaneously in the bodies of all the men, women and children in it. I took a chance cut through it, stopping here and there, picking up this or that object, gathering shells whose meaning was often obscure or illegible to me. I did not find anything which I would call Scotland; anything, that is to say, beyond the vague and wandering image already impressed upon me by memory.[83]

His 'chance cut' through the country can only allow for a series of 'impressions', a melancholy sense of fragmentation figured here in Muir's typically organic frame of reference, the Modern's experience figured as beach-combing, cut off from any real understanding of either the objects he finds or the environment he finds them in. In Muir's writing, processes of globalisation are acknowledged within the Scottish scene, with modern mass culture overwhelming the subtle, intuitive interrelationship between individual and place.

> The effect of all such innovations as the movies and the wireless is to make the place people stay in of less and less importance. Immediate environment has no longer, therefore, the shaping effect that it used to have . . . .[84]

Muir foresees the possibilities indicated by the continued proliferation of these 'innovations', since, he argues, 'variety and originality of character are produced by an immediate and specific environment; and that, in modern life, counts for less and less; it is being disintegrated on every side, and seems to be, indeed, a life-form of the past. It would be idle to regret this process, since it is inevitable'.[85]

Perhaps this is, as Michael Gardiner says, 'the scunneration for which Muir is famous'.[86] Certainly, Muir's writing about interwar Scotland has a despairing, fatalistic edge; as Gardiner notes, his awareness of the 'disintegration' of the links between character and local environment is related to the 'vast and terrifying disintegration' of the 'England of the organic community' F. R. Leavis and Denys Thompson wrote of in *Culture and Environment* (1932).[87] Muir's suggestion – which was a well-established one, for example, in the writings of Henry David Thoreau in the nineteenth century – was that as much as natural landscapes mould individual personalities, human communities in touch with nature create ecologically sound settlements:

> A town was once as natural an expression of a people's character as its landscape and its fields; it sprang up in response to a local and particular need; its houses, churches and streets were suited to the habits and nature of the people who lived in it. Industrialism, which is a mechanical cosmological power . . . has changed this.[88]

Leavis and Thompson pronounced a similar view on the rural towns of 'Old England', whose people 'themselves represented an adjustment to the environment; their ways of life reflected the rhythm of the seasons, and they were in close touch with the sources of their sustenance in the neighbouring soil'.[89]

The idea was a seductive one, but ultimately Gibbon and MacDiarmid sense that this needs to be resisted, not only due to the concept's susceptibility to the propaganda of right-wing ideologies, but also in order to avoid the invention of a sort of eco-Kailyard. Although he emphasises the unique identity of Shetland, Orkney and the Hebrides, MacDiarmid says he is 'all for the de-Tibetanisation of the Scottish Highlands and Islands'.[90]

'The real land': animism and bioregionalism

Geddes, who wrote that the town is an expression of the diversity of its region, would have disagreed with the assertion that an organic community could not exist in one of the larger provincial towns. Indeed, this question is interesting to consider in the light of Gibbon's *A Scots Quair* trilogy, which tracks a generation of workers from the country to the regional city. As Raymond Williams has suggested in *The Country and the City* (1973), what makes Gibbon significant in the context of the regional novel is that he expresses the fundamentally regional, rural roots of urban populations, of the people who had to leave the land and its associations for a life in the industrial centres.[91] Gibbon is an important novelist, Williams argues, because he represents the authentic 'experience of the country – in its whole reality, from a love of the land and its natural pleasures to the imposed pain of deprivation, heavy and low-paid labour, loss of work and place' – an experience which the folk who moved from farm to factory knew well, but which the wider world did not always appreciate or understand.[92] Gibbon's view emphasises his conviction of the innate 'peasant' connection with the soil, writing with pride of his background on the land and his sense that it was 'intimately mine', but he emphatically does not see 'back to nature' as either desirable or possible. Once again the cinema represents the average person's experience of modern global culture, juxtaposed with what would once have been a cosily familiar picture of rural life – and was indeed the image portrayed in much 'kailyard' literature – where 'the crofter may doze contentedly in the armchair in the ingleneuk'. While Gibbon feels a primal, instinctive connection with 'The Land' and its 'true, and unforgettable voice', he recognises the reality of 'narrowness and bitterness and heart-breaking toil in one of the most unkindly agricultural lands in the world' – an experience which, he suggests, while we are wise to remember, we are lucky is safely in the past.[93] For Gibbon, as for the average modern cinema-going, radio-listening town dweller, such a way of life would be 'alien and unendurable'.[94]

Part of this fascination with the land is the sense that it is 'only half inanimate', a view of the landscape which, as noted in Williams' study, is common to many regional novels of the period. MacDiarmid's poem, 'Tarras', part of the collection *Scots Unbound* (1932), plays with this idea of animism, with a lively representation of a sexualised bogland, an 'erotic description of the earth as mother', with the aim in mind, as Herbert suggests, of 'the synthesis of language and environment in an all-encompassing image of acceptance'.[95] 'Tarras', like 'Tam o' the Wilds', is symptomatic of a development in MacDiarmid's writing towards integration and comprehension – the aim for 'planetary consciousness' combined with attentive local knowledge which culminated in sequences such as the following extract from 'Direadh', encapsulating the textures and tangles of a hillside ecosystem in defence of 'our multiform, our infinite Scotland'.

> . . . not only the heather but blaeberries
> With bright green leaves and leaves already turned scarlet,
> Hiding ripe blue berries; and amongst the sage-green leaves
> Of the bog-myrtle the golden flowers of the tormentil shining;
>
> . . .
>
> And down in neglected peat-hags, not worked
> Within living memory, sphagnum moss in pastel shades
> Of yellow, green, and pink; sundew and butterwort
> Waiting with wide-open sticky leaves for their tiny winged prey[96]

This is partly intended as a metaphor for Scotland's potential cultural fecundity, resisting the reductive stereotype which sees Scotland as 'nothing but heather!'. In this respect it connects with *The Islands of Scotland*, a book Lyall has suggested can be read 'as a nationalist response to *A Journey to the Western Islands of Scotland* (1775), topographically extending yet ideologically troubling the assured Enlightenment metropolitanism of Johnson and Boswell's tour of lonely places incompatible with British civilisation'.[97] However, this lyric also bears a resemblance to Darwin's description of the 'entangled bank', the famous passage in *On the Origin of Species* (1859) which evokes the biodiversity of a section of vegetation, 'clothed with many plants of many kinds, with birds singing on the bushes, with various insects flitting about, and with worms crawling through the damp earth'.[98] MacDiarmid thus invokes Scottish biodiversity as a national metaphor.

Like the 'Direadh' sequences, it is likely that 'Tarras' was influenced by MacDiarmid's reading of his friend Sorley MacLean's Gaelic poetry, most notably 'The Cuillin' (published in his 1943 collection, *Dain do Eimhir*), which features an 'alien bogland' ('a' bhoglaich choimhich') representative of Western capitalism and the bourgeoisie, unlike MacDiarmid's 'Bolshevik bog'.[99] MacDiarmid's 'mother of usk and adder' is particularised, radical, and distanced from both culture and agriculture. The eroticised landscape, too, seems to be suggested by MacLean's poem, which finds feminised forms in the mountain itself:

> ri uchdaich nam fireach àrda
> 'nan creagan uamharra bàrcadh
> mar chìochan-màthar am t'saoghail
> stòite 's an cruinne-cé ri gaoladh.
>
> the heaving chest of the high mountain bluffs
> surging in proud crags
> like the mother-breasts of the world
> erect with the universe's concupiscence.[100]

However, MacDiarmid's excitement in 'Tarras' appears to stem more from the landscape's indifferent fecundity and half-animated *smeddum* – 'spirit, energy, drive, vigorous commonsense and resourcefulness' – than any sense of 'acceptance'.[101]

> Ah, woman-fondlin'! What is that to this?
> Saft hair to birssy heather, warm kiss
> To cauld black waters' suction
> Nae ardent breists' erection
> But the stark hills![102]

Although MacDiarmid finds distorted versions of female anatomy in this landscape, the gender of the bog-land is ambiguous, the speaker seeing at times his own bodily likenesses in the tangle of heather and moss, where 'laithsome parodies appear | O' my body's secrets in this oorie growth'. MacDiarmid's view sees all the diverse interrelations of the bog-land, barren for human purposes but necessary for the wider 'purpose o' life'.

Such animistic representations of the 'earth mother' have their parallels in the work of North East regional novelists such as Lewis Grassic Gibbon, Neil Gunn and Nan Shepherd. The land, in *A Scots Quair*, is neither male or female, although the paralleling in *Sunset Song* between the developing sexuality of Chris Guthrie and the processes of 'Ploughing', 'Drilling', 'Seed-time' and 'Harvest' – the titles of four of the five sections comprising *Sunset Song* – would seem to allude to the old idea of the agricultural land as feminised. Indeed, the figures which most frequently mediate the relationship between human communities and the land in Gibbon's work tend to be strong-minded women, like Chris in *A Scots Quair*, or Margaret Menzies in the short story, 'Smeddum'. Whilst the women's relationship with the land is an intimate one, the men's experience of the land can lead to obsession and the destruction of human relationships, as with John Guthrie, Chris's father, in *Sunset Song*, and Rob Galt in 'Clay'.

MacDiarmid's animistic, defiant peatbog is further paralleled by figures such as dark Mhairi, a survivor of the Highland Clearances, in Neil Gunn's *Butcher's Broom* (1934), in which she is pictured as 'the human mother carrying on her ancient solitary business with the earth'.[103] Such bonds of strength between women and the landscape abound in regional writing. Sorley MacLean writes that the 'uniquely robust and materialistic' poetry of Mary MacDonald, the poetess of the nineteenth-century Highland Land League, stems from the fact that 'her own land . . . is in her blood and every loved name is charged with memories of her youth, her own agony'.[104] A similar robustness can be detected in the work of Nan Shepherd, the Grampian novelist, who was herself an accomplished and resourceful hillwalker. Shepherd's female role models range from city-working mountaineers to elderly crofters in remote places; in her 1946 review of *Mountain Holidays* by Janet Adam Smith, Shepherd admires the resilience and adaptability of 'the girl who can walk out of a London office, spend a long night in a train, and then walk home through the Cairngorms from Spey to Dee'.[105] Similarly, in an essay on 'The Old Wives' of the Grampians, she speaks of old country women who 'last longer than the men. Or better', who 'rise before the light, make fires, milk cows . . . drag firewood from the hill, stew tea and drink it – black as peat, strong as their own sinewy selves'.[106] Shepherd describes one woman in particular, Betsy, as 'hoarse, and black. Her nails are encrusted with earth . . . [her] harsh voice exalts you like a dram'.[107] Roderick Watson has called attention to Shepherd's 'vivid sense of the material and social realities' faced by rural women, but also an awareness of her own – and other women's – ability to tap into a 'potent sense of spiritual being' through contact with elemental nature.[108] It is true that novels such as *The Weatherhouse* feature startling imagery of correspondence between individuals, often women, and the natural world:

> She had a feeling as though some huge elemental mass were towering over her, rock and earth, earthen smelling. Miss Barbara's tweeds had been sodden so long with the rains and matted with the dusts of her land, that they too seemed elemental. Her face was tufted with coarse black hairs, her naked hands that clutched the fabric of Lindsay's dress were hard, ingrained with black from wet wood and earth. 'She's not like a person, she's like a thing,' Lindsay thought.[109]

In some ways, the animism present in the works of these regional writers inverts the notion of the 'pathetic fallacy', finding human emotions originating in the natural environment rather than layering Romantic meanings or correspondences onto the landscape. Significantly, such viewpoints see the land as an active participant in human activities, rather than a passive commodity – and offer criticism when the primitive sense of connection is eroded by economic or political factors, as in *Sunset Song*. Gibbon's writing evokes the closely-felt correspondences between human biological processes and the earth. In *Sunset Song*, the land itself influences the actions and emotions of humans, whose lives are shown to be as closely interwoven with the cycle of natural rhythms as the animals and plants around them. John Guthrie's lust which emerges in the late summer with 'the harvest in his blood', and Chris's desire for Rob after completing the harvest, which 'came on her silently, secretly, out of the earth itself' demonstrate this connection.[110] Chris's body is 'as fine and natural and comely as a cow or a rose'; a part of nature, and not privileged above these other elements of the natural world.[111] This sense is most acutely felt during her pregnancy, where she senses that 'the sap that swelled in branch and twig were one with the blood that swelled the new life below her navel'.[112] As with MacDiarmid, this sense of bodily connection with the land extends into language itself, as Chris finds herself divided in two, with 'two Chrisses . . . that fought for her heart and tormented her':

> You hated the land and the coarse speak of the folk and learning was brave and fine one day and the next you'd waken with the peewits crying across the hills, deep and deep, crying in the heart of you and the smell of the earth in your face, you'd almost cry for that, the beauty of it and the sweetness of the Scottish land and skies.[113]

The divide between cultivation of the mind and cultivation of the land is extended to a divide within the psyche itself, organised along the divisions of language. The 'Scots words' speak of the connection with the land and its people, 'the toil of their days and unendingly their fight', in opposition to English vocabulary, with its 'sharp and clean' words which 'slid smooth from your throat' but which ultimately seem to be meaningless, dislocated from the land and its life. Language is hence seen to be inseparable from the human relationship with the land, whether this be one of closeness, typified here by Scots words, or distance, the 'modern' English.

This ecological sense, however, is under threat. The traditional ways of 'dwelling' on the land are shown in *Sunset Song* to be slipping away; the small crofters are displaced or killed by the machinations of the First World War, 'the madness beyond the hills' whose approach heralds the dissolution of the old ways of life. The War's effects are shown to be disastrous throughout the bioregion of Kinraddie; an old farmer goes mad; the woodland is cleared from the hills; the arable smallholdings are taken over for sheep grazing:

> And faith! The land looked unco woe with all its woods gone, even in the thin-sun-glimmer there came a cold shiver up over the parks of the Knapp and Blawearie folk said that the land had gone cold and wet right up to the very Mains.[114]

The land itself shivers with the cold, bare to the elements now that the woods are gone. The road leading from the land towards the terror of the Great War is an emblem of the technology which threatens the old ways of life, an 'ill road that flung its evil white ribbon down the dusk'.[115] Local, bioregional concerns are superseded by the demands of national and international politics, and the economic aspirations of big business – the global machinations of capitalism. Thus the cynical and exploitative 'greed of place and possession and great estate' overrides the peasant-farmer's local, more ecologically minded wish for 'the kindness of friends and the warmth of toil and the peace of rest'. In prophetic tones, the narrator warns:

> Great machines come soon to till the land, and the great herds come to feed on it, the crofter has gone, the man with the house and the steading of his own and the land closer to his heart than the flesh of his body.[116]

This sense of connection with the land is deeply engrained, pre-lingual, subconscious, and eminently physical; the young ploughmen, who will be superseded by the 'great machines', are conscious of 'something that vexed and tore at them, it belonged to times they had no knowing of'.[117] The collective memory of the land with 'the sweat of two thousand years in it' is transmitted to its inhabitants, an 'admission of dwelling' which endures despite the 'enframing' tactics of modern technology – ideas which would be important in the post-war work of Edwin Muir and later writers such as Ian Hamilton Finlay and George Mackay Brown, considered in Chapter 4. *Sunset Song* can be read ecologically as an attempt to draw the reader into the experience of dwelling in a network of humans and nature, what might be termed a bioregional narrative:

> Informed by an ecologist's sense of the interdependence and interconnectedness of all living systems and the process of constant adaptation in individual environments, bioregional writers picture specific localities as complex, multilayered palimpsests of geology, meteorology, history, myth, etymology, family genealogy, agricultural practice, storytelling, and regional folkways.[118]

The slipping away of the old ways of life through the remainder of the *Scots Quair* trilogy, the madness of the Great War replaced by other madnesses associated with modernity, is viewed with compassion and unflinching realism. Each stage of the trilogy, from the croft at Blawearie, the Segget manse, and the boarding house in Duncairn, demonstrates how regional life is profoundly affected by trans-national concerns. Just as the shadow of the First World War is cast over *Sunset Song*, *Cloud Howe* analyses the aftermath of that war, the unemployment, social deprivation, and crisis of faith which faced many on their return, with the minister Robert Colquohoun as much a victim of war as the ploughman-turned-soldier Ewan Tavendale. *Grey Granite*'s depiction of communist movements and civil discontent in the Scottish city suggests an ever more global outlook, with the young Ewan's experience of police brutality transforming him into a suffering 'Everyman'. The universal nature of human suffering had been explored in Gibbon's 1933 novel, *Spartacus*, where the figure of Christ and Spartacus's slave revolt are drawn into parallel. Hugh MacDiarmid's early lyric, 'The Innumerable Christ', explores a similar sense of cosmic humanity, the Earth appears as a distant twinkling star, a message of despair as much as of hope, foretelling the birth of countless 'fateful bairnies' who will grow up to become 'endless Christs'.[119] *Grey Granite*, dedicated to Hugh MacDiarmid, seeks but does not find the elemental qualities of human existence, unless this consists of ceaseless change whilst only the earth endures. It is possible to see this novel as a counterpart to MacDiarmid's geological poetry; the names of the sub-sections, drawn from geological terminologies, are the sort of glinting, abstract vocabulary MacDiarmid employs in 'On a Raised Beach', where he too insists on the solid realities of the earth, the need to make contact with elemental nature, to accept the non-human. Gibbon also contemplates this possibility, but finds himself drawn back to speculation on the presence of the folk:

> Perhaps this is the real land; not those furrows that haunt me as animate. This is the land, unstirred and greatly untouched by men, unknowing ploughing or crops or the coming of the scythe. Yet even those hills were not always thus. The Archaic Civilisation came here and terraced great sections of those hills . . . They are so tenuous and yet so real, those folk – and how they haunted me years ago![120]

Scottish Scene; *A Scots Quair*; *Scottish Journey*: the titles of these works might seem to invoke an obsession with nationhood and political territory, maps and boundary lines rather than the Geddesian bioregion. But for MacDiarmid, Gibbon and Muir, a holistic idea of the nation, if it is possible at all, can only be built upon an association of authentic (bio)regional identities. Reading Wordsworth's 'national' poetry, Bate has asserted that 'regional specificity' leads to a different kind of national identity, a 'federal' rather than imperial view, which 'begins at the periphery, not at the centre'.[121] Something of this can be recognised in MacDiarmid's approach:

> It pleases my patriotism . . . and flatters my Scotist [sic] love for minute distinctions, that Scotland has so many islands. Above all, they are useful nowadays because an island is almost startlingly an entire thing, in these days of the subdivision, of the atomisation, of life.[122]

Through his contact with Geddes and his participation in 'provincial' modernism, MacDiarmid saw that the regional, national and the global were interdependent. This is, in essence, the Scottish 'take' on the globe: ecological lyricism which fuses universal and local geographies, universal and local human experience. In this way, it was the land under their feet, and by extension, the earth itself, that was important for Scottish 'regional' novelists like Lewis Grassic Gibbon, a concern which is also reflected in Hugh MacDiarmid's poetry, and something which would become even more crucial for MacDiarmid's mature work and the writings of his contemporaries in the post-war, post-atomic world, which is the subject of the next chapter.

Notes

1. Hugh MacDiarmid, 'A Theory of Scots Letters', in Alan Riach (ed.), *Selected Prose* (Manchester: Carcanet, 1992), pp. 16–33; 22.
2. Ibid., p. 23.
3. Ibid., p. 24.
4. MacDiarmid, 'Introducing Hugh M'Diarmid', *Selected Prose*, p. 11.

5. Gavin Sprott, 'Lowland Country Life', in T. M. Devine and R. J. Finlay (eds), *Scotland in the Twentieth Century* (Edinburgh: Edinburgh University Press, 1996), pp. 170–87; p. 171.
6. Hugh MacDiarmid, *The Scottish National*, 15 May 1923, quoted by W. N. Herbert, *To Circumjack MacDiarmid* (Oxford: Clarendon Press, 1992), p. 27.
7. See Hugh MacDiarmid, 'A New Movement in Scottish Literature', in Alan Riach (ed.), *Selected Prose* (Manchester: Carcanet, 1992) p. 6, and Patrick Geddes, 'The Scots Renascence', *Evergreen: A Northern Seasonal*, Spring 1895, pp. 136–7.
8. Hugh MacDiarmid, 'Introducing Hugh M'Diarmid', *Selected Prose*, p. 10.
9. Herbert, pp. 33–4.
10. Scott Lyall, *Hugh MacDiarmid's Poetry and Politics of Place: Imagining a Scottish Republic* (Edinburgh: Edinburgh University Press, 2006), p. 116.
11. Robert Crawford, 'MacDiarmid in Montrose', in Alex David and Lee Margaret Jenkins (eds), *Locations of Literary Modernism: Region and Nation in British and American Modernist Poetry* (Cambridge: Cambridge University Press, 2000), p. 33. See also the chapter on 'Modernism as Provincialism' in Robert Crawford, *Devolving English Literature*, 2nd edn (Edinburgh: Edinburgh University Press, 2000), pp. 216–70.
12. Hugh MacDiarmid, *Lucky Poet: A Self Study in Literature and Political Ideas* (1943; reprint Manchester: Carcanet, 1994), p. 310.
13. Hugh MacDiarmid, 'The Future', *Scottish Scene or The Intelligent Man's Guide to Albyn* (London: Jarrolds Publishers Ltd, 1934), p. 336.
14. Kenneth White, 'The Alban Project', *On Scottish Ground: Selected Essays* (Edinburgh: Polygon, 1998), pp. 13–14.
15. Charles Murray, 'Gin I Was God', *Hamewith: The Complete Poems of Charles Murray* (Aberdeen: Aberdeen University Press for the Charles Murray Memorial Trust, 1979), p. 101; Thomas Hardy, *Collected Poems* (London: Macmillan, 1930).
16. Kenneth Buthlay, *Hugh MacDiarmid*, p. 28.
17. Hugh MacDiarmid, 'Au Clair de la Lune', in Michael Grieve and W. R. Aitken (eds), *Complete Poems 1920–1976*, vol. 1 (London: Martin, Brian and O'Keefe, 1993–1994), pp. 23–5.
18. *Concise Scots Dictionary*; Gloss, Hugh MacDiarmid, *Selected Poetry*, ed. Alan Riach (London: Penguin Books, 1992).
19. See Herbert, p. 161.
20. Patrick Geddes, 'Nature Study and Geographical Education', *Scottish Geographical Magazine*, vol. XIX (1903), pp. 525–36; p. 526.
21. Hugh MacDiarmid, 'In Memoriam James Joyce', *Selected Prose*, p. 224.
22. Hugh MacDiarmid, 'The Politics and Poetry of Hugh MacDiarmid', *Selected Prose*, p. 209.
23. Hugh MacDiarmid, 'Metaphysics and Poetry: An Interview with Walter Perrie', *Selected Prose*, p. 278.
24. Hugh MacDiarmid, 'Beyond Meaning', *The Raucle Tongue*, vol. I, pp. 162–71; p. 164.

25. MacDiarmid, 'A Theory of Scots Letters', p. 19.
26. Hugh MacDiarmid, 'Beyond Meaning', p. 170.
27. Hugh MacDiarmid, 'Science and Poetry', *Complete Poems*, vol. 2, p. 1220.
28. Kenneth Buthlay, *Hugh MacDiarmid* (Edinburgh: Scottish Academic Press, 1982), p. 29.
29. Catherine Kerrigan, *Whaur Extremes Meet: The Poetry of Hugh MacDiarmid, 1920–1934* (Edinburgh: Thin, 1983), p. 71.
30. Alan Riach, *Hugh MacDiarmid's Epic Poetry* (Edinburgh: Edinburgh University Press, 1991), p. 166.
31. Nancy Gish, *Hugh MacDiarmid: The Man and His Work* (London: Macmillan, 1984), p. 40.
32. Aldo Leopold, 'The Land Ethic', quoted by Peter J. Bowler in *The Norton History of the Environmental Sciences* (New York: W. W. Norton and Company, 1992), p. 515.
33. James Leslie Mitchell / Lewis Grassic Gibbon, *Hanno, or The Future of Exploration* (London and New York, 1928); *Nine Against the Unknown* (1934; reprint Edinburgh: Polygon, 2000).
34. A. J. Herbertson, Letter to Patrick Geddes, quoted by Morag Bell in 'Reshaping Boundaries: International Ethics and Environmental Consciousness in the Early Twentieth Century', *Transactions of the Institute of British Geographers*, 23(2), 1998, pp. 151–75; Patrick Geddes, 'The Mapping of Life', *The Sociological Review*, vol. XVI (July 1924), p. 194
35. Tim Ingold, *The Perception of the Environment: Essays in Livelihood, Dwelling and Skill* (London: Routledge, 2000), p. 242.
36. Patrick Geddes, 'Notes for an Introductory Course of Geography given at University College Dundee' (Spring 1898), Geddes Papers, National Library of Scotland, MS 10619.
37. A. J. Herbertson, 'Geography in the University', *Scottish Geographical Magazine*, 1902, p. 126.
38. Patrick Geddes, *A Study in City Development: Park, Gardens, and Culture-Institutes* (Dunfermline: The Riverside Press, 1904), p. 113.
39. Marshall Stalley (ed.), *Patrick Geddes: Spokesman for Man and the Environment* (New Brunswick, NJ: Rutgers University Press, 1972).
40. W. Iain Stevenson, *Patrick Geddes and Geography: A Bibliographical Study*, Occasional Paper No. 27 (University College London, March 1975), p. 4.
41. Patrick Geddes, 'Life and its Science', *The Evergreen: A Northern Seasonal*, Spring 1895, 29–37, p. 31. See John Veitch, *The Feeling for Nature in Scottish Poetry*, Vol. I (Edinburgh: William Blackwood & Sons, 1887), p. 3.
42. Hugh MacDiarmid, 'Letter to George Ogilvie, June 1918', in Alan Bold (ed.), *Collected Letters* (London: Hamilton, 1984), p. 26.
43. Hugh MacDiarmid, 'The Politics and Poetry of Hugh MacDiarmid', p. 203. Under the pseudonym of Arthur Leslie, MacDiarmid says that he 'submitted a series of brilliant memoranda which formed part of the joint volume *The Rural Problem* [London: Constable, 1913]'.
44. Hugh MacDiarmid, *The Company I've Kept* (London: Hutchinson, 1966), p. 79.

45. Ibid., pp. 80–1.
46. Hugh MacDiarmid, 'The Outlook Tower', *The Raucle Tongue: Selected Essays, Journalism and Interviews*, vol. 1, p. 131.
47. See Robert Crawford, 'MacDiarmid and English Identity', in R. P. Draper (ed.), *The Literature of Region and Nation* (London: Macmillan Press, 1989), p. 149.
48. See W. Iain Stevenson, *Patrick Geddes and Geography*, p. 2.
49. Volker M. Welter, *Biopolis: Patrick Geddes and the City of Life* (Cambridge, MA: MIT Press, 2002), pp. 61–3.
50. Geddes, *A Study in City Development*, p. 216.
51. Patrick Geddes, 'Talks from the Outlook Tower: The Third Talk – The Valley Plan of Civilisation', *Patrick Geddes: Spokesman for Man and the Environment*, pp. 321–33. See also Patrick Geddes, 'Edinburgh and its Region, Geographic and Historical', *Scottish Geographical Magazine*, vol. XIX (1903), pp. 302–12.
52. See Welter, pp. 60–6.
53. Thomas Crawford, 'The View from the North', *The Literature of Region and Nation* (London: Macmillan Press, 1989), p. 112.
54. Discussed by Douglas Gifford in *Neil M. Gunn and Lewis Grassic Gibbon* (Edinburgh: Oliver and Boyd, 1983), p. 11.
55. See Welter, pp. 31–3.
56. Patrick Geddes, 'Note on a Draft Plan for Institute of Geography', *Scottish Geographical Magazine*, vol. XVIII (1902), p. 143. The globe was part of an ongoing project, separate from the plans for the geographical institute. Geddes provides further details of the globe project in his obituary for Reclus: '1895–96 – *Projet de Construction d'un Globe Terrestre* on the scale of 1:100,000'. See Patrick Geddes, 'A Great Geographer: Elisée Reclus, 1830–1905', *Scottish Geographical Magazine*, vol. XXI (1905), p. 554.
57. Geddes, cited in Welter, p. 179; Ingold, p. 210.
58. Hugh MacDiarmid, 'Whither Scotland?' *The Raucle Tongue*, vol. 3, pp. 256–93.
59. A. J. Herbertson, 'Geography in the University', *Scottish Geographical Magazine*, no. III (1902), pp. 124–32; p. 131.
60. Jonathan Bate, *The Song of the Earth* (London: Picador, 2000), p. 234.
61. Ibid., p. 234.
62. Robert Crawford, *Devolving English Literature* (Edinburgh: Edinburgh University Press, 2000), p. 216.
63. Hugh MacDiarmid, 'Arne Garborg, Mr Joyce, and Mr M'Diarmid', *The Raucle Tongue*, vol. 1, p. 234.
64. Hugh MacDiarmid, 'Scotland', *Scottish Scene*, pp. 13–16; repr. *Complete Poems 1920–1976*, vol. I, p. 365.
65. MacDiarmid, 'The Future', *Scottish Scene*, p. 335.
66. MacDiarmid, 'The Modern Scene', *Scottish Scene*, pp. 37–57; p. 39.
67. Hugh MacDiarmid, *The Islands of Scotland* (London: B.T. Batsford Ltd, 1939), pp. xi.
68. Ibid., p. xii.
69. Ibid., p. 18.
70. Ibid., p. 43.

71. Neil Gunn, 'Surveying the Highlands', Neil Gunn Papers, National Library of Scotland (Dep. 209), p. 3.
72. MacDiarmid, 'Scotland', *Complete Poems*, Vol. I, p. 652.
73. MacDiarmid, 'On a Raised Beach', *Complete Poems*, vol. I, pp. 422–33.
74. MacDiarmid, *The Islands of Scotland*, pp. 1–2.
75. Ibid., p. 55.
76. Hugh MacDiarmid, 'Tam o' the Wilds and the Many-Faced Mystery', *Scottish Scene*, pp. 167–77; reprinted in *Complete Poems*, pp. 368–79; p. 377.
77. Ibid., p. 372.
78. Hugh MacDiarmid, 'Memorial to William Stewart' (1948), *The Raucle Tongue*, vol. III, pp. 133–6; p. 134.
79. Ibid., p. 134.
80. Hugh MacDiarmid, *Lucky Poet*, p. 282.
81. Ibid., p. 255.
82. Hugh MacDiarmid, 'Scotland', *Complete Poems*, vol. I, pp. 366–7.
83. Edwin Muir, *Scottish Journey* (Edinburgh: Mainstream Publishing, 1999), p. 243.
84. Ibid., p. 24.
85. Ibid., p. 25.
86. Michael Gardiner, *From Trocchi to Trainspotting: Scottish Critical Theory since 1960* (Edinburgh: Edinburgh University Press, 2006), p. 32.
87. F. R. Leavis and Denys Thompson, 'The Organic Community', in Laurence Coupe (ed.), *The Green Studies Reader: from Romanticism to Ecocriticism* (London and New York: Routledge, 2000), pp. 73–6; p. 73.
88. Muir, *Scottish Journey*, p. 21.
89. Leavis and Thompson, 'The Organic Community', p. 74.
90. Hugh MacDiarmid, *The Islands of Scotland*, p. 18.
91. Raymond Williams, *The Country and the City* (London: Chatto and Windus, 1973), pp. 264–71.
92. Ibid., p. 271.
93. Lewis Grassic Gibbon, 'The Land', in Valentina Bold (ed.), *Smeddum: A Lewis Grassic Gibbon Anthology* (Edinburgh: Canongate Classics, 2001), p. 84.
94. Gibbon, 'The Land', pp. 81–97; p. 85.
95. Herbert, p. 114.
96. MacDiarmid, 'Direadh I', *Complete Poems*, vol. II, pp. 1170–1.
97. Lyall, p. 136.
98. Charles Darwin, *On the Origin of Species* (London: Wordsworth Classics of World Literature, 1998), p. 368.
99. Sorley Maclean / Somhairle MacGill-Eain, 'The Cuillin / An Cuilthionn', *O Choille gu Bearradh / From Wood to Ridge: Collected Poems in Gaelic and in English translation* (Manchester and Edinburgh: Carcanet/Birlinn, 1999), pp. 64–131.
100. Ibid., p. 79.
101. *Concise Scottish Dictionary*.
102. Hugh MacDiarmid, 'Tarras', *Complete Poems*, vol. I, pp. 337–9; p. 338.
103. Neil Gunn, *Butcher's Broom* (Edinburgh: Porpoise Press, 1934), p. 426.

104. See Sorley MacLean, 'Màiri Mhór nan Oran', *Ris a' Bhruthaich: Criticism and Prose Writings*, Ed. William Gillies (Stornoway: Acair Ltd, 1985), pp. 250–7.
105. Nan Shepherd, 'Review of *Mountain Holidays* by Janet Adam Smith', Nan Shepherd Papers, National Library of Scotland, MS.27443.
106. Nan Shepherd, 'The Old Wives' (n.d.), Nan Shepherd Papers, National Library of Scotland, MS.27443. f.40.
107. Ibid.
108. Roderick Watson, '"To Know Being": Substance and Spirit in the Work of Nan Shepherd', in Douglas Gifford and Dorothy McMillan (eds), *A History of Scottish Women's Writing* (Edinburgh: Edinburgh University Press, 1997), pp. 416–27; p. 425.
109. Nan Shepherd, *The Weatherhouse*, in Roderick Watson (ed.), *The Grampian Quartet* (Edinburgh: Canongate Classics, 2001), p. 27.
110. Lewis Grassic Gibbon, *A Scots Quair* (London: Penguin Books, 1986), p. 89; p. 175.
111. Ibid., p. 141.
112. Ibid., p. 143.
113. Ibid., p. 37.
114. Ibid., p. 191.
115. Ibid., p. 176.
116. Ibid., p. 193.
117. Ibid., p. 194.
118. Michael Kowalewski, 'Bioregional Perspectives in American Literature', in David Jordan (ed.), *Regionalism Reconsidered* (New York: Garland Publishing, 1994), p. 41.
119. Hugh MacDiarmid, 'The Innumerable Christ', *Complete Poems*, vol. I, p. 32.
120. Gibbon, 'The Land', pp. 90–1.
121. Bate, pp. 216–25.
122. MacDiarmnid, *The Islands of Scotland*, p. 26.

Chapter 4

Dear Green Places

A difficult country, and our home

If the experience of war, urbanisation and technological innovation in earlier decades of the twentieth century had provoked a mixture of excitement and apprehension in Scottish writing, the events of the Second World War and its aftermath brought concerns about place, community and technology into even sharper focus. Personal experience of wartime Europe and fears about the atomic age, paralleled by a sense of expanding possibility in a world increasingly mediated by technology, led Edwin Muir in 1956 to question how 'progress' affects not only everyday life but, perhaps more fundamentally, the poetic imagination.

> Two hundred years ago, in the civilization then natural to man, the farmer grew his own wheat and corn, ground it at the neighbouring mill, killed and cut up his own pigs and oxen, and lived a poor, coarse, but self-sufficient life. He knew the value of bread, knowing how hard and precarious was the work of producing it, and was careful to look after his horses and cattle because their labour and their meat were necessary to him. His valuation of them was therefore a true valuation. In the same way the craftsman knew the material he fashioned and watched it changing under his hands from its rough to its finished state. He could tell good work from bad, and put a value on it. Now that we buy in shops shoulders of beef, loaves, chairs, beds, pots and pans, automobiles, and refrigerators, almost everything that has become necessary or convenient for us, we are eased of a great deal of labour, and have lost touch with a world of experience. I am not advocating a return to a past that has gone forever, or romanticising the coarseness of peasant life, or its poverty and hardship. All I want to suggest is that the vast dissemination of secondary objects isolates us from the natural world in a way which is new to mankind, and that this cannot help affecting our sensibilities and our imagination.[1]

By contrasting craft with mass-production, and linking this to the imagination, Muir echoes Heidegger's concept of craft as *techne*, a mode of creative revelation or *poiesis*, fundamentally distinct from modern technology which, as Jonathan Bate explains, '[obliterates] the unconcealed being-there of particular things . . . a mode of revealing which produces a styrofoam cup rather than a silver chalice'.[2] Contending, as in the poem 'The Last War', that 'our help is in all that is full-grown | In nature, and all that is with hands well-made', Muir suggests that this modern dissocation, the loss of 'a world of experience', extends to a psychological division which alters and devalues the role of the poet in modern society.[3]

In the 1960s, Edwin Morgan also identified this 'strange communicative gap' between poet and audience. However, by experimenting with new poetic forms and subjects drawn from science, even science fiction, Morgan's answer to the problem was for poetry to embrace technology. Scottish literature was 'being held back', he argued, by 'a desperate unwillingness to move out into the world . . . of television and sputniks, automation and LPs, electronic music and multi-storey flats'.[4] If poetry was to remain relevant to modern culture, Morgan contended, poets needed to radically alter both their outlook and their technical approach: 'although writers can struggle on for a time on language, on myth, on nature, on "eternal emotions" . . . there comes a day of reckoning when they realise that they are not speaking the same terms as their audience'.[5]

Morgan's critique of Scottish literary technophobia is brought into focus in his consideration of Edwin Muir and his apparent retreat from modernity which culminates in a vision of 'returning all post-atomic mankind to an Orkney farm' in Muir's 1956 poem, 'The Horses', which T.S. Eliot had called 'that terrifying poem of the "atomic age"'.[6] Portraying a remote farming community struggling to come to terms with the aftermath of nuclear war, 'the seven days war that put the world to sleep', Muir's poem imagines the mysterious return of plough horses to the farms, a reversal of the process which had replaced traditional agricultural methods with machinery in the first half of the twentieth century:

> In the first moment we had never a thought
> That they were creatures to be owned and used.
> Among them were some half-a-dozen colts
> Dropped in some wilderness of the broken world,
> Yet new as if they had come from their own Eden.
> Since then they have pulled our ploughs and borne our loads
> But that free servitude still can pierce our hearts.
> Our life is changed; their coming our beginning.[7]

Margery McCulloch notes that Muir's poetic warning was ahead of its time, as 'one of the earliest artistic statements of the horrors that nuclear war would bring'.⁸ However, for Morgan, this vision of 'a post-devastational return to primitive pastoral life [which] might restore man to the protection of the earth' is fundamentally suspect.⁹ While it is necessary to acknowledge the fears and anxieties evinced by cold war modernity, pastoral responses (and this includes post-war 'back to nature' movements in the UK) are a 'kind of retreat or escape from things which are not to be escaped from'. The solution, for Morgan, is 'not to go back to the organic world of nature and forget about the machine, but to do something about the aspects of machines that displeases you, and in order to do this you have to use science and technology'.¹⁰

This criticism highlights a common enough post-war perspective, namely that 'regional' or 'rural' writing is out of step with modern life, an escapist vision in contrast to the gritty social realities of the industrial city – what Terry Gifford describes as 'the contemporary sense of pastoral as a pejorative term'.¹¹ A sense of uneasiness about being branded an 'escapist' is evident in a number of Scottish writers. Douglas Dunn has voiced the predicament of the would-be 'quasi-mystical nature poet', for whom 'Romantic Sleep' exists in eternal tension with 'Social Responsibility'.¹² Kenneth White has also noted how 'the nostalgia for unity and unitive experience', which he sees as a 'desire of a whole world', may seem to run contra to modernity; this 'can only appear as mad and aberrant in a civilization which, while it satisfies many desires (most of which it has previously fabricated) leaves unsatisfied the one fundamental need'.¹³ However, writing about nature or the rural 'periphery' need not always be a guilt-ridden occupation. If it is important for literature to acknowledge the diverse experience of post-war modernity, part of that acknowledgement involves tackling the dissociations and environmental problems generated by modernity, and considering the role of poetry and writing in resisting or counteracting such dissociation. In this way, one can begin to see work by writers like Muir and Mackay Brown not as pastoral escapism but as an attempt to make sense of physical, imaginative and psychological displacement.

Despite Morgan's rousing polemics and poetic experimentation, not all post-war Scottish writers rallied to the call to 'put the machine in its full human context' – at least not in the way he might have envisaged.¹⁴ Morgan and the Orkney poet George Mackay Brown (a friend and former pupil of Muir) were publishing work at the same time and even in the same places, in magazines such as Ian Hamilton Finlay's *Poor. Old. Tired. Horse.* However, their preoccupations were radically different; while in 1968 Morgan was producing poems inspired by computer programming, such as 'The Computer's First Christmas Card', Mackay Brown's *An Orkney Tapestry* (1969), a book about the history and cultural identity of the Orkney Islands, offered a critique of 'rootless, utilitarian' progress, personified as 'some huge computer figure' dispensing 'food, sex, excitement' to a human world made infantile and superficial, overcome by 'a mania to create secondary objects that become increasingly shinier and shoddier and uglier'.[15] A litany of man-made objects cannot, for Mackay Brown, replace the ancient heraldic touchstones drawn from the farmers, fishers, monks and rulers of the Orkney Islands.[16] Instead, his work speaks of a faith in the constants of humanity and the earth: 'a circle has no beginning or end. The symbol holds. People in AD 2000 are essentially the same as the stone-breakers and horizon-breakers of 3000 BC'.[17]

The new experiences offered by the world of 'television and sputniks' may have irrevocably altered everyday life in the 1960s, but this was also the decade in which political environmentalism took hold in popular culture, alongside civil rights and women's liberation. The eco-historian, Donald Worster, suggests that the modern 'age of ecology' began with the explosion of the atomic bomb in 1945, and that the 'new moral consciousness' of environmentalism was confirmed in the 1960s, with the first glimpses of the earth from outer space.[18] The twentieth-century experience of war and technological destruction galvanised the environmental debate, highlighting the importance of questions about 'place' and 'home', about belonging and displacement. Post-war life promised a starry future but it also threatened crisis, even disaster, the possibility of atomic war and widespread environmental devastation. Not only that, it questioned some of the foundational premises of modernity itself:

> The bomb cast doubt on the entire project of the domination of nature that had been at the heart of modern history. It raised doubts about the moral legitimacy of science, about the tumultuous pace of technology, and about the Enlightenment dream of replacing religious faith with human rationality as the basis of material welfare and virtue.[19]

While Morgan was disappointed in Muir for his failure to meet 'the wonderful challenge which the apparent menace of the scientific and political future has thrown down to us mid-century', Muir certainly believed that this menace existed, and his prose work, which includes the Glasgow novel *Poor Tom* (1932) and the travelogue, *Scottish Journey* (1935), attempted to document the first rumblings of that threat. Morgan's outlook on Muir becomes more intriguing if one considers Muir's view of Walter Scott in the 1936 polemical study of Scottish culture, *Scott and Scotland*, which criticises Scott for retreating into the past, mythologising Scotland's history instead of interrogating Scotland's present. Muir suggests that 'Scott can find a real image of

Scotland only in the past, and knows that the nation which should have formed both his theme and his living environment as a writer is irremediably melting away around him'.[20] One might equally apply this argument to Muir's own work; but here, the difficulty in finding a 'real image' of home is not only a specific cultural one, but a problem endemic to the modern world as a whole.

Heidegger viewed the human predicament in terms of 'ontological homelessness, meaning that we have no abiding home, since we are not embedded in the world as a part of nature', and suggested that, in the twentieth century, 'Spellbound and pulled onward by all this [technology], humanity is, as it were, in a process of emigration':

> [Humanity] is emigrating from what is homely [*Heimisch*] to what is unhomely [*Unheimisch*]. There is a danger that what was once called home [*Heimat*] will dissolve and disappear. The power of the unhomely seems to have so overpowered humanity that it can no longer pit itself against it.[21]

One might point out here that this migration to the 'unhomely' was nowhere more evident than in the holocaust perpetrated by the Nazi party, of which Heidegger was a member in the 1930s. However, this philosophy of home and exile is certainly relevant to the foundational premise of ecological criticism, that ways need to be found to circumvent our fundamental alienation from nature, to somehow reconnect us with the earth. In this way, ecological theory links up with both postcolonial anxieties and the discourses of phenomenological philosophy, linking lost Edens with displaced humans.[22] Like 'exile', 'belonging' has become something of a loaded term in considerations of post-war culture, with its associations of home, community, and the dual possibility of inclusion or exclusion.[23] Such concepts had to be radically reassessed in the aftermath of the two world wars, with the knowledge of what 'blood and soil' ideologies of home and homeland could mean. The continuing relevance of these questions has been demonstrated more recently, by the use of 'belonging' to denote the idea of ecological 'dwelling' in Jonathan Bate's work, or to express John Burnside's view that there is a need for communal inclusiveness in the face of political patriotism, re-enfranchising 'the non-belongers, the flag-less'.[24] The sense of 'belonging' is, for modern ecotheory, an important part of 'being in the world'.

Belonging is also the title of Willa Muir's memoir, published in 1968. Although essentially a book about marriage, *Belonging* opens with a lengthy consideration of the importance of place in the early lives of both Muirs. For Willa Muir, who had been born in the Shetlands in 1890 but moved with her family to Montrose as a young child, 'belonging' in the everyday sense was defined by language. She notes that her 'first words were in the Norse dialect of Shetland, which was not valid outside our front door', which led to a fundamental sense that she 'did not feel that [she] belonged whole-heartedly to Montrose'. Similar questions about language and identity had been explored in the work of Lewis Grassic Gibbon, whose representation of the dilemma between homely 'Scots words to tell to your heart', rooted in the land and its people, and foreign, dislocated 'cool and clean' English vocabulary, is part of a wider debate within 1930s Scottish culture about language, folk-memory and cultural identity – a debate which was made explicit by the publication of Muir's *Scott and Scotland*.[25] However, in Willa Muir's memoir, this sense of cultural displacement is compensated for by a more universal sense of 'belonging':

> The 'feeling' came upon me like a tide floating me out and up into the wide greening sky – into the Universe, I told myself. That was the secret name I gave it: Belonging to the Universe. Like Thoreau, I found myself 'grandly related'.[26]

This is a reference to Thoreau's *Journal*, which records that, 'alone in the distant woods or fields . . . I come to myself, I once more feel myself grandly related, and that cold and solitude are friends of mine'.[27] This is a solitary sort of belonging, which has affinities both with nineteenth-century American transcendentalism and the 'sublime' of European Romanticism. However, this concept of 'belonging' is not simply a Romantic reflex. Having studied psychological and sociological thought as a postgraduate student, and having co-translated, with Edwin, the novels of Franz Kafka, Hermann Broch and other German-language modernists, Willa Muir was no naïve theorist. Her use of the term 'belonging' is qualified by her awareness of geographical, cultural and psychological estrangement. When she describes Edwin Muir as a 'displaced person', she not only indicates his exile from the Orkney Islands, but is all too aware that the term applies to real refugees, people driven from their homelands by war or political oppression. Muir had, after all, worked on educational projects with refugees in Edinburgh during the war years, and the writer, Hermann Broch, stayed with the couple after fleeing Austria at the outbreak of the war. For both Willa and Edwin Muir, displacement is a historical and political phenomenon, but it is also linked to a wider concept of psychological alienation.

Edwin Muir was born in 1887 and brought up on a farm on the Orkney island of Wyre. Increasing rents forced the family off the land, and they eventually settled in Glasgow when Muir was fourteen. The 'chaos' of Glasgow formed a stark contrast to Muir's memory of an

Orcadian life of 'legend, folk-song . . . [and] customs which sanctioned . . . instinctive feelings for the earth', and within a just few years Muir's parents and two of his brothers had died – a tragedy which he attributed to the 'violence' of displacement.[28] This experience is at the core of his imagination; as Mackay Brown suggests, Muir's autobiographical writings present 'a unique account of the head-on clash between the pastoral and the industrial', a conflict which, he maintains, 'broke Edwin Muir's life apart'.[29] Significantly, Muir frames this conflict in terms of both geographical and temporal dislocation:

> I was born before the Industrial Revolution, and am now about two hundred years old . . . in 1751 I set out from Orkney for Glasgow. When I arrived I found that it was 1901, and that a hundred and fifty years had been burned up in my two days' journey . . . All my life I have been trying to overhaul that invisible leeway.[30]

The key factor here is the Industrial Revolution – also a central point of tension in the work of the English Romantics. However, this telling passage reveals how technological 'progress' is, for Muir, central to modern exile. Morgan, reviewing Willa Muir's *Belonging*, rationalised the Muirs' perpetual rootlessness as a symptom of the times: 'They were transients in an age of transients, displaced persons in an age of technically "displaced persons", and much of the sense of wholeness in the poetry is owed to this fact'.[31] But while Muir's experience of exile is, as evidenced by his autobiography, linked to contemporary geopolitics, the roots of this sense of transience stretch back into Scottish history, aligned with the eighteenth- and nineteenth-century clearances of the Highlands and Islands – a painful history of 'displaced persons' emanating from rural Scotland.[32] Such personal and ideological transience, as many of Muir's critics have noted, contrasts markedly with the 'timeless', 'eternal' properties of Muir's childhood Orkney, as represented in the poetry.[33] The titles of his collections – *Journeys and Places* (1937), *The Narrow Place* (1943), *The Voyage* (1946), *The Labyrinth* (1949) and finally, *One Foot in Eden* (1956) – above all emphasise place and movement. Indeed, Muir's life was characterised by a certain restlessness, moving from Orkney to Glasgow and London, then, shortly after the war, to Prague and Rome. While, as Eliot observed, Muir's work is underpinned by the 'sensibility of the remote islander', it is also characterised by his contact with 'the modern world of the metropolis . . . and finally the realities of central Europe'.[34]

Muir held on to an idyllic image of Orkney free from the troubles of modern society but 'he knew well that this was an image, which even in Orkney was broken'.[35] Despite being conscious of his Orcadian mythologising, his 'childhood all a myth | Enacted on a distant isle', the abstraction of the pastoral ideal appeals to Muir's imagination, and his memory of the islands is co-opted to form the visionary landscape of his poetry, which also draws on the folk and ballad traditions of the Orkney Islands and rural Scotland.[36] Even these, Muir laments, are dissolving: 'Our old songs are lost, | Our sons are newspapermen | At the singers' cost'.[37] There are important values of harmony with the natural world in the traditions of the 'old songs', which Willa Muir wrote about in *Living With Ballads* (1965):

> Men, animals, birds, trees and rivers appear to be all on the same footing, all intensely alive and aware of each other, all belonging to the same world in a common flow of feeling. There seems to be little or no turning back to reflective self-consciousness, as if the tides of human feeling ran out unchecked to fill the whole visible universe.[38]

From this point of view, newspapers, mass-produced and mass-distributed, seem estranged from the localised folk-world of traditional culture – a view shared by Heidegger, who objected to modern mass media for its propagation of 'the one-sided view', a 'univocity of concepts . . . [which] has the same essential origins [as] the precision of the technological process'.[39] Mackay Brown took up this idea, warning that 'A community like Orkney dare not cut itself off from its roots and sources. Places like Rackwick and Eynhallow have no meaning if you try to describe or evaluate them in terms of a newspaper article'.[40] Writing with disdain about people whose opinions are 'regurgitate[d]' from 'some discussion they heard on TV the night before, or read in the *Daily Express*', he observes the disappearance of the 'old stories', which 'vanished with the horses and the tinkers . . . [the] surrealist folk [who] walked our roads and streets, Dickensian figures with earth and salt in them'.[41] One might argue that journalism is as much about telling stories as the Ballads or the Sagas are, and not antithetical to poetry – Hugh MacDiarmid having managed to combine the two occupations successfully (and incestuously, by virtue of his multiple pseudonyms) for a number of years. But for Mackay Brown, the newspaper report is a linguistic and cultural simplification; the aggressive gaze of the journalist skims over the hidden complex of tradition and place. Here, devoid of community, mass media becomes an instance of the clash between the mechanistic and the biocentric, and threatens the dissolution of an authentic sense of place.

Such sensations of 'harmony' or 'completeness', opposed to 'contradiction', are explored in Muir's *An Autobiography*, with the child's 'original vision of the world' posited as:

> a state in which the earth, the houses on the earth, and the life of every human being are related to the sky overarching them; as if the sky fitted the earth. Certain dreams convince me that a child has this vision, in which there

is a completer harmony of all things with each other than he will ever know again.[42]

This vision of interrelatedness bears a resemblance to Gaston Bachelard's phenomenological image of 'the immense sky resting on the immense earth' as a bird protects the eggs in its nest, related to the idea of the world as house or refuge which the etymology of the word 'ecology' (house study) presupposes.[43] A similar image recurs in 'Scotland 1941', in which Muir offers us a vision of rural harmony, an eternal 'rustic day' 'roofed in' by a 'simple sky'.[44] While this harmonious feeling might suggest a proto-ecological consciousness, and seems to recall Willa Muir's 'belonging to the Universe', Edwin Muir's portrayal of childhood experience is deeply problematic, expressing not contentment, as might be expected, but a deep sense of alienation. Following a spell of ill health, he experienced 'a passion of fear and guilt', which resulted in a sense of alienation from the people and the landscape around him, a world where 'every object was touched with fear . . . a sort of parallel world divided by an endless, unbreakable sheet of glass from the actual world'.[45]

It is, for Muir, as if a sense of deracination is fundamental to human experience, whether one lives on a farm or in a slum, suggesting that 'There comes a moment (the moment at which childhood passes into boyhood or girlhood) when this image [of harmony] is broken and contradiction enters life'.[46] While this idea is surely related to Blakean 'innocence and experience', the idea of the 'broken image' is of course one which T. S. Eliot, a major influence on Muir's writing, employed in *The Waste Land*, asking 'What are the roots that clutch, what branches grow | Out of this stony rubbish?' with no answer but 'A heap of broken images, where the sun beats | And the dead tree gives no shelter'.[47] Muir's work connects Romanticism with Modernism, and demonstrates that, in questions of home and belonging at least, they have similar preoccupations. As noted earlier, 'Modernism' tends to be viewed as a guilty, anthropocentric malady in the eyes of the ecocritic.[48] However, it is important to realise that Modernist poetry asks questions about 'being-in-the-world' which are interesting for ecological theory. Eliot's poem makes use of the archetypal visionary landscape, the desert, to symbolise what he senses as the intrinsic alienation of modern life. In this context, Muir's status as a 'displaced person' is not unique, and his melancholic sense of division and fragmentation is perhaps typical of the twentieth-century intellectual; as Adorno suggests, 'Home, wherever and for however long we find it, is, by its very nature, provisional and tainted'.[49]

Muir symbolises this idea as a 'crack . . . through our hearthstone' in a poem entitled 'The Refugees', published in *The Narrow Place*

(1943). Here, war is merely the ultimate manifestation of the 'power of the unhomely' already prevalent in our society. For decades we watched with 'non-committal faces' the 'nationless and nameless' refugees of Europe; now 'Tenement roofs and towers | Will fall upon the kind and the unkind | Without election'.[50] Similar ideas are explored in 'The Good Town' (1949), which presents a settlement devastated by war, reduced to 'mounds of rubble', a 'patch of raw and angry earth | Where the new concrete houses sit and stare'.[51] These ruins might be read as an echo of Wordsworth's 'The Ruined Cottage', in which a picturesque ruin reveals its sad history of a rural family destroyed by war.[52] However, Muir's approach to the subject does not indulge in pleasurable Romantic melancholy. While Muir is not exactly a Modernist, he is more than just a latent Romantic, or as MacDiarmid would have it, a practitioner of 'a sort of Emersonian transcendentalism'.[53] As Thomas Crawford notes, Muir's work contains a significant political element, which 'forces us to reject or at least seriously to qualify the view that sees him primarily as an escapist poet, immersed in an arcane subjectivism'.[54] Indeed, where Wordsworth had sketched an overgrown garden as an image of 'desolation', Muir presents us with a 'patch of raw and angry earth', where homes once used to be. The once-quiet landscape is now literally scarred by war, the demolished buildings representative of wider societal fragmentation, whilst the replacement 'concrete houses' offer no possibility of authentic 'dwelling'. Although some of the original homes still survive, 'what once | Lived there and drew a strength from memory' has gone. Again, Muir suggests that the 'inexhaustible' chaotic, destructive force of war, apparently originating from the 'outside' world, might be traced back to the community itself: 'Could it have come from us? Was our peace peace? | Our goodness goodness?'[55] For Muir, as for Heidegger, the need to counteract the 'power of the unhomely' is the central challenge facing modern humanity. Now the task is to build on this knowledge, to 'shape . . . a new philosophy', questioning whether we can bring ourselves to 'build a house here, make friends with the mangled stumps | And splintered stones, not looking too closely | At one another?'[56] This symbolic waste land sounds very much like some parts of Eliot's famous poem. But where Eliot despairs, Muir, perhaps surprisingly, asks about the possibility of house-building. Picking up the pieces, finding some way back to an authentic interrelationship between individuals, communities and the land on which they depend, is Muir's main project in his post-war poetry – a quest to discover 'where we came from, where we are going, and, since we are not alone, but members of a countless family, how we should live with one another'.[57]

An early intellectual fascination with Nietzsche contributed to Muir's sense of deracination – as Edward Said says, 'Nietzsche taught us to feel uncomfortable with tradition'.[58] However, working for A. R. Orage at *The New Age* in 1920s London, Muir underwent Jungian psychotherapy, and was introduced to a possible remedy in Jung's theory of archetypes and the 'collective unconscious', ideas which offered some kind of unifying myth in the face of displacement and fragmentation. As if in answer to Heidegger's assertion that we are no longer 'embedded in the world of nature', Jung's approach offered a biological link to the past and to the world of nature, contending that 'All those factors . . . that were essential to our near and remote ancestors will also be essential to us, for they are embedded in the inherited organic system'.[59] It seems likely that such ideas reactivated Muir's faith in his Orkney heritage, since a striking characteristic of his work is that, despite a keen awareness of alienation and dissociation, his emphasis remains on community and inclusiveness. Even the title of his most Nietzschean work, *We Moderns* (1918), speaks of this ambivalence, as do poems like 'Scotland, 1941', which begins 'We were a tribe, a family, a people'.[60] Even while Muir's poetry laments the loss of an authentic traditional community, by the use of these inclusive pronouns – 'we', 'our', 'us' – his poems suggest that some sort of community still exists, even if this is merely a community of outcasts. The sense of inclusive identity migrates to the present tense in the 1956 poem, 'The Difficult Land', another echo of *The Waste Land*. Despite the modern potential for alienation, symbolised by the difficulty of cultivating a land afflicted by 'spring floods and summer droughts: our fields | Mile after mile of soft and useless dust', where frustrated farmers 'shake our fists and kick the ground in anger', a community endures through the 'continuance of fold and hearth | Our names and callings, work and rest and sleep'.[61]

No longer taken for granted, community becomes the focus for a conceptual 'belonging' or 'dwelling-place', underpinned by collective memory. Behind the modern experience of displacement lie the Jungian archetypes of Adam and Eve, transformed in Muir's poetry into simple farmers – perhaps his own mother and father, whom he later reflects on as 'saints' for their 'goodness, their gentleness, their submission to their simple lot'.[62] Such ideas are reflected in the title of the first version of his autobiography, *The Story and the Fable* (1939), which refers to his Jungian-derived notion of the 'story' of an individual life and its context within the wider mythic narrative of human experience.[63] 'The Sufficient Place' (1937) provides a symbol of this belief, an archetype of home at the core of fragmented modern experience: 'From end to end of the world is tumult. Yet | These roads do not turn in here but writhe on |

Round the wild earth forever'.[64] As with Lewis Grassic Gibbon's striking image of the road that leads to war in *Sunset Song*, which 'flung its evil white ribbon down in the dust', the roads in Muir's poem also symbolise technology and the restlessness of modern life – a contrast with the symbolic potential of roads in the work of Robert Louis Stevenson or Walt Whitman.[65] World wars and international politics had darkened the potential of such images; their association with the machinery of a frightening modernity makes them appear, not as a dwelling place as in Stevenson, but as part of what Heidegger called an instance of 'enframing', a utilitarian intrusion into the landscape rather than the natural expression of human community and interconnection.[66]

Machinery, Heidegger contends, 'frames its material as ready for use, and thus reduces the material to its usefulness or serviceability', whereas traditional ways of relating to the natural world have more in common with art than with technology, in which the world 'is not "used up" or reduced to "usefulness" but is re-presented in a new aspect'.[67] Muir's thoughts on machinery – always containing the latent potential for violence, a capacity which culminates in the destructive force of the atomic bomb – can be related to such post-war philosophical critiques of technology. The cold war change in perspective from local to global, from a concern with 'the community or country we live in' to the 'single, disunited world' is, Muir says 'a dilemma . . . we must all solve together or on which we must all be impaled together'.

> This world was set going when we began to make nature serve us, hoping that we should eventually reach a stage where we would not have to adapt ourselves at all: machinery would save the trouble. We did not foresee that the machinery would grow into a great impersonal power, that we should have to serve it instead of co-operating with nature as our fathers did.[68]

The need to counteract this 'impersonal power' is the reason for the frequent appearance of both visionary and realistic animals in Muir's poetry and writings, and the central motivation behind 'The Horses' – silencing the metallic voice of the radio, abandoning 'that old bad world that swallowed its children quick'.[69] Muir's poetic representations of animals are both a continuation of the tradition of the mediaeval bestiary, in which animals represent certain cultural or moral concepts, and an assimilation of the psychological symbolism of animal forms, suggested by the practice of psychoanalysis. As co-translators of Kafka, the Muirs would have been familiar with Kafka's story, 'Metamorphosis', where a man awakes to find himself transformed into a giant insect.[70] Such disturbing distortions of human and animal bodies appeared in Muir's own dreams and feature in poems such as 'The Combat', a vision of an endless battle between a ferocious heraldic 'crested animal' and 'A soft round beast brown as clay'.[71] But this modern horror is also based on ancient guilt, and the denial of our reliance on the non-human world, as Muir acknowledges that he too has 'suppressed the animal in myself'.[72] Although we still depend on animal life for our survival, 'the personal relation is gone, and with it the very ideas of necessity and guilt. The animals we eat are killed by thousands in slaughter-houses which we never see'.[73] Again, this theory of dissociation relates to Heideggerean philosophy, contrasting the activity of the traditional farmer, who 'places the seed in the keeping of the forces of growth and watches over its increase' and modern agriculture, which has become 'the mechanised food industry'.[74] To bridge this psychological divide, Muir suggests, we need to recognise that:

> At the heart of human civilization is the byre, the barn, and the midden. When my father led out the bull to serve a cow brought by one of our neighbours it was a ritual act of the tradition in which we have lived for thousands of years, possessing the obviousness of a long dream from which there is no awaking. When a neighbour came to stick the pig it was a ceremony as objective as the rising and setting of the sun; and though the thought never entered his mind that without that act civilization, with its fabric of customs and ideas and faiths, could not exist – the church, the school, the council chamber, the drawing-room, the library, the city – he did it as a thing that had always been done, and done in a certain way. There was a necessity in the copulation and the killing which took away the sin, or at least, by the ritual act, transformed it into a sad, sanctioned duty.[75]

Strikingly, in these works, Muir is arguing for the centrality of what modern civilisation tends to view as peripheral. The farm is the symbolic, and the actual, centre of human civilisation. This reflects early twentieth-century anthropological theory, the idea of 'diffusionism' also explored by Lewis Grassic Gibbon, which stressed the importance of agriculture as a foundation of civilisation.[76] But Muir goes further, claiming that even in the modern world of the city, of 'televisions and sputniks', the natural world is central to human life; that our domination of and dissociation from nature has political and social consequences as well as psychological and moral implications.[77] What makes Muir interesting from an ecological point of view is that he adapts his Orcadian environmental consciousness to generalise about the plight of modern humanity. While, unlike MacDiarmid, Muir never uses the word 'ecology', his contemplation of the ancient interconnections between human and animal life implies an awareness of what might be called an 'ecological' relationship of interdependence, in contrast to the predominantly economical value attached to farm animals in modern day society – as 'creatures to be owned and used'.[78] 'The Horses' counteracts the 'enframing' of animal life by asserting the 'long-lost archaic companionship' of domesticated farm animals; indeed, the community's lack of familiarity with the animals is the fact which permits the possibility of redemption, or reconciliation, the sense of a miracle revealed and an understanding of the value of human dependence on the animal world. Of course, this is a utopian vision, but 'The Horses' is significant as an ecopoem because it imagines a reconciliation for modern humans with both the natural world and ancient tradition, mediated by an acceptance of and a respect for animal life – a vision which might ameliorate 'our blood-guiltiness towards the animals'.[79]

Knowledge, mystery and phenomenology

The psychological need to reconnect with the roots of human community, and to re-establish a sense of 'archaic companionship' with the natural world was also recognised by Muir's contemporary, the novelist Neil Gunn. This idea of the ritualised 'rite of passage' which acknowledges our dependence on, as well as our guilt towards, the natural world is also present in Gunn's novels; in the symbolic killing of the butterfly, 'God's fool', by the young Finn in *The Silver Darlings* (1941), or the triumphant struggle with the salmon which memorably opens *Highland River* (1937).[80] In *Highland River*, the protagonist Kenn's development from boyhood to adulthood is paralleled with a quest for the 'source' of his local river, as both physical environment and, as Douglas Gifford has shown, a symbol of ancestral continuity informed by Jungian theory, not only for the small Highland community but for modern humanity as a whole. Like Muir, Gunn's work contemplates the possibility of wholeness in a fragmented modern world, and includes representations of animal life as mediators in the relationship between the human individual and the environment. However, here it is the physical, phenomenological aspect of the animals which is most important, stressing the kinship of the boy and the animal life he finds so fascinating:

> The snug warmth of the hollow in the bed where he lay all curled up would sometimes induce a feeling of extraordinary glee, so that he would breathe under the blankets and laugh wide-mouthed and huskily. Hah-haa! he would chuckle, gathering all his body into a ball and touching his knees with his chin. Hah-hah-haa! softly, so that no one would hear . . . It was great fun to be so safe in this warm hole, while the dark, cold river rolled on its way to the distant thunder of the sea . . . All things with warm life in them were curled up, like himself and heard, waking or in sleep, the rushing of the river.[81]

This imaginative identification and delight with the sleeping animals recalls John Muir's talk of the 'divine radium' of all creatures, which must have 'lots of fun in them' – the essential joy of all living things, a concept which would later become important to Gunn in his study of Zen philosophy.[82] In *Highland River*, Kenn's vivid imagination allows him to pass 'from beast to beast . . . understanding best, however, those that were curled up in a den', a sense of gleeful 'intimacy'.[83] This physical pleasure of refuge, imaginatively sympathising with the experience of the animals in their dens, is the 'primal image' of refuge the phenomenological philosopher Gaston Bachelard relates to human inhabitation:

> Physically, the creature endowed with a sense of refuge, huddles up to itself, takes to cover, hides away, lies snug, concealed. If we were to look among the wealth of our vocabulary for verbs that express the dynamics of retreat, we should find images based on animal movements of withdrawal, movements that are engraved in our muscles . . . what a quantity of animal beings are there in the being of man![84]

Gunn and Shepherd combine their intuitive feelings of being 'at home' in the wild landscape with a phenomenological viewpoint which relies on close, reverent attention to the physical aspects of the world around them. Scientific observation and practical knowledge are combined with an acute sense of the sacred, and a fundamental respect for the natural environment which is informed not only by Romanticism and Eastern mysticism, but by scientific enquiry itself. Nan Shepherd's *The Living Mountain* was eventually published in 1977, but, as she reveals in the preface, it was 'written during the latter years of the Second War and those just after'.[85] She goes on to reflect, 'In that disturbed and uncertain world it was my secret place of ease'.[86] Shepherd's book, together with works such as Gunn's *Highland River* or his collection of wartime essays, *Highland Pack* (1939), offer as a counterpoint to the depersonalisation of war what might be called a phenomenology of wildness, focusing on the experience and sensations evoked by direct physical contact with the natural world.

For Shepherd, the sensation of delighted 'belonging' was focused on the Scottish mountain landscape of the Cairngorms. A 'forbidden country' during her childhood, Shepherd's early contact with the expansive 'glittering white' plateau high up in the mountains led to a lifelong fascination with and longing for the landscape.[87] This desire, while rooted in physical experience, is complex, and emphatically not a question of 'Munro-bagging':

> There is more in the lust for a mountain top than a perfect physiological adjustment. What more there is lies within the mountain. Something moves

between me and it. Place and a mind may interpenetrate till the nature of both is altered.[88]

This recalls John Muir's description of his experiences in the North American wilderness, where, immersed in the circle of 'plain, sky and mountains', 'you lose consciousness of your own separate existence: you blend with the landscape, and become part and parcel of nature'.[89] Similarly, in *Highland River*, Kenn's body and imagination are so in tune with the environment of the strath that he is 'unable to know where his own spirit ends and the wood begins'.[90]

Much of Gunn's writing about the Highlands is characterised by a physical enjoyment of what he sees as the 'fundamentals' of rural life – hunting and observing wild animals. This physical sympathy is connected in Gunn's work to a strong sense of ancient folk culture and folk laughter, symbolised by artefacts such as the broch. For Kenn in *Highland River*, at the core of life lies 'a wise pagan laughter . . . cunning and evasive . . . hard as a tree knot', which he sees as the essence of the 'folk'.[91] Such folk laughter is essential to Mikhail Bakhtin's theory of 'carnival ambivalence', the bodily aesthetic of mediaeval folk culture which undercuts the seriousness and hierarchical control of 'officialdom'.[92] This may alert us to an aspect of Gunn, where contemplation of physical bodies attempts to formulate a way of establishing the basis for human attitudes towards the natural world. Like John Muir, Gunn recognises the playful, almost visceral relationship between rural children and the animal world, but the young Kenn's attitudes to wildlife in *Highland River* also seems linked back to this idea of wise pagan culture, linking with the Bakhtinian aspect of the 'grotesque', observing the 'faint movement' in the fur of a sleeping animal, 'a fascinating, crawling movement, like the slow ripple he had seen in the warm gut of a disembowelled rabbit'.[93]

Highland River, like Gunn's other novels, makes rich use of Highland folk myths and their implied ancient pagan roots. In such myths, the salmon is imaginatively identified with the serpent, and the landing of the first salmon of the season is supposed to confer 'wisdom' on the fisher. Wisdom, in this novel, is figured as 'secret knowledge'; a combination of local knowledge and self-discovery, all achieved for Kenn through the physical or imaginative exploration of the river.[94] While Kenn grows up to become a nuclear physicist, what might be seen as the apotheosis of modern scientific progress, at times the novel betrays a certain ambivalence about scientific knowledge in the face of folk wisdom. There is a suggestion that reductive science might dissolve the solid reality of the landscape, negating the phenomenological apprehension of reality, alienating the human body from a world made abstract and fragmented. Revisiting the pool where he had caught the salmon as a young child, Kenn feels 'that if the boulders were to become geological rocks, the water a chemical compound, and the salmon a polarised amalgam of tissues reacting to the play of certain stimuli, the adventure in the pool would be given its cosmic application and the mirth would break on an abrupt laugh'.[95]

By contrast, in Nan Shepherd's meditation on the mountain she is attempting 'to know its essential nature', but this knowledge does not exclude the validity of science.

> The more one learns of this intricate interplay of soil, altitude, weather, and the living tissues of plant and insect (an intricacy that has its astonishing moments, as when sundew and butterwort eat the insects), the more the mystery deepens. Knowledge does not dispel mystery.[96]

Ways of observing, ways of looking, become more and more important for post-war Scottish writers. Gunn says in a letter to Shepherd that 'without a certain eye many a scene would be unspeakably bleak and boring' but remarks that in her writing, the reader can find a 'momentary apprehension of the primordial sense of life, alert, quick-eyed'.[97] Both writers value this alert sensitivity to the material world, as Shepherd notes how merely changing the 'focus in the eye, moving the eye itself when looking at things that do not move, deepens one's sense of outer reality'.[98] By experimenting with different ways of looking, she suggests, the human can perceive the inanimate in 'the act of becoming':

> In no other way have I seen of my own unaided sight that the earth is round. As I watch, it arches its back, and each layer of the landscape bristles – though bristles is a word of too much commotion for it. Details are no longer part of a grouping in a picture of which I am the focal point, the focal point is everywhere. Nothing has reference to me, the looker. This is how the earth must see itself.[99]

This search for an altered viewpoint is reminiscent of Dorothy Wordsworth's methods of viewing landscapes, going off the beaten track to view a Highland mountain from a different angle, eclipsing the egotistical sublime to offer an alternative, less self-conscious view of the natural world. Gunn and Shepherd are not simply belated Romantics, but are aware of modifying what they see as Romantic impulses in the face of modern politics and technologies, continually searching for modes of observation and expression which evolve away from the conventional Romantic response to natural environments, into something more meaningful, more 'pure'. What Shepherd experiences on the mountain 'is not ecstasy, that leap out of the self that makes man like a god'. Instead, 'I am not out of myself, but in myself. I am. To know Being, this is the final grace accorded from the mountain'.[100]

The body is not made negligible, but paramount. Flesh is not annihilated but fulfilled. One is not bodiless, but essential body . . . It is therefore when the body is keyed to its highest potential and controlled to a profound harmony deepening into something that resembles trance, that I discover most nearly what it is to be. I have walked out of the body and into the mountain. I am a manifestation of its total life, as is the starry saxifrage or the white-winged ptarmigan.[101]

The phenomenological encounter with nature resolves the dualism suggested by the Cartesian approach, breaking away from the Western mode of thinking, which Gunn describes as 'linear, one-dimensional, continues like a straight line, adding to itself until it is stopped by a QED', in contrast to the Eastern approach, 'somehow three dimensional and organismal'.[102]

Such questions are explored in Gunn's essays, relating real encounters with Highland animals and landscapes to Zen philosophy and poetics. Stopped in his tracks at the side of a river, Gunn presents an almost trancelike vision of the heron, where a 'solitary bird, almost to its knees in the water, still as a slender tree stump, fishing, its size magnified in the fading light', is transformed into the Zen painting, or the haiku.[103] Gunn is struck by such static images. In 'Pictures in the Air', an essay from *Highland Pack*, Gunn relates his encounter with an old apple tree in winter, 'festooned with snow', yet 'laden with golden fruit' – fruit which turns out to be a flock of yellow hammers, 'each with its breast to the sun and still as the tree itself'. Gunn notes that he did not observe the moment when they flew off, giving his memory of the scene a 'static quality that time and change can never affect'.[104] Again, this recalls Bachelard, who suggests that 'real images are *engravings*, for it is the imagination that engraves them on our memories. They deepen the recollections we have experienced, which they replace, thus becoming imagined recollections . . . "phenomenological reverberation" obliterates all mediocre resonances'.[105] For Gunn, the encounter with the animal, and the transformation of this experience into an image which evokes 'phenomenological reverberation', fosters a sense of wholeness:

> Here was no destruction, no slightest apprehension of it. The very opposite. Not broken bits falling apart, but a calm cohering whole. Not fear but assurance. Not terror but delight. Not an internal subjective mess but an external objective scene, cool as the evening, held in a clarity that bathed the eyes and made them see as they had never seen.[106]

This Zen-inspired poetics of wildness seeks to avoid the pitfalls of Western expressions, with 'our unending torrents of words, our philosophical systems, our gargantuan Joycean outpourings'.[107] Instead, a calm, contemplative mode of perception allows a sense of harmony and wholeness, with the viewer's eyes made to 'see as they had never seen', and in place of an 'internal subjective mess' there appears an 'external objective scene'. Gunn suggests that this altered perception requires a different kind of writing:

> Such economy of means, each stroke so inevitable, so final . . . Can this wonder, and the serenity in which it lingers, be caught in words? Can it be set down, written, with the ultimate inspired simplicity, economy, of the single brush stroke?[108]

Gunn finds the 'haiku' or 'ideogramme' as the most suitable vehicle for such directness of observation – the three line form the Imagists loved for its verbal brevity and visual purity.

'In Talk with Duncan Ban MacIntyre': exploring the limits of poetry

Ideals of visual purity were certainly central to the work of other Scottish writers – and some who, like MacDiarmid and more recently Kenneth White, came to see the Highlands as the ground on which to build a renewed sense of Scottish identity, identifying the need 'to establish a new relationship to it, way outside anything like the rural bucolics of, say, England'.[109] Iain Crichton Smith writes of the 'visual hardness' of Duncan Ban MacIntyre's Gaelic poetry, his 'fidelity of observation' and his 'knowledge of subject matter'.[110] These attributes are also valued by Sorley Maclean, who calls for a recognition of Gaelic poetic tradition as radically distinct from English Romanticism:

> I know the world 'realism' is now chiefly applied to prose literature, and that its special modern connotation is naturalism as manifested in much of the European novel since Zola's time. But there is no necessity to limit the word thus. I see no reason why it cannot yet be applied to poetry to denote the opposite of romance, escapism, fantasy, and their concomitants, affectation, fancifulness, far-fetchedness, and falseness . . . As its matter, poetry has the life of man or external nature, and thus poetry may embrace all knowledge.[111]

Arguing that Gaelic poetry, in its clear-sighted approach to the natural world, is 'inconsistent with the pathetic fallacy', MacLean goes on to suggest that this cultural distinctiveness, which manages to avoid the limiting conventions of Romanticism, is a valuable alternative method of viewing landscape and nature.[112] For MacLean, MacIntyre's lively portrait of a Highland mountain and its wildlife, 'The Praise of Ben Dorain', 'makes no pretension to metaphysical content; actually its realization of dynamic nature makes its essential philosophic value as far superior to Wordsworth's poetry as it is in pure technique'.[113]

This distinction between Gaelic and English modes of thought and poetic conventions was also pursued by Hugh MacDiarmid, whose later work, partly inspired by his contact with younger Gaelic writers such as MacLean and George Campbell Hay, sought to establish an 'Ur-Gaelic initiative' as the 'impetus to civilisation'. Significantly, MacDiarmid aligned this 'Gaelic Idea' with Eastern thought – a connection which was also pursued by White in his 1960s and 70s approach to Zen, finding in Celtic poetry a delight 'in flickerings, scatterings, dissolvings, shudderings, all kind of sharp, momentary movements and sudden glimpses'.[114] Connecting his ideal of a 'poetry of facts' with Gaelic poetics, MacDiarmid claims that he 'dropped the romantic imagination in the thirties', and that 'Cartesian dualism had all gone from . . . [his] later work' in favour of 'materialism'.[115] As part of this project, MacDiarmid produced a series of imaginary conversations with Duncan Ban MacIntyre – 'In Talk with Donnchadh Bàn Mac an t'Saoir' and 'Further Talk with Donnchadh Bàn Mac an t'Saoir' – which were evidently written around or just after the time MacDiarmid had been translating MacIntyre's 'The Praise of Ben Dorain'.[116] In an epigraph to the first of these poems, MacDiarmid quotes Aldous Huxley's assertion that D. H. Lawrence 'could get inside the skin of an animal and tell you in the most convincing detail how it felt, and how, dimly, inhumanly, it thought'.[117] In doing so, he sets up a deliberate series of contrasts between the nature observation of the eighteenth-century Gaelic poet, who represents the 'Gaelic genius' which MacDiarmid was hyping-up elsewhere, and Lawrence's much-praised poetry of animals, such as those of *Birds Beasts and Flowers* (1923). MacDiarmid characterises Ban MacIntyre as a sort of Gaelic 'Pan', a pastoral bard whose poetry expresses 'The speech of one neither man nor animal – or both – | Yet not monster; a being in whom both races meet | On friendly ground'. Here, the natural world is 'kneaded | Into one substance with the kindred qualities in human nature, | Trees, grass, flowers, streams, cattle, deer and unsophisticated man'.[118] Probably MacDiarmid was thinking of Lawrence's writings on 'The Great God Pan', which emphasises 'the lived relatedness between man and his universe: sun, moon, stars, earth, trees, flowers, birds, animals, men everything'.[119] It is also possible, given MacDiarmid's contact with the folklorist F. Marian MacNeill, that this 'sylvan' creature is a peculiarly Gaelic version of Pan, the half-man, half-beast *Urisk* or *Uruisg*, said to haunt Ben Dorain in Gaelic folklore.

> Nature needed, and still needs, this beautiful creature
> Standing betwixt man and animal, sympathising with each,
> Comprehending the speech of either race, and interpreting
> The whole existence of one to the other.[120]

This liminal 'beautiful creature', positioned 'on the verge of nature', is a metaphor for *poiesis* itself, a means of connecting the human and natural worlds. Here MacDiarmid anticipates the idea of 'ecopoetics' developed by Jonathan Bate, who suggests that *poiesis* 'is language's most direct path or return to the *oikos*, the place of dwelling'.[121]

W. N. Herbert has commented that this portrait of MacIntyre is 'impersonal' and that it is his 'capacity to store information as much as the cultural value of the information stored that impresses MacDiarmid'.[122] Personal portraits are perhaps not MacDiarmid's main concern in this poem – although I would suggest that he does indeed see a cultural value in the ecological knowledge encoded in MacIntyre's poetry. Sorley MacLean's acknowledgement that the poetry of Gaels such as MacIntyre is 'deficient in explicit humanity' seems to correspond to Herbert's criticism of MacDiarmid's 'Scotland Small' lyric from his 'Direadh' poems, that 'it is a poem which concerns itself, however, magnificently, with shrubbery, not with humanity'.[123] Central to an understanding of MacDiarmid's engagement with MacIntyre is the surprising fact of his reliance on the ecologist Frank Fraser Darling's research on deer. The epigraph taken from Fraser Darling's pioneering ecological study, *A Herd of Red Deer: A Study in Animal Behaviour* (1937), states that 'It is very difficult for an active mind stuffed with the matter of 'Education' to play its part effectively in stalking wild animals':

> If you are going to observe an animal well you must know it well, and this statement is not such a glimpse of the obvious as it appears at first. It is necessary intellectually to soak in the environmental complex of the animal to be studied until you have a facility with it which keeps you as it were one move ahead. You must become intimate with the animal.[124]

Fraser Darling's notion of 'intimacy' is picked up by MacDiarmid in 'In Talk . . .', with a consideration of the 'intimate, initiating experience' of observing deer in the wild, through the medium of MacIntyre's poetry. This poetic virtual deer-stalking leads to a state of almost visionary perception, somewhat like the feelings described by Nan Shepherd in *The Living Mountain*, as MacDiarmid notes, 'The whole threshold of awareness was raised; the whole organism | Worked with unheard-of co-ordination'.[125] This phrase, which seems to appeal directly to a bardic, or shamanic, sense of raised consciousness, is in fact adapted from *A Herd of Red Deer*, in which Fraser Darling notes his sensations on discarding his shoes and socks in tracking the deer.

> I have been interested to note the reactions of my own senses. They all sharpened . . . The whole threshold of awareness was raised, I was never fatigued and stalking became very much easier. This ease in approaching animals was

something more than what was gained by leaving off heavy and possibly noisy shoes. The whole organism worked in better co-ordination.[126]

'Further Talk with Donnchadh Bàn Mac an t'Saoir' also draws on Fraser Darling's text, reflecting on 'weather conditions and insect pests' and 'meteorological changes' as factors influencing animal behaviour.[127] Whilst talk of the deer's 'growth-mechanism', or the phenomenon of 'orthogenesis', might, as Herbert suggests, have baffled MacIntyre, in a sense MacDiarmid wants his own modern Scottish writing to be seen to be carrying out the implications of the Gaelic poet's conclusion to 'The Praise of Ben Dorain', that:

> Is ged a thuirt mi beagan riu,
> Mun ìnnsinn uil' an dleasdnas orr',
> Chuireadh iad am bhreislich mi
> Le desimireachd chòmhraidh.[128]

> Though I've told a little of Ben Dorain here,
> Before I could tell all it deserves I would be
> In a delerium with the strange prolixity
> Of the talking called for, I fear.[129]

The linguistic layering and tireless cataloguing of details in the poetry of MacDiarmid's 'Mature Art' period does indeed amount, at times, to a delerium – and, some might argue, to 'prolixity' in the sense of 'tedious or tiresome lengthiness'.[130] But MacDiarmid's concern, in these poems written following his attempts at Gaelic translation, is with the possibility of a true poetic insight into the natural world, of bridging the gap between man and nature. In pursuit of this, he chose the verbosity of the epic as the only form which could encompass the 'enormous new perspective of the sciences', as opposed to the 'simplicity, economy, of the single brush stroke' Gunn identified in Zen poetics.[131] In his poetry of facts, MacDiarmid is aspiring to MacIntyre's capacity for what Maclean called Gaelic 'objective naturalist realism'. 'Only in *your* poetry,' MacDiarmid claims, do we experience:

> [. . .] the feeling of having reached that state
> All watchers of animals desire
> Of having dispensed with our physical presence
> [. . .]
> Or is that it? Is not really the bottom of our desire
> Not to be ignored but to be accepted?[132]

This possibility of acceptance – most importantly, the need for the human to accept the thing-in-itself – is an anxiety which runs through much post-war Scottish writing. Such possibilities were later questioned by Iain Crichton Smith in 'Deer on the High Hills' (1962). Smith, who had written his own fine translation of 'Ben Dorain', interrogates the central problem of 'knowing' the deer, of getting beyond the layers of cultural constructs and pathetic fallacies to the animals themselves.[133] Opening with some deliberately artificial similes, Smith says the deer are 'like debutantes on a smooth ballroom floor', or 'like Louis the Sixteenth | sustained in twilight on a marble plinth'.[134] Dismissing these images, he argues that in order to see the deer as they really are, 'you must build from there and not be circumvented by sunlight . . . or intuitions from the sky above | the deadly rock. Or even history'. Instead:

> You must build from the rain and stones
> till you can make
> a stylish deer on the high hills,
> and let its leaps be unpredictable![135]

While the gamekeeper-poet MacIntyre 'knew them intimately, was one of them', as Smith says, in 'a kind of Eden', 'Nevertheless he shot them also'. The difficult thing for the human to come to terms with is that the deer are an objective reality, separate from the human observer and, in Smith's view, unknowable, even meaningless, in purely objective terms. Humans can only know the natural world, he seems to suggest, subjectively, by imposing narratives upon it:

> What is the knowledge of the deer?
> Is there a philosophy of the hills?
> Do their heads peer into the live stars?
>
> . . .
>
> Are rivers stories, and are plains their prose?
> Are fountains poetry? And are rainbows the
> wistful smiles upon a dying face?
>
> Such symbols freeze upon my desolate lips![136]

Instead, we need to recognise the truth of the things-in-themselves, that 'there is no metaphor. The stone is stony. | The deer step out in isolated air'.[137]

This recalls MacDiarmid's contemplation, in 'On a Raised Beach', of the 'inconceivable discipline, courage, and endurance, | Self-purification and anti-humanity' required to fully know reality, suggesting that 'it is wrong to indulge in these illustrations | instead of just accepting the stones'.[138] To 'get into this stone world', to shake off the human tendency towards metaphor and anthropomorphism requires an 'Adamantine and inexorable' personality, but risks profound alienation, and it is questionable whether either MacDiarmid or Smith are able to sustain this stance in their own work. Instead, attentiveness and the development of linguistic representation are the tactics which MacDiarmid suggests can bring us closer to an understanding of other organisms. In the spirit of 'tell[ing] all it deserves', MacDiarmid muses about the possible outcomes of an exhaustive poetry of facts:

> It would be relatively easy to write the history
> Of a pair of nesting dab-chicks or of a day in their life,
> With a continuousness and exhaustiveness that might challenge comparison,
> Without breaks, a seamless garment,
> With the most accomplished and most dangerous works of modern fiction,
> Differing from them only in not pretending to know
> The birds' minds from the inside out, but hoping at best
> To get at their nature from their movements and write their odyssey
> By working from the outside in.[139]

The idea that the 'history | Of a pair of nesting dab-chicks' might rival 'the most . . . dangerous works of modern fiction' is a characteristic piece of MacDiarmidean rhetoric – recalling his claim for the 'moral resemblance' of Jamieson's *Etymological Dictionary of the Scottish Language* to James Joyce's *Ulysses*.[140] Despite the hype, such claims are surely what MacDiarmid's later poetic endeavours are all about – the poetry of verifiable scientific data, of materialism building on Romanticism. But the danger of subjectivity persists, as MacDiarmid notes: 'let us take nothing for granted. | Allen Upward used to warn us to learn | From things themselves, not from words about the things'.[141] The Imagist credo, glanced at by MacDiarmid's reference to Allen Upward, called for a 'direct treatment of the thing', a succinctness of description which aims for a visual clarity.[142] MacDiarmid elsewhere claims these properties for the Gaelic language and, by implication, for himself, 'that faculty of sheer description | Which not only tells *what* a thing is, but at least | Incidentally goes far towards telling *why*. | But beyond this how?'[143]

From Glasgow to Orkney (via Little Sparta)

Although the 1960s might seem to bring about a dislodging of the age of MacDiarmid and Muir, in fact the coming of 1960s 'countercultures' highlighted the significance of ecologically-minded aspects of writing in earlier twentieth-century Scotland, and provided the opportunity for these aspects to flourish in an international climate which was increasingly attuned to green issues. In many ways, it was Kenneth White who took up MacDiarmid's quest begun in 'On a Raised Beach', searching for a form of expression which might allow the human to 'get into this stone world'. By linking this quest for the fundamentals of existence, which White has theorised as 'geopoetics', with a search for an authentic culture 'grounded' through contact with essential nature, White's work also intersects with the likes of Muir and Mackay Brown.

> In my semantics, 'world' emerges from a contact between the human mind and the things, the lines, the rhythms of the earth. When this contact is sensitive, subtle, intelligent, you have 'a world' (a culture) in the strong, confirming and enlightening sense of the word. When that contact is insensitive, simplistic and stupid, you don't have a world at all, you have a non-world, a pseudo-culture, a dictatorial enclosure or a massness. Geopoetics is concerned with developing sensitive and intelligent contact, and with working out original ways to express that contact.[144]

White's geopoetics predates Bate's ecopoetics by some years and, while the two concepts share similar preoccupations, White's approach has broader aims (in its aim to fuse science, philosophy and poetry into a coherent school of thought) and is more politicised, directed towards a quest for cultural renewal, focused, in part, on Scottish national identity. As in MacDiarmid's work, there is a certain elitism in White's poetics, an elitism which is essentially a form of resistance, a belief in the power of geographical and cultural 'eccentricity'. White aligns himself with the figure of the 'intellectual nomad':

> . . . engaged, outside the glitzy or glaury compound of late modernity, in an area of complex co-ordinates. [The intellectual nomad] is trying to move out of pathological psycho-history, along uncoded paths, into fresh, existential, intellectual, poetic space.[145]

White, born in the Gorbals area of Glasgow in the 1930s, has lived for most of his adult life in France, participating in the intellectual life of Paris at the time of the student revolt of 1968. White draws on diverse sources, including eastern philosophies and, as Michael Gardiner has shown, the radical postmodern thought of French theorists such as Gilles Deleuze.[146] Since then, situated on the outermost periphery of Scottish culture and physically on the 'edge of Europe', as he characterises his home on the Breton coast, White has made this outsider status into a position of strength, establishing the International Institute of Geopoetics in 1989.

The geopoetic possibilities of life on the periphery are explored in *The Cold Wind of Dawn* (1966), and specifically in the poem, 'Ovid's Report', spoken in the persona of Ovid during his exile from Rome on the shores of the Black Sea. In contrast to MacDiarmid's exhaustive 'seamless garment', and conscious of Gunn's search for the economy of 'the single brushstroke', White proposes a poetry composed of 'quick notes'. As with the quality Sorley MacLean identifies in the work of

Gaelic poets, 'rich in image . . . [but] not very rich in metaphor', White's work is to involve 'no metaphor-mongering | no myth-malarkey'.[147] Instead, the poet is compelled to go beyond cultural convention, 'into | this new space':

> follow right through
> the transhuman road
> find, who knows, the source
> of another light.[148]

White notes that his early work was influenced by Neil Gunn's 'cold images . . . based on a triple notion of primordial contact, ecstatic experience and the search for a logic, a language to make it all last'.[149] The poem 'Cape Breton Uplight', first published in the 1979 collection, *Mahamudra*, speaks of this need for 'primordial contact', where, if 'the earth disappears | from the minds of the living | the real world is lost'.

> At the edge of the world
>   in the emptiness
>   maintaining the relations
>   the primordial contact
>   the principles by which
>   reality is formed
>   on the verge of the abstract[150]

To be able to evoke this experience involves, as it did for MacDiarmid, Gunn and Shepherd, a development away from conventional modes of expression, from anthropomorphism or romantic egoism. 'The Valley of Birches', first published as part of his 'Pyrenean Meditations' in *Atlantica: mouvements et méditations* (1986), traces a development in White's approach to the experiencing of and writing about a landscape. At first, the valley 'speaks to me like a memory', but, like MacDiarmid on the Shetlandic beach, White 'must enter this birch-world | and speak from within it' – a quest which involves a search for 'the necessary words' which will enable us 'to quietly | penetrate the reality'. Recalling Gunn's view of poetic insight involving 'sheer hard work, concentration, discipline, a hunch, and, with luck, an astonishment', the geopoetic quest, White suggests, is complex; partly intuitive, partly relying on discipline and patience – an approach which is influenced by Zen philosophy.[151]

> Before we can ever say anything . . . we must link ourselves, by a long silent process, to the reality. Only long hours of silence can lead us to our language, only long miles of strangeness can lead us to our home.[152]

Unlike Sorley Maclean's contemplation of the animistic birch wood in 'Hallaig', a perspective on place infused with human emotion and memory, White's geopoetic stance seeks to break away from history. What he is contemplating in these poems is a move from 'place' to 'space', taking 'the bird path', 'giving up all merely egoistic attachment and being open to "original nature"'.[153] White's work speaks of an essential distrust of narrative and history; here, the human markers of place present an obstacle to reaching the real world, the things-in-themselves. White believes that, in order to truly 'ground' ourselves and our culture, we need to '[move] out of history':

> the end of history as a primal reference, and as vector towards some longed-for absolute . . . the absence of any overriding story – mythic, religious, metaphysical, socio-historical. When you've got no story left, what is there? – the nature of things. The reading of that nature is inexhaustible. It's from the nature of things that real writing emerges, not from any I-Thou dialectic.[154]

This seems to be where the ideal exhaustive poetry of facts breaks down. Like Shepherd's assertion that 'Knowing another is endless', in place of a grand narrative or essential 'truth', White proposes a poetry constantly in flux: 'I have traced out the black on the white | like an unfinished poem – | always broken off, always recommenced'.[155]

The anxiety over history and the potential value – and limitations – of poetic representation extends to other writers of White's generation, perhaps most explicitly in the work of Edwin Morgan. As noted above, Morgan was sceptical about 'traditional' poetic subjects, arguing that poetry must grapple 'not only with the very slowly evolving nature of man but also with the very quickly evolving relation of man to his environment'.[156] In line with this aim, much of his poetry is localised within Scottish urban spaces and draws its energies from the life of the city. His sequence of 'Glasgow Sonnets', from the 1973 collection *From Glasgow to Saturn*, offers an interesting counterpoint to the Glasgow novel of the post-war period, transforming the politically-inflected concerns of the urban novelists into lyrics, striking not only for their artistry but for their representational power. Morgan's 'Glasgow Sonnets' contain little to suggest the natural world, little, indeed to suggest any sort of life other than abject urban poverty and despair. Animal life is functional or alienating: 'a shilpit dog fucks grimly by the close', whilst a 'cat's eyes glitter' from beneath an abandoned baby's pram.[157] Similarly, the only signs of vegetative life are 'roses of mould', and the only houses not homes, but condemned tenements. The only possibility of escape or transcendence here seems to be represented by the concrete flyovers' 'loops of light', not the empty promises of the 'Environmentalists, ecologists | and conservationists', whose plans for 'Pedestrianization' and 'riverside walks' are met with bitter sarcasm. Traditional poetic responses are also redundant: 'elegists can't hang themselves on fled- | from trees or poison a recycled cup'.[158]

Morgan's dismissal of the elegists and environmental campaigners reflects the conservative, middle-class aspect of popular environmentalism as it stood in 1960s and 70s Britain. Despite the origins of the idea in the nineteenth century, the concept of ecology had after all, only been in the domain of public consciousness for a relatively short period of time – although it is notable how quickly Hugh MacDiarmid picked up on its significance in the 1940s. Environmentalism and ecology had, for most of the century, gone about under the guise of geographical and biological sciences, and of regional planning, but to many people 'ecology' itself meant nothing more than stuffy conservationism, whilst the radical 'green' politics of ecological thought associated with American Beat poetry had not quite filtered into British environmental consciousness as an explicit movement.

While Morgan was interested in Beat innovation, it is also true that Hugh MacDiarmid occupied an important place in his theory of poetry. Morgan was conscious, in his own work on poetry and science, to be engaging with some of the issues MacDiarmid had grappled with in earlier decades. Writing in 1963, Morgan drew parallels between the startling perspectives on the planet earth gained by the first space mission and the need for new perspectives in poetry, exemplified by MacDiarmid's own work.

> When Yuri Gagarin was circling the earth in his spaceship Voztok he was not only exposed to a new physical and mental experience . . . he also received an aesthetic experience which no man had had before, and his reaction to the 'delicate and lovely' and 'hard-to-describe' blue aureole surrounding the globe . . . deserve to be noted both by non-scientists who say there is nothing 'human' to be gained from such experiments and by scientists who say that instruments would record everything better than men in any case. The fact is that man must react, as man, to his whole environment.[159]

In Morgan's poetry space explorers are frequently earth explorers. 'Memories of Earth', from *The New Divan* (1977) imagines a troop of such voyagers who are shrunk down in order to enter a stone and, at the sub-atomic level, find the planet earth, a 'speck of blue swirling with white' at its centre – as Colin Nicholson notes, Morgan's explorers literally fulfil MacDiarmid's quest to get into the 'stone world'.[160] Once on the planet's surface, they find earth time is non-linear, their experiences given only in flickering glimpses, 'a gabble in a wilderness of wires | an earth labouring in memories'. In an echo of Muir's heraldic image of 'fabulous steeds set on an ancient shield' in 'The Horses', the earth's memories appear as a series of tableaux, where 'rearing horses | foam at their jerked bits like an old frieze'. The aliens are horrified by the human history of cruelty, encapsulated in the 'acrid smoke' of the concentration camp, and contrasted with the image of the Scottish moorland of 'yellow broom' and 'swooping bird[s]' – a contrast which corresponds to Theodor Adorno's cold war belief that the 'real, wide world of grass and earthquakes and bullfinches' is forever separate from 'this human state – grief, and anger, and guilt'.[161] However, the poem contemplates the human ability not only to destroy but also to nurture. Opposed to the twentieth-century terror of the concentration camp's 'eerie furnaces', and a post-apocalyptic future where humanity is forced to abandon the earth, dispersed, 'like seeds' in a thousand spaceships, Morgan presents the image of a canoe. The tiny vessel in the middle of the vast ocean parallels the image of the earth in space, and is also a version of Noah's ark, laden with tattooed rowers, families, animals, coconuts brimming with 'fresh smiling milk'. Here, the boat symbolises the human capacity for endurance, the quest to find and make a home against the odds: 'that infinite hope | that forces a canoe upon the waters'.[162]

For Morgan, as for other post-war Scottish writers such as Alasdair Gray, science fiction presents an alternative way of exploring questions of heritage, homeland and dwelling.[163] True, Morgan attempts to make a radical distinction between himself and more 'traditional' poets, saying 'Good luck to Seamus Heaney . . . but I pushed out, and continue to push out, a different boat . . . a nuclear-powered icebreaker . . . a ship of space out there up there riding the solar wind'.[164] Despite such pyrotechnics, however, Morgan is also interested in the fundamental question of belonging, those 'primary laws of our nature' which, as Heaney suggests, impels us to 'make homes and search for our histories'.[165] Something of this can be seen from his translations from Anglo-Saxon poetry, where 'The soil grips hard. There a hundred | generations of people have dwindled and gone'.[166]

The late 1960s was a particularly fruitful time for Scottish literature, with poets and novelists including Edwin Morgan, Archie Hind, Ian Hamilton Finlay, George Mackay Brown, Iain Crichton Smith and Douglas Dunn all publishing work. However, despite MacDiarmid's poetic efforts, there was still an apparent division between rural and urban writing in Scotland. Practitioners of the 'Glasgow novel' such as Hind and George Friel were producing work with a politically hard edge which at first sight seems opposed to the likes of Crichton Smith and Mackay Brown, whose focus remained on the islands and rural environments of Scotland. The contrast would seem to be encapsulated in the near-simultaneous publication of Hind's *The Dear Green Place* (1966) and Mackay Brown's *The Calendar of Love* (1967) – although it is worth noting that both Hind and Mackay Brown were students of Edwin Muir at Newbattle Abbey College.

The fact that links between rural and urban environments were beginning to be questioned during this period is evident from the publication of both Leo Marx's *The Machine in the Garden* in 1964, and Raymond Williams' *The Country and the City* in 1973. Marx's book is the first in a tradition of American critical studies of cultural attitudes towards the natural world, and is useful in this context as a signifier of the changing attitudes to literature and ecology. Marx points out that American writers fail to design 'satisfactory resolutions for their pastoral fables', since the ideal of the American 'virgin' wilderness no longer exists. The recognition that the American pastoral 'ideal landscape' is an impossibility means that 'an inspiring vision of a humane community has been reduced to a token of individual survival . . . the old symbol of reconciliation is obsolete'.[167] The unsatisfactory nature of pastoral should not, he argues, be seen as the fault of the writer, since the writer is merely clarifying 'the root conflict of our culture'.[168] Williams also notes the disruption of pastoral modes of representation in the twentieth century, as traditional agricultural communities were broken up in the move towards increased industrialisation and urbanisation. However, he also suggests that narratives which recognise the long heritage of rural Britain combined within the context of modern urban life are of crucial importance:

> It is easy to separate the country and the city and then their modes of literature: the rural or regional; the urban or metropolitan . . . But there are always some writers who insist on the connections, and among these are a few who see the transition itself as decisive, in a complex interaction and conflict of values.[169]

In fact, the interaction between rural and urban environments had been acknowledged in Scottish fiction long before the 1960s, in novels such as Edwin Muir's *Poor Tom*, George Blake's *The Shipbuilders* (1935) and even Edward Gaitens' *Dance of the Apprentices* (1948).[170] The title of Archie Hind's Glasgow novel, *The Dear Green Place*, suggests the image of a pastoral landscape which belies its urban, industrial setting. Indeed, it is hard to think of a less appropriate name for a novel which opens with an overview of a Scottish industrial wasteland, and closes with its protagonist, trapped in a cycle of poverty and disappointment, vomiting on a Clyde ferry. Hind highlights this distinction by quoting a piece of well-known Glasgow doggerel, based on the city's coat-of-arms:

> This is the tree that never grew,
> This is the bird that never flew,
> This is the fish that never swam,
> This is the bell that never rang.[171]

While the naming of the novel is certainly intended as a sardonic swipe at the industrial decline and aesthetic dearth of the city in the 1960s, the reverberations of the name, which translates the Gaelic root of the word 'Glasgow' – 'Gles Chu', or 'dear green place' – are felt throughout the book, with the result that the ghost of the pastoral world is never far away. Others have commented on the novel's references to the Gaelic and agricultural origins of Glasgow, with the implied distance between the urban present and the pastoral past.[172] I would go further, however, and suggest that *The Dear Green Place* can itself be read as a kind of distorted pastoral, bringing the urban roots of pastoralism back to the flashpoint of tension itself, the industrial city.

The negative representations of urban environments to be found in works such as *The Dear Green Place* or Edwin Morgan's 'Glasgow Sonnets' owe as much to an engagement with ideas and ideals about the natural world and the legacy of pastoralism as they do to urban realism. Novels such as Hind's necessarily deal with the socio-economic realities of urban places, and have even been given a critical category of their own – 'The Glasgow novel' – which brings to mind these themes. However, *The Dear Green Place* is a novel as much about environmental impact and ideas about rurality as it is about urban experience. Take, for example, the following passage which considers the history of the river Clyde, that enduring symbol of Glasgow industry:

> The mossy slopes harden into packed banks of black hardened mud, the soft greenery is a *virid* colour from the stretches of soda waste, the rippling affluents gush from cast iron pipes, an oily chemical sediment; we hear now the din of machinery, the thumping of hammers and the hiss and blast of steam and gas. Then the din dies down to a rattle and we come to the idyllic spot where the gentle oxen crossed and the little Molendinar burn flowed into the broad shallows of the river; the spot which the Gaels named Gles Chu, the spot where as legend had it St. Mungo recovered his lost ring from the belly of a salmon. The little valley of the Molendinar is now stopped with two centuries of refuse – soap, tallow, cotton waste, slag, soda, bits of leather, broken pottery, tar and caoutchouc – the waste products of a dozen industries and a million lives, and it is built over with slums, yards, streets and factories.[173] [author's italics]

Originally meaning 'verdant', the term 'virid' – which appears in pastoral verses such as James Macpherson's *Poems of Ossian* – is a measure of the distance between Glasgow's pastoral past and its industrial present in Hind's novel.[174] It is difficult to read this narrative history of Glasgow presented by the novel's protagonist, Mat Craig, without also observing a history of environmental impact – the transformation of 'country' into 'city', the pollution of the once-pure Clyde, and the layers of 'waste products', 'slums' and 'factories' deliberately contrasted with the initial 'idyllic spot' denoted by Gaelic place-names. The original *strath* (valley) is presented as a pastoral idyll, with 'soft greenery' and 'thymy banks', the only sounds 'the hum of the wandering bee and the splash of water on stone', but, in an echo of Patrick Geddes's geographical model of the 'Valley Section', the surveying eye moves 'down from the idyllic and uncertain past into the reaches of the Clyde where the air begins to darken, the horizon is smudged, and intermingled with grazing fields, trees, farms and gardens are coal heaps, pit heads, corrugated iron sheds, foundries, machine shops, bings and mills'.[175]

Mat's attitude towards this transformation is, however, one of ambivalence, taking pleasure in the idea that the 'river had become something of a human artefact'.[176] The history of human interactions is *de facto* the natural history of the Clyde. Indeed, the boundaries between the supposedly separate categories of 'country' and 'city' are repeatedly blurred in this novel. In the unremitting detail of Hind's descriptions, it is almost as if nature is the alien factor in this landscape, polluting the concrete with dampness and greenery:

> It was a particular kind of landscape, a mixture of human and natural industry which intrigued him. Each aspect seemed to take on and mingle with some of the characteristics of the other. The grass and willows growing along the banks of the river were grey and sooty looking . . . the mud selvedge of the river showed rainbow tints from an oily sediment . . . the brick buildings were heavily marked from the weather, the power station had great damp streaks running down it, the pointing on the factory was all crumbled and the bricks eaten with damp and covered with a thin green mossy slime.[177]

The Dear Green Place is in many ways a novel about a boy's relationship with a river – the industrial, polluted Clyde – and in this sense it is a distorted, post-war reflection of Neil Gunn's *Highland River*.

> He knew every waste pipe that gushed its mucky sediment into the river, every path along its bank, every forsaken spot and lonely stretch where no one but children ever went, where between long factory walls and the river there were narrow paths that led merely from one open stretch of dumping ground to the next. Here he had played as a child in the oldest industrial landscape in the world, amongst the oldest factories in the world, and it had been through this landscape that he had walked when he had once felt so unaccountably happy.[178]

This, surely, is a strange adaptation of Hardy's concept of 'local knowledge'. It might seem incongruous that someone should describe the polluted stretches of the Clyde with the same fondness and intimacy experienced, for example, by Kenn in exploring the strath in *Highland River*. But to ignore the reality that most of the Scottish population does live in urban zones would be to pastoralise – or kailyardise – Scottish life and environment. Hind is certainly using irony to show the degradation of the Clydeside industrial wasteland, especially given the unemployment and poverty of 1960s Glasgow. Belonging to a generation of Scottish writers who grew up with Muir's *Autobiography* and the novels of Neil Gunn, Hind is also challenging the pretence that the emotions of the rural child exploring its environment are different, or any less significant, than for the urban child. This is not to say that Hind finds the countryside less attractive than the town, or that exploring a Highland burn is not more satisfying and pleasurable than exploring a polluted river, but it does lend the whole experience of growing up in this urban landscape a dignity which it has often been denied.

In contrast to the impact of the 'Glasgow novel' and its gritty realism, George Mackay Brown's work may seem an anachronism in the modern literary scene, with a possibly unhealthy obsession with the archaic, mythological history of the Orkneys, which seeks to deny the reality of contemporary life. Terry Gifford has criticised his poetry for its reliance on myth, its 'wish-fulfilment' form of pastoral. Commenting on the poet's use of 'archaic words', he wryly (and falsely) suggests that 'No one ever drinks beer in a Mackay Brown poem. Only 'ale' is served in Arcadia'.[179] This 'retreat from the adult complexities of life, even in contemporary Orkney', leads to a 'mythic fatalism in his nostalgia for Orkney life', an 'Arcadia [which] forces fewer moral questions than Muir's'.[180] But what Gifford is really criticising is the apparent lack of an explicitly 'green' political agenda, based on his reading of Brown's poetry as a 'pejorative pastoral', an example of a complacent idealisation of rural life.[181] It is significant, Gifford claims, that 'the one "green" poem that Mackay Brown has written, against the drilling for uranium in Orkney in the 1970s, he tried to suppress, refusing to republish it'.[182] In response to this, one might cite Jonathan Bate's argument that 'the role of *ecopoiesis* . . . is to engage *imaginatively* with the non-human', and that 'the cause of ecology may not necessarily be best served by poets taking the moral high ground and speaking from the point of view of ecological correctness'.[183] However, I would suggest that Gifford's commentary ignores the crucial element of resistance, the power of defiance, in Mackay Brown's writing, a defiance which is also evident in the work of other Scottish island and garden poets.

Christopher Whyte has noted the 'aestheticisation of violence' in Mackay Brown's poetry, which itself is so stylised as to seem 'deliberately set apart and cut off from the world in which it subsists'.[184] One might think here of the poet and artist Ian Hamilton Finlay's tanks, machine guns, grenades and guillotines in his poetry garden at Little Sparta, the sculpted bird tables which 'transform hungry birds into aircraft landing on and taking off from their carrier' – and note that Finlay had lived on Orkney in the 1950s, working as a shepherd and making his first concrete poems.[185] As Finlay has asserted, in one of his characteristic punning aphorisms, 'certain gardens are described as retreats when they are really attacks'.[186] Similarly, Iain Crichton Smith, who defended the status of the islander in the essay 'Real People in a Real Place', says that his community and its local, natural environment is 'a central concern for me, but beyond it there are echoes of war, injustices, violence, evil'.[187] The island or rural village, for Smith, is 'a home from which I can explore, and expatiate on that larger contemporary world'.[188] For Finlay, as for Mackay Brown and Crichton Smith, all of them 'wee bloke[s] on . . . Scottish hillside[s]', the garden or island is not an attempt to escape from the problems of modernity but a place where we can attempt to make sense of our place in the world.[189]

Little Sparta, Finlay's hillside farm, garden and poetry temple in Lanarkshire was named as a strategy of defiance following a protracted conflict with the local authority over the designation of the garden's public building as a 'temple'. Finlay's artistic practice takes place at the interface between the built and the natural environment, and at the meeting point of poetry, sculpture, architecture, and philosophy; his avant-garde experimentation in concrete poetry is often considered alongside Edwin Morgan or North American Beat or Black Mountain poets such as Robert Creeley. Finlay's work is, however, also a meaningful point of connection with the perspectives offered by Muir and Mackay Brown. Indeed, Creeley, whose work provided the title for Finlay's *Poor. Old. Tired. Horse.* magazine, values Finlay's 'commitment to wonder', supplying a necessary 'acknowledgement, a prayer, a faith, a place' for the recognition of the physical world.[190] Paralleling Mackay Brown's quest to recuperate elements of Orkney's 'ancient life-giving heraldry', the past 'from which it draws its continuing life, from which it cuts itself off at its peril', for Finlay, modern Western culture is 'condition[ed]' – and perhaps also condemned – by its 'separat[ion] from the past', with the result that 'there is no place for piety any longer'.[191] Piety, Finlay feels, is an essential component of an authentic culture; the lack of piety in modern Western societies, he suggests, 'is why so many things become incomprehensible, and therefore cannot be spoken about'. Piety implies reverence, faithfulness, but beyond that a sort of asceticism – a belief that art should embody 'order and some kind of ethical plainness'.[192]

This quest for piety and plainness of expression seems related to the way Finlay's poetic practice evolves. As Ken Cockburn observes, Finlay follows a rather unusual trajectory from the early short stories, not, as might be expected, to the 'expanses' of the novel, but into the confined and measured brevity of the lyric.[193] Through experimentations in concrete poetry – as in *Glasgow Beasts, An a Burd* (1961) – Finlay's methods are further refined; eventually the lyric is pared back to a single sentence, even a single word, and then set into the physical world itself, inscribed on wood, stone and other materials in public spaces or in the garden at Little Sparta. Finlay writes of this as the logical extension of a trajectory already set in motion:

> It seemed obvious to me that one could not have a literally one-word poem on the page, since any work must contain relationship; equally, one could (conceivably) have a one-word poem in a garden, if the surroundings were conceived as part of the poem.[194]

This is almost a crystallisation of Gunn's idea of the 'economy of the single brush-stroke', where the poem, transmuted into sculpture and set into the garden becomes a sort of contemplative, static image as well as poetic language, with its possibility for what Gaston Bachelard described as the 'phenomenological reverberation' of the isolated poetic image, 'the vocal importance . . . of a word'.[195]

Mackay Brown's poems frequently have this solid, runic quality about them, as though they too were carved or crafted artefacts. Indeed, some lyrics play with such associations, as in 'Hill Runes':

> *Kirkyard*
>   Between stone poem and skull
>   April
>   Touches rat, spade, daffodil[196]

Deliberate, resonant words and phrases are set out on the page; as Brown says of Orcadian speech in *An Orkney Tapestry*, 'few words [are] considerately placed like stones on a dyke'.[197] Mackay Brown's poems are always emphatically 'made' – this is the 'mannered', artificial quality, the 'fondness for epithets' which Whyte suggests verges on the 'kitsch', 'an aesthetic object'.[198] However, one might suggest that perhaps this is where the Orcadian rune meets the 'model, of order' which characterises Finlay's concrete poetry, a crafted object not, as Whyte suggests, cut off from its surroundings, but set in relation to them: a 'tangible image of goodness and sanity'.[199]

What Mackay Brown is aiming for is 'word, blossoming as legend, poem, story, secret', which 'holds a community together and gives a meaning to its life'.[200] Yves Abrioux has noted Finlay's reaction against 'the language of the administrative and judicial establishment, both elected and bureaucratic . . . Finlay's artistic response to the behaviour of hostile authorities challenges the discursive and constitutional propriety of their actions'; Finlay himself suggested that 'the bureaucratic battle is the language battle'.[201] Taking into consideration such wider concerns, a reading of Mackay Brown's work does not reveal a 'pejorative pastoral' but a representation of a regionally distinct community. His novel *Greenvoe* (1972) offers just such a representation, with no central 'hero' but a series of interwoven voices and interwoven lives of the small island community. Perhaps the nature of the vision of the Orkney Islands which he is trying to portray might best be understood through the application of Bakhtinian theory, which seeks to emphasise 'architectonics' or 'interrelationships', and is sympathetic to the ideas of both ecology and communities. In *Greenvoe*, the arrival of the bureaucratic 'guest' signifies division, the sinister stranger on the island bringing with him disruption and eventual devastation. But this is not to say that the Orkney Islands are represented as an enclosed space, hostile to strangers. The arrival of the Indian silk salesman, for instance, is seen to enrich the island, although individuals in the community may react with ambivalence towards him. The community in Mackay Brown's work, as in Lewis Grassic Gibbon's *A Scots Quair*, is not a univocal entity existing in some sort of idyllic vacuum, but a heteroglossic one; ambivalent, by turns harmonious or contradictory, the voices expressing the discord and disharmony of individuals which are subsumed within wider societal harmony – a concept which is represented in Mackay Brown's work as a 'seamless garment', interestingly recalling the similar image employed by MacDiarmid to symbolise by turns the unity of the Workers or the potentialities of poetic representation.[202]

Speech on the Orkney Islands varies from the 'heroic voices' of the 'gentry' to the crofters and fishermen whose speech is 'slow and wondering, like water lapping amongst stones'.[203] Mackay Brown does not need to explicitly express a moral judgement or political viewpoint in his creative work; he lets the heteroglossic nature of his writings do that for him – the combined voices of the Orkney islands themselves. As Kathleen Jamie has commented, Mackay Brown's writing 'enacts the ecology it describes . . . the soundscape of an interconnected, secure community'.[204] In contrast to this heteroglossic soundscape is the sinister 'guest', the bureaucrat who signifies the destruction of the island by the Black Star project. This stranger does not speak, does not interact with the woven voices of the island in any way. Even his name, scrawled in the guestbook at the inn, is unreadable, 'not a name, it was more a strange involuted squiggle, a sign or a hieroglyph out of the remote past or the remote future'.[205]

Bakhtin wrote that discourse is defined by certain 'speech genres' which the speakers must tacitly agree upon in order to engage in a dialogue. But the stranger's silence prevents such dialogue, and denies communal life:

> Men must dance to some music, answer to some utterance. For our worship is erected now, all over the world, in place of the Word, the Number. And the belly is filled with uniform increasingly tasteless bread, the hands cannot have enough of possessing, face by face by face comes from the same precise mould and gazes, a rigid numbered unseeing mask, into the golden future.[206]

The 'speech genre' of the bureaucrat is that of the 'number' rather than the 'word', an alien, cataloguing form of discourse which reduces the worth of the islanders to 'Black Star potential: 9' or 'Black Star potential: Nil' on an index card.[207] The 'number' is thus associated with everything that is not 'natural': technology, concrete, destruction – much the same unholy trinity which Muir feared in 'The Good Town'. Like Muir, Mackay Brown's antidote is focused on the concept of community, of belonging; but unlike Muir, by writing with a strong sense of local identity, Mackay Brown's defiance is perhaps more robust. Keeping in mind Bakhtin's argument about the power of folk culture, whose rituals reflect the cyclical aspects of the seasons, of birth, death and the body, Mackay Brown's focus on these cycles of destruction and renewal offer some hope. In his scenes involving the initiation rites of the crofters, the 'Ancient Mystery of the Horsemen' (notably, this is a concept which Edwin Morgan also employs in his 1972 collection of concrete and experimental poetry, *The Horseman's Word*) Mackay Brown offsets the daily trivial incidents of life with the ancient, pagan roots of agricultural knowledge and ritual – a version of Muir's universal 'fable' behind the individual 'story', as well as Gunn's idea of a unifying archaic folk culture. Mackay Brown consciously opposes folk culture with 'officialdom' in a way which relates to Bakhtin's idea of the carnivalesque:

> The feast is always essentially related to time, either to the recurrence of an event in the natural (cosmic) cycle, or to biological or historic timeliness. Moreover, through all the stages of historic development feasts were linked to moments of crisis, of breaking points in the cycle of nature or in the life of society and man. Moments of death and revival, or change and renewal, always led to a festive perception of the world.[208]

For Bakhtin, folk rituals offer an alternative 'second world and a second life outside officialdom'.[209] Mackay Brown seems to understand this idea of folk culture as an antidote to 'officialdom' and technology. Officialdom's 'intolerant, one-sided tone of seriousness' is countered, in the novel, by 'the people's unofficial truth', evident from the continuation of the 'very ancient brutal beautiful ceremony' of the Horseman's initiation.[210] If 'pastoralism' disenfranchises the 'real people' of the supposed idyll, then Mackay Brown's representations of the Orkney Islands can hardly be unproblematically pigeonholed as 'pastoral', even if he does rely on certain pastoral conventions and modes of expression. An idyll denies time and change, and erases the individual personality in preference for what Iain Crichton Smith called a 'vague' and 'misty' representation of rural people. But what emerges in Mackay Brown's writings is both a celebration of personalities and a history of change, with one wave after another of incomers to the island, each bringing with them their own traditions and technologies. The eviction of the crofters and fishermen of *Greenvoe* by the agents of sinister progress reflects the long history of violent evictions in the Highlands and Islands by wealthy landowners. Behind these human changes, though, lie the cycles of the seasons and the lives of the animals – echoing in prose what Edwin Muir had expressed in poetic myths and emblems.

Ancient human artefacts, such as the brochs which appear in both Gunn's and Mackay Brown's writings, or the 'eirdes' or 'earth-houses' described by Lewis Grassic Gibbon, are representative of a perceived ancient connection with the earth.[211] Rather than a sentimental or romanticised view of this primitive relationship, Mackay Brown introduces ideas of totemic sacrifice and ritual behaviour, which develops from Muir's abstracted classical, mediaeval and Christian influences into a more concrete, primitive concept of human-nature relationships. In many ways, Mackay Brown is a poet on the far side of that cycle of folk culture – a culture which he is concerned is coming to an end, even while he asserts that the fundamentals of human psychology are much the same as they were 5000 years ago. His concern does not arise merely out of a conservative wish for things always to stay the same, but for the worry that faceless progress will do away with individuality and personal freedoms. Mackay Brown's more concrete emphasis on folk culture and heritage draws both reader and author closer to the community and the earth on which it depends, rather than establishing the conceptual distance common to the idyllic pastoral.

But Mackay Brown's novels and poetry speak of the possibility of a connection with the natural world which defies – rather than denies – the intrusion of technology and mass culture. As White has suggested, 'a country is that which offers resistance . . . Post-colonial Scotland means getting back down to Alba, to original landscape-mindscape, and, connecting them, to wordscape'.[212] Viewed in the context of apparently more 'radical' writers like Finlay or White, George Mackay Brown is not the end of a tradition, but part of an ongoing debate in Scottish literature concerning the importance of myth and ritual in our relationship with the natural world, as well as the differing abilities of poetry and prose to maintain or transform this fundamental relationship.

Such fundamental concerns with community, environment and shared responsibility, both for the 'belongers' and the 'non-belongers', are perhaps more important now than they ever were: there has indeed, to borrow Morgan's words of 1962, been a 'day of reckoning' which recognises that 'language, myth, nature' are relevant precisely *because* we live in an age of technology.

Ultimately, what writers like Muir and Mackay Brown, Shepherd and Gunn, MacDiarmid, Finlay and White value above all is the human capacity for 'naming' and 'dwelling', and the ability for poetic language to, as Morgan suggests, fulfil its potential as 'the brilliant, vibrating interface between the human and the non-human'.[213] That is why their writings continue to matter, and why these works should be seen not just as some Scottish rural enclave, but as part of a wider literature which explores our relationship with the natural world in ways which are conscious of ecological theories and questions. Edwin Morgan has suggested that what matters for poetry is 'Biodiversity, whether vegetal, animal, human, geophysical, or astrophysical'.[214] John Burnside, Kathleen Jamie and Alan Warner are ensuring that a 'biodiverse' Scottish literature of the twenty-first century continues to discover new ways of exploring our crucial relationship with the natural world. It is their work which will be the subject of the next chapter.

Notes

1. Edwin Muir, *The Estate of Poetry* (London: The Hogarth Press, 1962), pp. 8–9.
2. Jonathan Bate, *The Song of the Earth* (London: Picador, 2000), p. 255.
3. Edwin Muir, *Collected Poems* (London: Faber and Faber, 1984), p. 284.
4. Edwin Morgan, 'The Beatnik in the Kailyard', *Essays* (Cheshire: Carcanet New Press, 1974), pp. 174–5.
5. Ibid.
6. T. S. Eliot, Preface to Edwin Muir, *Selected Poems* (London: Faber and Faber, 1965), p. 10.
7. Edwin Muir, 'The Horses', *Collected Poems*, p. 247.
8. Margery McCulloch, *Edwin Muir: Poet, Critic, Novelist* (Edinburgh: Edinburgh University Press, 1993), p. 116; Morgan, 'Edwin Muir', pp. 192–3.
9. Edwin Morgan, 'Edwin Muir', *Essays*, p. 193.
10. Edwin Morgan, 'Let's Go' (Interview with Marshall Walker, 1975), *Nothing Not Giving Messages*, ed. Hamish Whyte (Edinburgh: Polygon, 1990), p. 65.
11. Terry Gifford, *Pastoral* (London: Routledge, 1999), p. 71.
12. Douglas Dunn, quoted in Sean O'Brien, *The Deregulated Muse* (Newcastle: Bloodaxe Books, 1998), p. 65.

13. Kenneth White, 'Into the White World', *On Scottish Ground* (Edinburgh: Polygon, 1998), p. 61.
14. Ibid., p. 66.
15. George Mackay Brown, *An Orkney Tapestry* (London: Quartet Books, 1973), pp. 20–1.
16. George Mackay Brown, Letter to Willa Muir (18th April 1966), Willa Muir Papers, National Library of Scotland. Acc.10557/4.
17. George Mackay Brown, 'Brodgar Poems', *Selected Poems 1954–1992* (London: John Murray, 1996), p. 166.
18. Donald Worster, *Nature's Economy: A History of Ecological Ideas*, 2nd edn (Cambridge: Cambridge University Press, 1994), pp. 342–87.
19. Ibid., p. 343.
20. Edwin Muir, *Scott and Scotland: The Predicament of the Scottish Writer* (Edinburgh: Polygon, 1982), p. 87.
21. George Pattison, *The Later Heidegger* (London: Routledge, 2000), p. 9; Martin Heidegger, quoted in Pattison, p. 60.
22. Susie O'Brien, 'Articulating a World of Difference: Ecocriticism, Postcolonialism and Globalization', *Canadian Literature* 170/171 (2001): 140–61.
23. Julia Kristeva, *Nations without Nationalism* (New York: Columbia University Press, 1993).
24. Bate, *The Song of the Earth*, p. ix; John Burnside, 'Standards of Belief', *The Guardian*, Saturday January 25, 2003.
25. Lewis Grassic Gibbon, *A Scots Quair* (London: Penguin Books, 1986), p. 37.
26. Willa Muir, *Belonging: A Memoir* (London: Hogarth Press, 1968), p. 14.
27. Henry David Thoreau, Entry for 7th January 1857, in B. Torrey and F. H. Allen (eds), *The Journal of Henry David Thoreau*, 14 vols (Boston: Houghton Mifflin, 1906).
28. Edwin Muir, Peter Butter (eds), *An Autobiography* (Edinburgh: Canongate, 2000), p. 54.
29. George Mackay Brown, 'The Broken Heraldry', in Karl Miller (ed.), *Memoirs of a Modern Scotland* (London: Faber and Faber, 1970), p. 141.
30. Edwin Muir, *An Autobiography*, p. 289.
31. Edwin Morgan, 'On A Slow River: Review of Willa Muir's *Belonging*', *Times Literary Supplement*, Issue 3452, 25th April 1968, p. 412.
32. George Marshall, *In a Distant Isle: the Orkney Background of Edwin Muir* (Edinburgh: Scottish Academic Press, 1987), pp. 141–2.
33. See James Aitchison, *The Golden Harvester: The Vision of Edwin Muir* (Aberdeen: Aberdeen University Press, 1988), p. 3.
34. Eliot, Preface to Muir's *Selected Poems*, p. 10.
35. P. H. Butter, *Edwin Muir: Man and Poet* (Edinburgh: Oliver and Boyd, 1966), p. 4.
36. Edwin Muir, 'The Myth', *Collected Poems*, p. 144.
37. Muir, 'Complaint of the Dying Peasantry', *Collected Poems*, p. 262.
38. Willa Muir, *Living with Ballads* (London: The Hogarth Press, 1965), p. 53.
39. Heidegger, *The Question Concerning Technology*, quoted in Pattison, *The Later Heidegger*, p. 58.

40. George Mackay Brown, Letter to Willa Muir (6 May 1965), Willa Muir Papers, National Library of Scotland, Acc.10557/4.
41. Mackay Brown, *An Orkney Tapestry*, p. 21.
42. Muir, *An Autobiography*, p. 25.
43. Gaston Bachelard, *The Poetics of Space*, trans. Maria Jolas (Boston: Beacon Press, 1994), p. 104.
44. Muir, 'Scotland 1941', *Collected Poems*, p. 100.
45. Muir, *An Autobiography*, p. 25.
46. Edwin Muir, *The Story and the Fable: An Autobiography* (London: George G. Harrap, 1940), p. 36.
47. T.S. Eliot, 'The Waste Land', *Selected Poems* (London: Faber and Faber, 1961), p. 51.
48. Jonathan Bate, *The Song of the Earth* (London: Picador, 2000), p. 234.
49. Theodor Adorno, quoted by Edward Said, *Reflections on Exile: And Other Literary and Cultural Essays* (London: Granta, 2001), p. 305.
50. Muir, 'The Refugees', *Collected Poems*, pp. 95–6.
51. Muir, 'The Good Town', *Collected Poems*, pp. 173–6.
52. William Wordsworth, 'The Ruined Cottage', in Nicholas Roe (ed.), *Selected Poetry* (London: Penguin Books, 1992), pp. 5–19.
53. MacDiarmid, *The Raucle Tongue*, vol. III, p. 128.
54. Thomas Crawford, 'Edwin Muir as a Political Poet', in David Hewitt and Michael Spiller (eds), *Literature of the North* (Aberdeen: Aberdeen University Press, 1983), pp. 121–33; p. 131.
55. Muir, 'The Good Town', *Collected Poems*, pp. 173–6.
56. Muir, 'The Refugees', p. 96; Muir, 'Variations on a Time Theme', *Collected Poems*, pp. 49–62.
57. Muir, *An Autobiography*, p. 56.
58. Said, 'Reflections on Exile', p. 173.
59. C. G. Jung, quoted in Anthony Stevens, *Jung: A Very Short Introduction* (Oxford: Oxford University Press, 2001), pp. 47–51.
60. Edward Moore [Edwin Muir], *We Moderns: Enigmas and Guesses* (London: Allen and Unwin, 1918); Edwin Muir, 'Scotland, 1941', *Collected Poems*, p. 100.
61. Edwin Muir, 'The Difficult Land', *Collected Poems*, pp. 237–8.
62. Edwin Muir, *An Autobiography*, p. 293.
63. See C. G. Jung, *The Archetypes and the Collective Unconscious*, trans. R. F. C. Hull (London: Routledge and Kegan Paul, 1968).
64. Edwin Muir, 'The Sufficient Place', *Collected Poems*, p. 91.
65. Lewis Grassic Gibbon, *A Scots Quair* (London: Penguin Books, 1986), p. 176.
66. See Robert Louis Stevenson, 'Roads', *Essays of Travel* (London: Chatto and Windus, 1916).
67. Pattison, p. 53.
68. Ibid., p. 189.
69. Muir, 'The Horses', *Collected Poems*, p. 246.
70. Franz Kafka, 'Metamorphosis', in J. M. S. Pasley (ed.), *Short Stories* (London: Oxford University Press, 1963). The Muirs translated much of Kafka's fiction in the 1930s.
71. Edwin Muir, 'The Combat', *Collected Poems*, p. 179.

72. Edwin Muir, *An Autobiography*, p. 47
73. Edwin Muir, *The Story and the Fable*, p. 53.
74. Heidegger, 'The Question Concerning Technology', cited in Pattison, p. 54.
75. Muir, *The Story and the Fable*, p. 39.
76. See Lewis Grassic Gibbon, *Three Go Back* (Edinburgh: Polygon, 2000) and *Gay Hunter* (Edinburgh: Polygon, 1989).
77. For example, the Diffusionist theories which influenced both Lewis Grassic Gibbon and Edwin Muir. See Edwin Muir, 'Lewis Grassic Gibbon', *Uncollected Scottish Criticism* (London: Vision Press, 1982), pp. 251–3.
78. The term 'ecology' appears fairly frequently in MacDiarmid's prose writings. See, for example, *The Company I've Kept* (London: Hutchinson, 1966), p. 81, or 'Tom Robertson and "Human Ecology"' (1948), in Angus Calder, Glen Murray, and Alan Riach (eds), *The Raucle Tongue*, vol. III (Manchester: Carcanet, 1996–1998), pp. 168–71.
79. Muir, *An Autobiography*, p. 45.
80. Neil Gunn, *The Silver Darlings* (London: Faber and Faber, 1989), p. 100; Neil Gunn, *Highland River* (Edinburgh: Canongate Classics, 1991), pp. 5–9.
81. Gunn, *Highland River*, p. 71.
82. John Muir, 'The Story of My Boyhood and Youth', in Terry Gifford (ed.), *The Eight Wilderness Discovery Books* (London: Diadem Books, 1995), p. 81.
83. Gunn, *Highland River*, pp. 71–2.
84. Bachelard, *The Poetics of Space*, p. 91.
85. Nan Shepherd, *The Living Mountain* in *The Grampian Quartet* (Edinburgh: Canongate Books, 2001), p. iv.
86. Ibid., p. iv.
87. Shepherd, *The Living Mountain*, pp. 83–4.
88. Ibid., p. 6.
89. John Muir, 'A Thousand Mile Walk to the Gulf', in Terry Gifford (ed.), *The Eight Wilderness Discovery Books* (London: Diadem Books, 1995), p. 183.
90. Gunn, *Highland River*, p. 82.
91. Ibid., p. 218.
92. Mikhail Bakhtin, from *Rabelais and His World* (1965) in Pam Morris (ed.), *The Bakhtin Reader: Selected Writings of Bakhtin, Medvedev, Voloshinov* (London: Arnold Publishers, 1994), pp. 227–44.
93. Gunn, *Highland River*, p. 72.
94. Ibid., p. 131.
95. Ibid., p. 182.
96. Shepherd, *The Living Mountain*, p. 45.
97. Neil Gunn, Letter to Nan Shepherd (17 May 1940), in J. B. Pick (ed.), *Neil M. Gunn: Selected Letters* (Edinburgh: Polygon, 1987), pp. 62–3.
98. Shepherd, *The Living Mountain*, p. 8.
99. Ibid., p. 8.
100. Ibid., p. 84.
101. Ibid., p. 83.

102. Neil Gunn, 'The Flash', in Alistair McCleery (ed.), *Landscape and Light: Essays* (Aberdeen: Aberdeen University Press, 1987), p. 233.
103. Gunn, 'The Heron's Legs', *Landscape and Light*, p. 231.
104. Neil Gunn, *Highland Pack* (Glasgow: Richard Drew Publishing, 1989), pp. 64–5.
105. Bachelard, *The Poetics of Space*, p. 32.
106. Gunn, 'Eight Times Up', *Landscape and Light*, p. 240.
107. Gunn, 'The Flash', p. 235.
108. Gunn, 'The Heron's Legs', p. 231.
109. White, 'The Alban Project', *On Scottish Ground*, p. 14.
110. Crichton Smith, 'Real People in a Real Place', pp. 62–5.
111. Somhairle MacGill-Eain / Sorley MacLean, 'On Realism in Gaelic Poetry', in William Gillies (ed.), *Ris a' Bhruthaich: Criticism and Prose Writings* (Stornoway: Acair Ltd, 1985), p. 15.
112. Ibid., p. 34.
113. Ibid., p. 34.
114. White, 'The Birds of Kentigern', *On Scottish Ground*, p. 84.
115. 'The MacDiarmids – A Conversation: Hugh MacDiarmid and Duncan Glen with Valda Grieve and Arthur Thompson, 25 October 1968', *The Raucle Tongue*, Vol. III, p. 566.
116. MacDiarmid, 'In Talk with Donnchadh Bàn Mac an t'Saoir', in Michael Grieve and W. R. Aitken (eds), *Complete Poems 1920–1976*, vol. 2 (London: Martin, Brian and O'Keefe, 1993), pp. 1098–1102; 'Further Talk with Donnchadh Bàn Mac an t'Saoir', *Complete Poems*, vol. I, pp. 632–4.
117. MacDiarmid, 'In Talk . . .', p. 1098.
118. Ibid., p. 1099.
119. D. H. Lawrence, 'Remembering Pan', in Laurence Coupe (ed.), *The Green Studies Reader: From Romanticism to Ecocriticism* (London: Routledge, 2000), p. 72.
120. MacDiarmid, 'In Talk with . . .', p. 1099.
121. Bate, *The Song of the Earth*, p. 76.
122. W. N. Herbert, *To Circumjack MacDiarmid* (Oxford: Clarendon Press, 1992), p. 179.
123. Ibid., p. 197.
124. Frank Fraser Darling, *A Herd of Red Deer: A Study in Animal Behaviour* (London: Oxford University Press, 1941), p. 27.
125. MacDiarmid, 'In Talk . . .', p. 1101.
126. Fraser Darling, p. 27.
127. MacDiarmid. 'Further Talk . . .', p. 633.
128. Duncan Ban MacIntyre / Donnchadh Ban Mac An T-Saior, 'Moladh Beinn Dobhrain' / 'In Praise of Ben Dorain', in Roderick Watson (ed.), *The Poetry of Scotland: Gaelic, Scots and English, 1380–1980* (Edinburgh: Edinburgh University Press, 1995), p. 330.
129. Hugh MacDiarmid, 'The Praise of Ben Dorain', *Complete Poems*, vol. I, p. 600.
130. *Oxford English Dictionary*.
131. Hugh MacDiarmid, 'Metaphysics and Poetry: An Interview with Walter Perrie', *Selected Prose*, p. 278.
132. MacDiarmid, 'In Talk . . .', p. 1102.

133. Deer are an important motif of much twentieth-century Highland and Gaelic poetry. For example, see Somhairle MacGill-Eain / Sorley Maclean, 'Hallaig', *O Choille gu Bearradh / From Wood to Ridge: Collected Poems in Gaelic and in English translation* (Manchester and Edinburgh: Carcanet/Birlinn, 1999), pp. 226–31.
134. Iain Crichton Smith, 'Deer on the High Hills', *Collected Poems* (Manchester: Carcanet, 1995), p. 36.
135. Ibid., p. 39.
136. Ibid., pp. 40–6.
137. Ibid., p. 46.
138. Hugh MacDiarmid, 'On a Raised Beach', *Complete Poems*, vol. I, pp. 422–33; p. 429.
139. MacDiarmid, 'In Talk with . . .', p. 1100.
140. Hugh MacDiarmid, 'A Theory of Scots Letters', in Alan Riach (ed.), *Selected Prose* (Manchester: Carcanet, 1992), pp. 16–33; p. 20.
141. Hugh MacDiarmid, 'The Nature of a Bird's World', *Complete Poems*, vol. II, pp. 1352–7; p. 1352.
142. John T. Gage, *In the arresting eye: The Rhetoric of Imagism* (Baton Rouge, LA: Louisiana State University Press, c.1981), p. 11; Gunn, 'The Flash', *Landscape and Light*, p. 235.
143. MacDiarmid. 'In Talk . . .', p. 1099.
144. Kenneth White, cited in Tony McManus, 'Kenneth White: a Transcendental Scot', in Gavin Bowd, Charles Forsdick and Norman Bissell, *Grounding a World: Essays on the Work of Kenneth White* (Glasgow: Alba, 2005), p. 17.
145. Kenneth White, *The Wanderer and His Charts* (Edinburgh: Polygon, 2004), p. vi.
146. Michael Gardiner, *From Trocchi to Trainspotting: Scottish Critical Theory since 1960* (Edinburgh: Edinburgh University Press, 2006), p. 75.
147. Sorley MacLean, 'Mairi Mhor nan Oran', *Ris a' Bhruthaich*, p. 257.
148. Kenneth White, 'Ovid's Report', *The Bird Path: Collected Longer Poems 1964–1988* (Edinburgh: Mainstream Publishing, 1989), p. 40.
149. White, 'The Archaic Context', *On Scottish Ground*, p. 15.
150. White, 'Cape Breton Uplight', *The Bird Path*, p. 95.
151. Gunn, 'Eight Times Up', p. 238.
152. White, 'Valley of Birches', *The Bird Path*, p. 160.
153. White, 'The Archaic Context', p. 34.
154. White, *The Wanderer and his Charts*, p. 207.
155. White, *The Bird Path*, p. 160.
156. Morgan, 'A Glimpse of Petavius', *Essays*, p. 14.
157. Edwin Morgan, 'Glasgow Sonnets', *Collected Poems* (Manchester: Carcanet, 1990), pp. 289–92; p. 290.
158. Ibid., pp. 290; 291.
159. Morgan, 'A Glimpse of Petavius', p. 14.
160. Colin Nicholson, *Edwin Morgan: Inventions of Modernity* (Manchester: Manchester University Press, 2002), p. 120.
161. Theodor Adorno, quoted by Edward Said, *Reflections on Exile: And Other Literary and Cultural Essays* (London: Granta, 2001), p. 305.
162. Morgan, 'Memories of Earth', *Collected Poems*, pp. 330–40.

163. See Marshall Stalley, 'The Voyage Out and the Favoured Place: Edwin Morgan's Science Fiction', in Robert Crawford and Hamish Whyte (eds), *About Edwin Morgan* (Edinburgh: Edinburgh University Press, 1990), pp. 54–64.
164. Edwin Morgan. 'Roof of Fireflies' (1990), in W. N. Herbert and Matthew Hollis (eds), *Strong Words: Modern Poets on Modern Poetry* (Northumberland: Bloodaxe Books, 2000), p. 192
165. Seamus Heaney, 'The Sense of Place', *Preoccupations: Selected Prose, 1968–1978* (London: Faber, 1980), pp. 148–9.
166. Edwin Morgan, 'The Ruin', *Collected Poems*, p. 31.
167. Leo Marx, *The Machine in the Garden: Technology and the Pastoral Ideal in America* (New York: Oxford University Press, 1964), p. 364.
168. Ibid., p. 365.
169. Raymond Williams, *The Country and the City* (London: Chatto and Windus, 1973), p. 264.
170. Beat Witschi draws attention to glimpses of the natural world contrasted with urban experience in these novels in his study *Glasgow Urban Writing and Postmodernism: A Study of Alasdair Gray's Fiction* (Frankfurt am Main, Bern, New York, Paris: Peter Lang, 1991), pp. 44–50. See Edwin Muir, *Poor Tom* (Edinburgh: Harris, 1982); George Blake, *The Shipbuilders* (London: Faber, 1935); Edward Gaitens, *Dance of the Apprentices* (Glasgow: W. MacLellan, 1948).
171. Archie Hind, *The Dear Green Place* (Edinburgh: Polygon Books, 1984), p. 17.
172. Douglas Gifford, *The Dear Green Place? The Novel in the West of Scotland* (Glasgow: Third Eye Centre, 1984).
173. Hind, p. 20.
174. As in pastoral lines such as James Macpherson's 'there smiles the virid grass | While through the shaded green, rough murmuring, glides | A brook crystalline'. James Macpherson, 'The Hunter', Canto VII, ll.164–166, *Poems of Ossian* (1805; repr. Edinburgh: Thin, 1971).
175. Hind, p. 19.
176. Ibid., p. 19.
177. Ibid., p. 26.
178. Ibid., p. 21.
179. Terry Gifford, *Green Voices: Understanding Contemporary Nature Poetry* (Manchester: Manchester University Press, 1995), p. 33.
180. Ibid., p. 38; Terry Gifford, *Pastoral* (London: Routledge, 1999), p. 42.
181. Gifford, *Pastoral*, p. 2.
182. Ibid., p. 42.
183. Bate, p. 199.
184. Christopher Whyte, *Modern Scottish Poetry* (Edinburgh: Edinburgh University Press, 2004), pp. 167–8.
185. Yves Abrioux, *Ian Hamilton Finlay: A Visual Primer* (London: Reaktion Books, 1992), p. 167.
186. Ian Hamilton Finlay, 'Unconnected Sentences on Gardening', in Abrioux, p. 40.
187. Iain Crichton Smith, in Clare Brown and Don Paterson (eds), *Don't Ask Me What I Mean: Poets in their Own Words* (London: Picador, 2003), p. 271.

188. Ibid., p. 272.
189. Hamilton Finlay, cited in Sue Innes, 'Man of Sparta', in Alec Finlay (ed.), *Wood Notes Wild: Essays on the Poetry and Art of Ian Hamilton Finlay* (Edinburgh: Polygon, 1995), p. 14.
190. Robert Creeley, Foreword to Ian Hamilton Finlay, in Ken Cockburn (ed.), *The Dancers Inherit the Party: Early Stories, Plays and Poems* (Edinburgh: Polygon, 2004), p. xii.
191. George Mackay Brown, *An Orkney Tapestry*, p. 23.
192. Ian Hamilton Finlay, 'The Death of Piety: Ian Hamilton Finlay in conversation with Nagy Rashwan', *Jacket 15*, December 2001, http://jacketmagazine.com/15/rash-iv-finlay.html [accessed 1 June 2007]; Ken Cockburn, Introduction to Ian Hamilton Finlay, *The Dancers Inherit the Party* and *Glasgow Beasts, an' a Burd* (Edinburgh: Polygon, 2004), p. xxii.
193. Cockburn, p. xxii.
194. Abrioux, p. 13.
195. Bachelard, p. xxvii; p. xx.
196. George Mackay Brown, 'Hill Runes', *Selected Poems 1954–1992*, p. 74.
197. Mackay Brown, *An Orkney Tapestry*, p. 13.
198. Whyte, pp. 168–9.
199. Hamilton Finlay, cited in Yves Abrioux, *Ian Hamilton Finlay: A Visual Primer*, p. 167.
200. *An Orkney Tapestry*, p. 21.
201. Abrioux, p. 220.
202. See George Mackay Brown, *Magnus* (Edinburgh: Canongate, 2000); Hugh MacDiarmid, 'A Seamless Garment', *Complete Poems*, vol. I, pp. 311–14.
203. George Mackay Brown, *Greenvoe* (London: Longman, 1977), p. 7.
204. Kathleen Jamie, 'Primal Seam', The Scotsman, 30 July 2005, http://living.scotsman.com/books.cfm?ca=1702392005 [accessed January 2006]
205. Mackay Brown, *Greenvoe*, p. 40.
206. Ibid., p. 87.
207. Ibid., p. 228.
208. Mikhail Bakhtin, from *Rabelais and His World* (1965) in *The Bakhtin Reader: Selected Writings of Bakhtin, Medvedev, Voloshinov*, pp. 198–9.
209. Ibid., p. 197.
210. Ibid., pp. 208–9; Letter from George Mackay Brown to Willa Muir, 21st June 1969, Willa Muir Papers, National Library of Scotland, Acc.10557/4.
211. See Lewis Grassic Gibbon, 'Clay', *Smeddum: A Lewis Grassic Gibbon Anthology*, pp. 69–81; p. 79.
212. White, 'The Alban Project', *On Scottish Ground*, p. 3.
213. Morgan, 'Roof of Fireflies', p. 192.
214. Ibid., p. 192.

Chapter 5

Lines of Defence

> poetry's a line of defence; poetry's not very good at getting out there fighting, but it's very good at holding a last line of defence . . . And it could be that poetry is holding a very good line of defence here against the intrusions of globalisation, the mass market, the ecological threat . . . [1] Kathleen Jamie

Re-defining 'nature poetry'

John Burnside, Kathleen Jamie and Alan Warner are three younger Scottish writers who are not only reviewing human relationships with nature, but also the role writing has to play in exploring and strengthening that relationship – helping to determine the ecological 'value' of poetry and fiction. What I want to argue in this final chapter is that in Scotland, contemporary poetry, and lyricism more generally, constitute an ecological 'line of defence', providing a space in which reader and author can examine their relationship to the world around them. While these writers do not form a conscious 'school' or affiliation, they share in common a lucid and intelligent lyrical vision which seeks to re-centre and redefine concepts of nature and rural environments – an outlook which is crucial in an age of growing ecological crisis. John Burnside recently endorsed this view, stating:

> I think more people are realising that the relationship we have with the natural world, the whole natural world, not just green woods and verges and stuff, but with other things, cockroaches and other people, is the main thing we should be exploring right now.[2]

It has been suggested that Kathleen Jamie could be viewed as 'a nature poet who has been sidetracked by "issues"' – meaning issues of gender, culture and national identity which have, to date, been the main contexts in which her poetry has been viewed.[3] This comment, however, implicitly suggests that to write about the natural world is to avoid an engagement with political 'issues' – an assertion with which both Jamie and Burnside would vehemently disagree. Burnside criticises this view in his essay 'Strong Words', finding himself 'dismayed by the common misapprehension that a poet who makes such a choice – the choice of a quest, as it were, as opposed to a settlement – has no political or social interests or usefulness'.[4]

Burnside evades labelling of all forms, but that did not prevent him from being described as the 'token nature poet' of the Arts Council 'New Generation' promotion in the early 1990s. The term 'nature poet', he feels, is outmoded, derogatory and marginalising, 'a term of dismissal'.[5] Similarly, feeling 'irritated and . . . confined' by the twin labels of 'woman writer' and 'Scottish writer', Jamie has left them behind – 'deliberately and consciously wanting to change the direction of [her] work'.[6] It is likely that she would resist the limitations of the term 'nature poet' as strongly as Burnside has. 'At the moment,' she recently stated, 'I'm writing a lot "toward" the natural world'.[7] That cautious word, 'toward', echoes Burnside's expression of a similar distinction, that he is writing 'poems with flowers in them, but they're not *about* flowers'.[8] As Burnside and Maurice Riordan argue in *Wild Reckoning* (2004), the constricting label of 'nature poetry' needs to be reconsidered, and in order to understand poets who choose to write about the natural world, we should 'return to the original meaning of the word ecology . . . its delineation of a *Logos* of dwelling, a *Logos* which is neither exclusively "science" nor "art"'.[9]

It is clear that for Burnside and Jamie at least, the idea of the natural world they are exploring in their poetry and other writings is a philosophical and political matter of vital importance, with poetry as a crucial 'line of defence'. Partly inspired by the work of American writers such as Gary Snyder or Barry Lopez, Burnside has begun to talk about ecology and environmental issues in a more mainstream context through criticism and journalistic activity. Like more overtly 'political' poets such as Tony Harrison, Burnside uses broadsheet newspapers to get his message across, whether this is a prose polemic against the intrusions of corporate golf in Scottish rural areas or a poem about the noise pollution of a military air base.[10] However, questions of style and craft are also important if poetry is to be an effective political tool. Recognising that writing poems which 'ask important questions' inevitably 'change[s] your relationship to craft', Burnside admits to feeling frustrated with the British 'attachment to the craft side of [poetry]' which, he feels, is 'part of the deal that poets shouldn't get too big for their boots, the idea that poetry doesn't change anything and all that'. By contrast, he cites the importance of writers who have been prepared to 'pare . . . work down' in order to make it 'direct and challenging' and are therefore able to communicate to 'as big an audience as possible'.[11] When poets like Burnside and Jamie talk about poetry as 'a line of defence', they are not exactly taking up Shelley's argument about poets being unacknowledged legislators, but they are suggesting that poetic modes of observation and expression are important for the 'world out there', with important questions to ask about how we live in that world.

In exploring these questions Kathleen Jamie, like Burnside, rejects traditional systems of belief, instead searching for new ways of celebrating and understanding existence.

> I don't believe in God. I believe in spiders, alveoli, starlings . . . I might suggest that prayer-in-the-world isn't supplication, but the quality of attention we can bring to a task, the intensity of listening, through the instruments we have designed for the purpose. It might be the outermost reaches of the Universe, the innermost changes at the bottom of a lung, the words on a page, or a smear of blood on a slide. I think it's about repairing and maintaining the web of our noticing, a way of being in the world. Or is that worship?[12]

This reverence for details is part of a developing poetic manifesto, a search for ways in which to express 'the true and the good and the sacred' – concepts which she is aware might sound a bit old-fashioned or trite, to some ears. In her essay, 'Holding Fast – Truth and Change in Poetry', Jamie expresses her fundamental belief that 'A poem is an approach to truth'. This might suggest the transcendent 'eternal truth' pursued by the Romantic poets, or that she is developing a poetic creed based on the importance of external objects, and aligned with scientific observation, provable fact. Neither of these options is quite what Jamie is talking about; despite 'what the ecologists and scientists will tell you . . . there are things which cannot be said – not by scientists anyway'.[13] Essentially, she is working out a theory of the 'sacred' – a word that seems to hover at the edges of her essay, and something which she is characteristically self-conscious about pinning down. This poetry of 'truth' bears some similarities to the 'poetry of facts' MacDiarmid wanted to develop, but the exhaustive cataloguing of MacDiarmid's late poetry is not the tool Jamie chooses to employ, despite her fondness for litanies and lists in poems like 'Lucky Bag'.[14] Recognising the complications which might arise from such ideals, she says poems are often 'witty, quirky and sly . . . mischievous, tricksterish. Their truths don't sound like the truths of the court-room or inquest'. All this leads her to wonder, 'Can we say . . . that truth itself is a shape-shifter?'[15] This train of thought steers towards Martin Heidegger's idea of 'truth' as 'dynamic'; that the revelation of truth in a poem or work of art is an active process, open to constant re-interpretation – not a static statement of 'fact'. The poem, as an art-form, is 'an instance of *techne*, of bringing-forth from unconcealment', which is 'not the presentation of a finished product with a determinate significance . . . but an active bringing-forth, a process of unconcealment'.[16] This suggestion of poetry as an active process rather than a finished product brings in the reader as a creative participant in *poiesis*, and ultimately leads Heidegger to the assertion that 'Truth is un-truth', in that the 'truth' of a poem is not immediately available to the reader.

Heidegger's provocative philosophical stance problematises concepts of truth and representation in ways which are particularly fruitful for all three writers considered here. Blurring the categories of 'truth' and 'untruth' opens up the possibility for a poetry – or prose – which is at once ambiguous and 'shape-shifting' but also mysterious and reverential. Such possibilities are a recurrent topic for meditation in Burnside's poetry and fiction, certainly influenced by his interest in Heidegger and other phenomenological philosophers such as Gaston Bachelard. Paul, the protagonist in Burnside's novel, *The Locust Room* (2002), is a photographer searching for the perfect image, haunted by the tension between perception and revelation. He desires 'a photography of the night, of the gaps between the hidden and the revealed, that would more closely resemble natural history than anything that might be called "art"'.[17] This difficulty of representing the world is also contemplated in Burnside's poetry:

> He had his camera
>   but couldn't take
> the picture he wanted
>   the one he thinks of now
> as perfect
>   – he couldn't betray
> that animal silence
>   the threadwork of grass through the hide
> the dwelling place
>   inherent in the spine[18]

Striking a balance between a flat record of the 'facts' – a concept which, like Jamie, Burnside mistrusts – and the self-conscious 'art-form', which is also a distortion of the 'real', is a quest central to much of Burnside's writing. In *The Locust Room*, it leads Paul to develop a theory of 'Orphic' art, which is based on taking an original, unsullied look at the world, 'the essential creative act . . . of seeing, and making seen, for the first time, the true nature of the world'.[19] This is a reverence for the objects themselves, an approach which parallels Jamie's belief in noticing or 'paying heed' as 'a kind of prayer' in her own poetic theory.[20] In *Findings* (2005), Jamie offers a series of finely-observed contemplations on aspects of Scottish heritage, landscape and ecology, and describes an attempt to fine-tune this observational ability. While watching local birds of prey, she tells herself to 'learn again to look, to listen', to 'hold [the experience] in your head, bring it home intact'.[21] Although Jamie has only recently articulated her belief in attentiveness as an ecopoetic ideal, a quality of sensitive observation has been a defining feature of her work throughout her career. In the poem, 'Mr and Mrs Scotland Are Dead', Jamie's tender attentiveness to the ephemeral nature of household objects, out of their domestic contexts and forlorn on the council rubbish-heap, endows them with a certain numinous aspect. She treats them reverentially, attentively, reading the postcards 'spew[ed]' from the dead woman's 'stiff | old ladies' bags, open mouthed', noting the 'tired handles' of a man's joiners' tools, stamped with 'SCOTLAND, SCOTLAND'.[22] This kind of contemplation allows for the construction of narratives based on a supposed history of the objects encountered, but perhaps more importantly, it also enables the viewer or poet to hone their observational skills.

In *The Locust Room*, photography, the ultimate 'Orphic art form' is an art capable of bringing 'us back to the things themselves' – and what enables it to do this is a capacity to make the familiar strange, 'other', 'picturing the world from which all invested meaning had been stripped away, a neutral, and so natural act'.[23] Viewed through the camera lens, objects:

> possessed, or were possessed of, that quality of estrangement that seemed to allow the things to move away from the viewer's gaze, to set each thing, each pebble and plank and scab of weed, in its own inviolable space, not as a mere object, but as something respected, something loved and so left to be itself, beyond possession, beyond comprehension.[24]

This is an interpretation of Kant's idea of the 'thing-in-itself', the real, unmediated object, as opposed to the 'thing-for-us'. In this novel, Paul's first theory of an ideal photography reveals the 'thing-in-itself' by a process which removes the creative self from the picture, erasing the ego – an ability which Jamie admires in Heidegger's favourite poet, Holderlin.[25] This necessary distance facilitates a revelation of 'the no man's land between the real and fantasy – the mystery in the commonplace – the uncommonness of the commonplace', a concept which has haunted Burnside's writing since the phrase 'the mystery in the commonplace' appeared in his first poetry collection, *The Hoop* (1988).[26] However, as a record of the 'phenomenon of the encounter' which involves 'an awareness . . . both of the subject and the self' in which 'one almost becomes the other' suggests a more Wordsworthian encounter with the natural object, a continuum between mind and nature in which awareness of the self is necessary to evoke the mystery of the subject.[27] The problem of how human perception always intercedes between self and world provokes, in Burnside's thought, a shift to a philosophy of phenomenology, to the discovery of 'primary virtues' which 'go beyond the problems of description'.[28] For Burnside, this can also mean paring down language and the most obvious markers of poetic 'craft' to a bare minimum, creating a simplicity which effaces the ego and rids poetry of the flourishes which declare the presence of the writer – Coleridge's 'eternal I AM'. Instead, Burnside argues, 'interesting poetry . . . asks questions about the quality of experience. What did you really hear? What did you really see? What did you really taste? . . . Poems that make us pay attention. Poems with an ecological heart'.[29]

The differing potential of the visual arts as opposed to language or poetry to 'reveal' truths about the world is an important issue for Burnside, whose poetry is itself characterised by a strongly visual, sensuous style. Limitations are discovered in both methods. In the poem, 'Taxonomy', the speaker finds it difficult to describe the precise colour of foliage he is observing, 'nothing like baize | or polished jade', it exists in the 'gap' between one name and another. This 'unknown' aspect of the world is 'looking always worked towards a word: | trading the limits of speech | for the unsaid presence'. Unsaid and unsayable presences abound in Burnside's work, whose acute sense of the mysterious forms the still centre of much of his poetry. He considers the ways in which language is fundamentally limited in evoking the 'real', a mode of representation or exploration which is always provisional or compromised. For Burnside, there is no possibility of complete description or of complete detachment, implying a deeply-held suspicion of pretensions to ideals of precision or accuracy which modern science might claim.

> and the magic
> that speech performs
> is all
>
> continuum: the given and the named
> discovered and invented
> one more time,
>
> with each new bud or tendril that unfolds
> upon the revelation
> of the known.[30]

Kathleen Jamie experiences similar descriptive dilemmas. In her book about her travels in Pakistan, *The Golden Peak* (1994), reissued with new chapters as *Among Muslims* (2002), Jamie is aware of how important precision and deftness are in literary representations. In describing a Himalayan landscape, she finds nuances of colour and form which demand a thoughtful, considered lyricism:

> There are words we reach for out of habit, like desolate, bare, barren, colourless, but these are not true. There were colours, but subtle, just a breath of pale blues and snow-greys, a smudgy brown denoting a village at the riverside. Above the river and villages, mountains slammed upward, young, hasty, sharp-edged.[31]

Thinking more deeply about such linguistic issues, Jamie has recently said she used to believe 'that language was what got in the way . . . that it was a screen, a dark glass. That you could not get at the world because you were stuck with language, but now I think that's wrong. Now I think language is what connects us to the world'.[32] This contention parallels Jonathan Bate's case for 'ecopoetics' in *The Song of the Earth* (2000), writing which helps us 'to live . . . with thoughtfulness and attentiveness, an attunement to both words and the world, and so to acknowledge that, although we make sense of things by way of words, we do not live apart from the world'.[33] However, while Jamie ardently believes in language's capacity to bring us closer to the natural world, she is forced to admit there are limitations. Significantly, *The Tree House* (2004), a book which is above all characterised by Jamie's own form of 'ecopoetics', closes by contemplating how a water bird's 'supple, undammable song' cannot be put into words by the poet: the song simply 'isn't mine to give'.[34]

Burnside considers such difficulties of representation towards the end of *The Locust Room*, as Paul shifts his stance, recognising that his ideal of the 'detached observer' is 'an improbable fantasy' which is replaced by a quest for a 'form of alchemy . . . to become a participant, or celebrant, rather than a witness' – a stance which recalls Hugh MacDiarmid's almost religious desire 'not to be ignored but accepted' when observing deer in the poem 'In Talk with Duncan Ban MacIntyre'.[35] Such concepts are the starting point for poems meditating on the theme of 'Habitat' in Burnside's 2002 collection, *The Light Trap*. Here, an epigraph from the ecological philosopher, Paul Shepard, suggests the existence of 'something more mutually and functionally interdependent between mind and terrain, an organic relationship between the environment and the unconscious'.[36] This idea is reflected by Paul's wish in *The Locust Room* to emulate the symbolic creativity of the Orpheus myth, where the god sings animals into existence. Orpheus has long been associated with poetry – particularly lyric poetry – but Burnside's contemplation of the myth deepens the mystery of the continuum between subject, language and object. In this version, Orpheus's singing liberates the animals from their status as 'mere objects, named and forgotten and shrouded in the contempt bred of familiarity', as they emerge 'alive, shining, made other in the poet's song'.[37]

For both Burnside and Jamie, the ambiguities of language or the 'shape-shifting' aspect of poetry seem most likely to be capable of revealing the 'mystery in the commonplace'. In support of this, Burnside's poem 'Sense Data' invites us to think about the limitations of scientific measurement, 'observed migrations, rainfalls, frequencies':

> and somewhere behind it all, in private realms
> of gulls' eggs and stones and things I couldn't name,
>
> another world of charge and borderline,
> an earth-tide in the spine, the nightlong
> guesswork of old voices in the mind.[38]

'Guesswork' is revealed as a vital element in understanding the world which science has taught us to consider as quantifiable, nameable and understandable. For Burnside, our ways of knowing the natural world are by their very nature provisional, subsisting on 'guesswork and hope', where we must acknowledge 'a world we do not know | and name the things | one object at a time'.[39] In the novel *Living Nowhere* (2004), the protagonist Francis gains access to this other way of seeing the world through the eyes of his friend, Jan. At first, to Francis, the world:

> was a static affair: buildings, steelworks, trees, water, gaps, tracks – everything was given, nothing had history, nothing seemed to change. But you had another way of looking at it all. You subsisted on guesswork; you lived by hypothesis and inference.[40]

In such a world of 'flux', where the world itself is a 'changing text' which must be 'scried', mystery becomes possible, as in Jamie's poem 'Skeins o Geese', which evokes the conflicting desire and inability for us to 'read' the world: 'Whit dae birds write on the dusk? A word nivir spoken nor read'.[41] This aspect of the 'sacred', most often found in conjunction with meditations on the natural world, is a concept which recurs continually in Burnside's poetry and prose, and seems allied to Jamie's search for a heightened, reverential 'quality of attention'.

The revelation of such mysteries in Burnside's work, however, seems to depend upon the elision of the self. In his poetic manifesto, 'Strong Words', he argues that 'the lyrical impulse begins at the point of self-forgetting', a freedom which allows creativity, *poiesis*, to occur. Effacements of the self, of personal identity and rootedness in place, recur continually in Burnside's fiction, with fantasies of invisibility, disappearance, effacement or estrangement comprising a psychological trait common to many of his characters and personae. In *The Locust Room*, Paul reaches the conclusion that 'estrangement' from society is the route to his concept of the perfect work of art, which is itself a way of experiencing an authentic 'being in the world':

> this quality – of estrangement, rather than alienation – was the best asset he had. It was the starting point for a process that led inevitably to invisibility. To care nothing at all for being seen. The grace of the forgotten: the tree that falls in the woods.[42]

This point is reiterated in *The Light Trap*'s 'After Lucretius', where 'nothing matters less | than being seen'.[43] Social invisibility, the 'grace of the forgotten' leads inevitably to a confrontation with concepts of the 'other' – indeed, it is his chance encounter with a fox on a woodland path which brings about Paul's epiphany. Paul realises that opting out of the social world, in which he is an outsider anyway, brings him closer to the world of the fox, a world of animals and physical objects which have their own intrinsic mystery. Similarly, in *Living Nowhere*, disappearing, escaping and being forgotten are experienced as somehow liberating for Francis, another character on the periphery of society. Following the funeral of his murdered friend, Jan, Francis sees a gap in a hedge at the perimeter of the cemetery, and simply walks through it:

> It was the kind of gap animals use, deer coming in from the fields to browse the graveyard roses, foxes following a path they had used for generations, ignoring the lines of human settlement . . .[44]

Crossing boundaries the way animals do, Francis denies the allegiances of human-defined territories, and in so doing, denies the possibility of 'home'. The hedge is an intriguing borderline, a human marker of territory, as well as a natural habitat – in many ways a liminal space between culture and nature, which Francis must inevitably cross as a rite of passage.

Burnside's fiction often meditates on the idea of getting 'clean away', of simply leaving home, with no fidelity to place, family, community or possessions. 'Of course we escape,' he says in *The Good Neighbour* (2005), a collection literally divided into the poetry of 'Here' and 'There', with homeland and belonging considered from both local and global perspectives. This can mean 'Turning aside forever | or just for the moment, | crossing a lawn and slipping away through a hedge'.[45] 'It was a necessary ritual, this process of erasure,' Francis explains in *Living Nowhere*, 'I had to become myself again, a non-person, someone with no defined identity, without family or friends, or fixed abode'.[46] In a way, *Living Nowhere* is indeed 'only the story of some | local, who went out one afternoon | and strayed home decades later, | much the same as when he left'.⁴⁷ At times, it seems that Burnside's male characters are a population of loners, drifters, would-be escapists, searching for an elusive way of 'being in the world', and recognising something Edward Said suggested:

> The exile knows that in a secular and contingent world, homes are always provisional. Borders and barriers, which enclose us within the safety of familiar territory, can also become prisons, and are often defended beyond reason or necessity. Exiles cross borders, break barriers of thought and experience.⁴⁸

Exile, in Burnside's novels, is accompanied by a blurring of identity and selfhood – the 'self-forgetting' he contends is necessary for the lyrical act to occur. Such effacements of the self are also performed in his shorter fiction. In 'The Invisible Husband', a short story in *Burning Elvis* (2000), a relationship between a married couple dissolves when the wife, Laura, having experienced some form of mental breakdown, conjures a phantom husband to replace her real one. The illusion is seductive, disturbing, and begins inform the real husband's thoughts, breaking down his own sense of identity, producing 'a dizzying sense of myself as imagined, as transient and insubstantial as any ghost', which leads him to reject the entire fabric of his life as illusory, and to leave, effecting 'an escape, not only from the place that had held him for so long, but also from the sheer mass of his life, the bearable pretences of marriage and work and home'.⁴⁹ In so doing he is 'searching . . . for a stillness in his own mind, a new way of being that doesn't involve maintenance'.⁵⁰ Similarly, the sinister protagonist of *The Dumb House* (1997) toys with the idea of 'becoming someone else', of 'getting into the car and driving away . . . vanishing from the world I had inhabited all my life'.⁵¹ The 'liberation' of such escapes and self-forgettings perhaps risks what Said described as 'a fetish of exile, a practice that distances [the exiled person] from all connections and commitments. To live as if everything around you were temporary and perhaps trivial'.⁵²

The idea of 'dwelling', derived from Heideggerean philosophy and employed as an ecological concept in Burnside's work and in recent criticism such as Bate's *The Song of the Earth*, is revealed to be a difficult term. In *Living Nowhere*, Alma, a 'displaced person' who traces her roots back to a shadowy childhood homeland of Latvia, is reminded by her husband of the dual aspect of 'dwelling'. It can mean 'to live, to have a house, to be sheltered, but it also meant this other thing, this dwelling on, this being caught up in something and unable to move on'.⁵³ It is this second aspect of 'dwelling' which inspires Francis to leave Corby. On the road, he feels both 'at home' and 'joyfully lost', 'free, blown in the wind, unburdened'.⁵⁴ Such ideas link up with key concerns about home and belonging in the work of prominent post-war theorists such as Edward Said or Theodor Adorno, who argued:

> This is a world where nobody should feel altogether at home, this is a world where no honest person can feel he belongs – or not altogether. In a world like this – not the real, wide world of grass and earthquakes and bullfinches, but this world, this human state – grief, and anger, and guilt for that matter, are only natural. Home, wherever and for however long we find it, is, by its very nature, provisional and tainted.[55]

Such impulses might suggest an intrinsic state of exile, the idea that 'dwelling . . . is now impossible', that our homes 'have grown intolerable: each trait of comfort in them is paid for with a betrayal of knowledge'.[56] However, while 'home' is sometimes a philosophical and political problem for modern writers, it need not always be viewed in such bleak terms. In *Identifying Poets*, Robert Crawford argues that 'home' is in fact central to modern poetry, with the figure of the 'identifying poet', that is, a poet who explicitly identifies himself or herself with a particular terrain or territory, as a valid and illuminating way of interpreting poetic work. Home, he says, is 'a topic which pervades contemporary verse' and was 'one of the great themes of the poetry of the 1980s . . .' and, he suggests, is particularly important in the work of modern Scottish writers such as John Burnside and Kathleen Jamie.[57] Reading the former's poetry, Crawford points out that the title of Burnside's 1991 poetry collection, *Common Knowledge*, was originally to have been *Home*, and that 'the concerns about the uncertainties of identity and homing glimpsed in an explicitly Scottish context in "Exile's Return" are central to Burnside's imagination'.[58]

Erasures and disappearances are, however, more than just an escape from social norms and expectations in Burnside's work; they are part of his questioning of the philosophical idea of 'home' or 'belonging' which is, for him, one of the central concerns of ecology. Informed by his reading of Heidegger, Burnside is haunted by the possibilities of 'dwelling', of an authentic way of 'being in the world'. An epigraph from Heidegger's influential lecture, 'Building Dwelling Thinking' (1951) sets the tone for Burnside's *The Asylum Dance* (2000). Heidegger suggests that while the human condition is one of intrinsic 'homelessness', the search for a true home, for a way of 'dwelling' on the earth, is central to human experience:

> The proper dwelling plight lies in this, that mortals ever search anew for the essence of dwelling, that they must ever learn to dwell. What if man's homelessness consisted in this, that man still does not even think of the proper plight of dwelling as the plight? Yet as soon as man gives thought to his homelessness, it is a misery no longer. Rightly considered and kept well in mind, it is the sole summons that calls mortals to their dwelling.[59]

In other words, acknowledging and thinking about the problem brings us closer to authenticity, closer to the possibility of 'home'. I would like to argue that this ecological philosophy of 'home' is what Burnside has been pursuing throughout his literary career. My point here is that 'home', for contemporary Scottish writers, has taken on new meanings, beyond questions of 'nationalism' or 'Scottishness'. 'Home' is not only about that sort of political allegiance, but needs to take into consideration broader questions of how we can live as 'good neighbours', both to other people and to the natural world. The need to be taught 'a way to live | on this damp ambiguous earth' is openly considered in the poetry of both Jamie and Burnside.[60] Burnside has said that he is seeking a 'view of identity that sets terrain and habitat before tribal allegiance', admitting that his 'natural influence' is probably 'an anarchist influence. I don't really want to belong to a country. I want to belong to a local community, to a region'.[61] This is a different concept of 'home' than, say, Stevenson wrote about when he was missing Scotland.

Homes and homelands

While exploring such ecological aspirations, contemporary Scottish writers are also forced to acknowledge the difficulty of 'belonging' in an increasingly urban and globalised world. Alan Warner is a Highland novelist who, despite knowing and admiring Iain Crichton Smith, has more often been associated with the urban counter-cultural novelists of the 1990s such as Irvine Welsh. Warner's *The Man Who Walks* (2004) considers the motives behind travel and outlooks on home. 'We are not always travelling to places, often we are escaping,' the mysterious Man Who Walks writes: 'Anschluss and exodus are the common movements of our time'.[62] As if in defiance of his rejection by the West Coast 'Settled Community', the Nephew describes a community of pan-European tree-dwelling gypsies, 'old ladies who made tea for me up in their tree houses', their grandchildren at the fiestas, 'dancing all night, and leaping through the bonfires with crowns of jasmine'.[63] Whether or not this idyll is a fiction, like the wandering narratives of his Uncle discovered inscribed on a tangle of typewriter ribbon, is not clear – and it is notable that such reveries tend to occur under the influence of drugs or alcohol. The possibility of 'dwelling' in this way is, however, under threat, as the old travelling ways of life begin to die out. Realising this, the Nephew wonders if 'The Man Who Walks is the only traveller walking under these purple, then dark skies?'[64] Like Robert Louis Stevenson's discovery that the experience of emigration does not live up to the romance of the 'storybook imagination', the Nephew feels that travel is also something to be suspicious of:

> We should all be sick of it. Always moving from A to B. Only a legacy of worn boots. The longing just for stillness. Eyes rest on nothing long enough for meditation upon it. We go through those gateways of transformation: airports; and we come back unchanged. When did travel last change someone? In what century?[65]

The Nephew himself entertains fantasies of escape, however: 'what a place, the Nephew thought, if only I could get out. To where? I'll tell you where: to some place proper, if only!' At other times he claims that we 'should despise and distrust travel' – and it seems that it is the secular, tawdry aspect of modern travel to which he objects, complaining that 'travel has to be a fetish and mystified and sold and finally trivialised'.[66] Touristic, modern travel negates the possibility of a 'rite of passage' or a pilgrimage.

Nevertheless, escape and exile have retained their fascination for Scottish writers like Warner, Jamie and Burnside. Writing in 1993, Crawford suggested that one problem with home is that it is sometimes 'smug' and 'constricting', and that 'the poetic celebrants of home at the moment tend not to be women'.[67] The constrictions of home do indeed appear to be a motive for Jamie's early travel writings; the tension between the desire to be on the road and the expectations of gender (home, babies, a settled life) are fully explored in *Among Muslims*, as well as her poetry.

> I could have children, and maybe no worries. But I was a person walking down a track in Baltistan all alone on a Wednesday morning. I was capable; and sometimes, a glimpse of what we could be opens in our minds like the fearsome blue crevasses I'd seen on glaciers. I could be a person who lives here . . . a wandering monkish figure gone native.[68]

But to be a permanent wanderer would mean 'forgoing the children, and the shadowy figure that filled the vacuum when they asked, "Where is your husband?"'[69] 'Wee Baby' speaks of this dilemma, a 'glimpse' of the possibility of pregnancy which follows her around. At home or abroad, the baby is a choice yet to be made: 'She blows about the desert in a sand-pram, | O traveller' since 'the kingdom of Wee Baby is within'.[70] Similarly, domesticity becomes internalised and personified by 'Wee Wifey', who exists 'in the household of my skull', constricting and infuriating at times, but 'sad to note | that without | WEE WIFEY | I shall live long and lonely as a tossing cork'.[71] These are issues which also confront male wanderers, as Francis in *Living Nowhere* is met with questions about his unmarried, childless state, returning home after twenty years' absence, 'both son and stranger'.[72]

There are aspects of home which retain a distinctive Scottish accent in Jamie's work, considered in the soft cadences of Scots, but she makes it clear that her own concerns about home and family life, phrased in Scots words in her poetry, extend to the women she meets on her travels, saying in *Among Muslims* that the duty of a travel-writer 'is to our common humanity. Travel-writing is less about place than people, it describes people's lives'.[73] But travel itself is undertaken for more complex reasons, part of the tension between home and the search for somewhere else which Stevenson and others experienced more than a century ago. The impulse to travel while at home is suggested from the 'Twitter of swallows and swifts: | *"tickets and visas, visas and tickets"'* while, wandering abroad, ideas of home seem an inextricable part of consciousness, given by a lapse into a soft, sibilant Scots:

> . . . her heid
> achin wi the weicht o so much saun
> the weicht o the desert that waits every morn
> an blackly dogs her back.[74]

Jamie, identifying with two historical characters on her journeys across Tibet and China, speaks for herself as much as for them, 'on a suddenty mindit: A'm far fae hame, | I hae crossed China'.[75]

The equivocal idea of home, and associated philosophical questions about 'dwelling' in the modern world, are played out to their fullest extents in Burnside's poetry. A recurrent motif in Burnside's work is the elemental erasure of the ordinary human world which compasses everyday life, othered by the action of fog, snow, even darkness. In 'Lost', 'home was unremarkable until | it disappeared into the hinterland | behind our practised blindness', while in *The Good Neighbour* Burnside notes how a dense sea fog transforms the town in which he lives, 'tracing a path of erasure back to the house | where all I possess is laid up'.[76] At times such natural effects take on a quasi-spiritual significance; at others, they serve to highlight the natural world's indifference to human lives, and the difficulty of sustaining a sense of belonging in the face of impassive yet powerful natural processes. Burnside's prose poem, 'Suburbs', considers how night changes the daytime identity of the suburb, destabilising the secure 'commonplace' aspect of everyday life. At night,

> the garden is stolen by foxes rooting in turned dustbins, emptiness takes form and approaches from the centre of the lawn, a white devil, smiling out of the dark, and the realisation dawns that I live in an invented place whose only purpose is avoidance, and what I would avoid, I carry with me, always.[77]

The suburbs may appear as an illusory, artificial place, constructed to avoid the question of 'dwelling' and creating some sort of 'non-place', or 'nowhere'. Marc Auge has suggested that there is a radical difference between what used to be called 'modernity', the 'willed coexistence of two different worlds . . . chimneys alongside spires' which Baudelaire explored in his poetry, and what might be called 'supermodernity' in which 'the individual consciousness' is subjected to 'ordeals of solitude, directly linked with the appearance and proliferation of non-places'.[78] Non-places are what 'we inhabit when we are driving down the motorway, wandering through the supermarket or sitting in an airport lounge' which inscribe the individual with a commodified meaning, becoming 'no more than what he does or experiences in the role of passenger, customer or driver'.[79] 'The space of non-place creates neither singular identity nor relations; only solitude, similitude'.[80] Non-places, in other words, conspire in a super-modern culture of identity loss which is a solitary experience, an effacement of self which is not the same thing as Baudelaire's anonymous *flâneur* or man-of-the-crowd.

Although the simplistic categorisation of such spaces as 'non-places' would likely be denigrated by attentive, observant poets like Jamie and Burnside, this concept of the 'non-place' does seem relevant to Burnside's portrayal of suburbia. Liminal spaces are the location for much of Burnside's poems, and it is the permeable, porous aspect of the suburbs which haunts his work. The suburb appears as a buffer zone or liminal space between the urban and the rural, 'where everything is implied: city, warehouse district, night stop, woods emerging from mist'.[81] This metamorphic status is what confers its non-identity, making it a 'nowhere' and suggesting to the inhabitants 'that nothing is solid at all, and the suburb is no more substantial than a mirage in a blizzard'.[82] The inauthenticity of this way of living is far from the ecological ideal of 'dwelling', and Burnside explores the possibility that this kind of settlement is in fact a form of escapism, of 'avoidance', running away from the emptiness at the heart of a modern life which separates itself from the authentic, natural world. The speaker acknowledges the home-like aspects of living in these suburban houses, the 'primitive identity' of the place which allows some gestures towards authentic 'dwelling': the ability to cultivate plants, or the pleasure in sitting undisturbed in its 'warm kitchen'. Such gestures are part of this concept of a 'primitive identity' which echoes the phenomenological 'primary virtues' or 'original shell' of inhabiting which Bachelard tries to uncover in *The Poetics of Space*.[83] However, in these poems at least, such intimations of normal inhabitance seem merely to be part of a well-constructed illusion.

Similar anxieties about authenticity and artificiality appear in Jamie's poetry. In 'Fountain', she asks 'What are we doing when we toss a coin,

| just a 5p piece into the shallow dish | of the fountain in the city-centre | shopping arcade?' Thinking about the irony of shop-names like 'Athena, Argos, Olympus' and the modern reality of women laden with polythene bags sipping 'coffee in . . . polystyrene cup[s]', she admits 'We know it's all false'. But Jamie's ironic, playful viewpoint remains optimistic, offering the tantalising possibility of a re-connection with some ancient tradition, some dislocated pagan sensibility, 'a nod | toward a goddess we almost sense | in the verdant plastic'.[84]

Tuning in to some vestige of the authentic, of the 'real', is a paramount concern for both writers. Ideals of authenticity, for Burnside especially, are related to the philosophy of Existentialism, which developed as a reaction to modernity, and stressed the importance of 'authentic' life, as opposed to the 'bad faith' of the masses, or the 'herd', as Nietzsche called them. There are, perhaps, implicit suggestions of superiority in such a doctrine of authenticity – although Jamie's poetry, which focuses on the democratic voice as much as the importance of an individual, solitary relationship with the world, might be exempt from such an analysis. Burnside's work, on the other hand, does contain traces of suspicion or derision for the 'masses'. However, following the birth of his son, there is a subtle adjustment in his approach, becoming concerned not only with how he as an individual is to relate to the natural world around him, but how his son can enjoy and understand that world. Kite-flying, for Burnside, incorporates some elements of the 'dowser's twitch'. The poem, 'History' meditates on 'the problem: how to be alive | in all this gazed-upon and cherished world | and do no harm'. Written in the aftermath of September 11th 2001, Burnside finds himself 'dizzy with the fear | of losing everything – the sea, the sky, | all living creatures, forests, estuaries'. The toddler on the beach represents an innocent way of seeing the world, 'puzzled by the pattern on a shell', their different ways of exploring and experiencing the 'other' that is the natural world allows for some hope:

> his parents on the dune slacks with a kite
> plugged into the sky
>   all nerve and line
>
> patient; afraid; but still, through everything
> attentive to the irredeemable.[85]

Kite-flying is also a motif in *The Locust Room*, where Paul's father uses as it a means of mediation between self and nature, discovering a sense of belonging through the physical engagement with the sky, 'a subtle, responsive thing, like skin'. 'It was a correspondence, of sorts, a kind of dialogue. Sometimes, he would think that the sky was the only thing to which he was certain he belonged'.[86] This way of 'plugging in' to the natural world is predicated not on sight but on bodily sensation, 'to do with feeling, with tension and movement flowing back through the nerves and into the spine and the belly'.[87]

The search for such methods of mediation is a central theme in *Living Nowhere*, perhaps Burnside's most explicitly 'ecological' prose work to date. At first set in the industrial, polluted environment of Corby, the novel falls into four sections, corresponding to the four ancient 'elements' – 'The Perfection of Water', 'Keeping Fire', 'The Air of the Door' and 'Earth Light'. The title of the novel is itself ambiguous, suggesting both pessimism and idealism – 'nowhere' resonates with connotations of utopia, literally 'nowhere', perhaps recalling the idealistic, anti-industrial future imagined in William Morris's *News from Nowhere* (1890). The 'nowhere' of the northern industrial town, however, is closer to purgatory than to any utopian idyll. The inhabitants of the town find themselves 'steeped in a miasma of steel and carbon and ore . . . drenched in the stink of coke and ammonia and that lingering undertow, part-carbon, part-iron, that was everywhere – in the soil and the water, on the air . . . in the flesh of the living and the bones of the dead'.[88] Corby suffers from some of the same problems that the 'non-place' of the suburbs faces, with half-hearted attempts by the town planners to keep a few elements of nature in the industrial landscape, leaving room for 'narrow strips of dusty woods, mysterious angles and recesses of greenery and brackish water'. These areas fail in their intention to prettify the town, instead 'reminding everyone of what had been there before The Works arrived'; 'remnants of ancient forest, the dusty ghosts of what had once been clear ponds and rivers full of carp or pike, occasional clumps of wildflowers in woodland clearings, their blossoms impossibly blue, or gold, or blood-red'.[89]

Children and adults alike dream of alternative homes, away from the town. 'People here were always talking about home, and they always meant some other place, somewhere in the past or the future, a place they had come from, a place they were going to'.[90] Home is never the 'here and now' for the residents of Corby, but a 'home' they fondly remember from childhood or a destination they fantasise about retiring to. Their children realise what they do not, that 'the mythical communities they dreamed about were just estates and tenements', places no different from Corby, except that they now existed in the mind, idealised.[91] Younger characters like Alina, Francis or Derek dream of escapes, possible lives which are not rooted in memories of elsewhere. Such dreams are known to be unreal, but in this case it is the value of imagination itself that is prized:

All that mattered was that she could imagine somewhere outside this smoky, poisoned town: light; empty woods; deer crossing a country road in the dusk. This imagined place, this country which did not exist, was *home* for her.[92]

It seems that escape to a conceptual dwelling place, a place which can only be inhabited by the mind, is the only 'true' habitation possible in this novel. If exile can be viewed as an internalised condition, a state of mind, then perhaps 'home' is too. Alina discovers a way of tuning in to the world first by using acid, which enables her to recognise what Bachelard would call the 'primary essence' of the objects around her, which confers upon them a sense of magic, of numinosity. An apple tree in someone's garden is revealed, to Alina's altered mental state, as 'bedecked with tiny golden apples that seemed lit from within, lit and warm, still alive, the seeds still liquid in the sleeping core'. The drug use allows her to recognise how much she 'belongs' to her body, how much it is possible to feel 'at home' in the body – a sensation which returns when she later walks out onto a frozen lake, heading for the 'vivid white space', a 'magical zone' at its centre. Walking on the ice, her senses are heightened, noticing:

> her breath going in and out like this: the world, herself, the world, warmth and cold and warmth again, a constant measured exchange till it was impossible to say where one thing ended and the other began. A body in the world, breathing. A centre of balance, a breath of air.[93]

This breakdown of self/other or subject/object relationships is important, positing the possibility of a continuum, a 'world that was continuous with her body'.[94] This seems closely related to Burnside's statement in 'Strong Words', where he notes his central fascination with 'what is 'real' (as opposed to merely factual, i.e. 'true'); what is the relationship between self and other (and why do we feel obliged to make such a distinction); and what do we mean when we talk about the spirit[?]'.[95]

Encountering the 'other'

Thinking about 'self' and 'other', as Foucault demonstrated in *The Order of Things*, is predicated upon taxonomies, systems of linguistic categorisation that divide the perceived world into distinctive, comprehensible objects. However, such systems, the 'ordered surfaces . . . with which we are accustomed to tame the wild profusion of existing things' are liable to collapse, threatening to disintegrate the 'age-old distinction between the Same and the Other'.[96] As Octavio Paz suggests, Western thought has for centuries promoted the idea of a 'world of the clear and trenchant distinction between what is and what is not', which, it has been suggested, has sidelined mysticism and poetry into a 'subsidiary, clandestine and diminished life'.[97] In defiance of this, poetry 'not only proclaims the dynamic and necessary co-existence of opposites, but also their ultimate identity'.[98] This potential for poetry – and poetic prose – to negotiate the boundaries of categorisation is important for Burnside, as it is for Jamie and Warner. Such boundaries are constantly collapsed or rendered ambiguous in these writers' representations of individuals and the natural world, recognising the most fundamental construction of 'Other' as the natural world itself. By deliberately blurring the gaps between 'self' and 'other', 'human' and 'nature', Burnside invites the reader to join him in deconstructing these binary oppositions, which he feels are misleading and constrictive, exploring the liminal world which exists at the edges of such categories.

The 'liminal' or the 'borderline' has long been an important concept for post-colonial theory, giving a voice to the marginalised racial or geographical 'other', and it is clear that a similar process can be applied to the natural world, which has been similarly marginalised, exploited or 'spoken for' in modern Western societies. Burnside is certainly aware of these theoretical implications, pointing out the correspondences between ecological theory and the post-structuralist discourses of post-colonialism and feminism.[99] The social anthropologist Victor Turner theorised that 'liminal people fall in the interstices of the social structure, are on its margins, or occupy its lowest rungs', and that they are often associated with death, or the underworld.[100] Burnside's depiction of the relationship between Francis and Jan in *Living Nowhere* plays upon such constructions. Jan's death is certainly the catalyst for Francis's abandonment of his previous life, and following his exit through the cemetery hedge, the remainder of the novel takes the form of an autobiographical narrative, comprising a series of letters written by Francis to his dead friend. Jan is in many respects a sort of ethereal 'twin' for Francis, and the relationship between the two friends displaces Francis's real brother, Derek. Jan chooses to opt out of normal social interaction, providing the 'alchemy of studied absence' to family snapshots, 'a blur at the edge of the picture like snowfall . . . he was the boy who never existed, the boy who spent his free time with phantoms'.[101] After his death, his presence continues to haunt Francis, becoming the conceptual or spiritual 'brother' Francis confides in, writing a series of letters to his dead friend but never writing home to his family in Corby.

The 'double' or 'doppelgänger' has certainly been a recurring motif in the work of Scottish writers – James Hogg's *Memoirs and Confessions of a Justified Sinner* and Robert Louis Stevenson's *The Strange Case of*

Dr Jekyll and Mr Hyde are two striking examples. Burnside's work is full of strange twinnings, relationships between real and imagined brothers, distorted versions of the self which seem to be both psychological and mysteriously 'organic'. Cases 'of wolf-boys, calf-children, infants raised by gazelles, pigs, bears and leopards' are contemplated in *The Dumb House*, whilst Paul encounters a mysterious, fierce boy in the woods keeping watch over birds' nests in *The Locust Room*.[102] In the poem 'Heatwave', the awakening sexuality of a boy watching a woman bathe in the river manifests itself as 'a darker presence, rising from the stream, | to match my every move, my every breath. | Eel black and cold'.[103] Elsewhere, Burnside contemplates fairytales of metamorphosis, the frog in which he sees 'another self: | the changeling I might have been'.[104] In the poems, 'Animism' and 'Animals' in *The Light Trap*, we discover the animal half-life of houses which 'contained a presence', 'a kindred shape | more animal than ghost'. Inhabitants wake up to discover 'a slickness of musk and fur | on our sleep-washed skins' which suggests 'not the continuity we understand | as self, but life, beyond the life we live | on purpose'.[105] Individual psychology is necessarily part of this perception, as when one of the characters in *The Locust Room* suffers some form of mental breakdown, encountering a indeterminate figure, who looks like 'he belonged to the woods', not 'even a man at all, but something else . . . he had risen up out of the earth one day, like those people in fairy stories', his clothes that 'might have been part of his body . . . made of fur or hair'.[106]

This borderland between self and other, human and nature is, however, morally ambiguous, belonging as much to the rapist in *The Locust Room* as it does to the sensitive personae of Burnside's poetry. The masked rapist reveals a close, intuitive relationship with some kinds of animals – he identifies with stealthy or vicious hunters, realising 'he should have been an animal – a polecat or a wolverine'. What he senses is not the subject-object relationship which might exist between an owner and his pet, but 'something closer and, at the same time, more respectful: a recognition; more of a secret kinship than an understanding'.[107] Part of this animal identity leads to a sense of 'dwelling' on the margins of human life, belonging 'to that borderline of cool air at the window, to the half-life of greenery and rain . . . to the places that other people treated as dead space, to attics and stairwells and narrow rooms at the back of the house'.[108] There do indeed appear to be a clutch of images and ideas which Burnside returns to again and again, in both his prose and his poetry: twins, liminal spaces, strange encounters with wild animals, points at which the environment and the self fade in or out, and intermingle.

The liminal, alchemical processes of poetry – or poetic prose – extend to the shifting boundaries between self and other. In 'The Myth of the Twin', the title poem of Burnside's 1994 collection, the speaker is aware of some presence mirroring the human, 'out in the snow | meshed with the birdsong and light':

> . . . not
> the revelation of a foreign place,
> but emptiness, a stillness in the frost,
> the silence that stands in the birchwoods, the common
> soul.[109]

The experience of the unnameable 'other' provokes, as in *Living Nowhere*, a sense of continuum between self and world, a 'common soul'. A more concrete encounter with the 'other' is evoked in 'September evening; deer at Big Basin', a poem which bears some resemblances to MacDiarmid's 'In Talk with Duncan Ban MacIntyre' or Iain Crichton Smith's 'Deer on the High Hills'. The deer, 'bound to the silence', make the human observers aware of their own 'otherness'. This encounter conveys the unexpected 'gift of an alien country', 'a story that gives us the questions we wanted to ask, | and a sense of our presence as creatures, | about to be touched'.[110] Being able to acknowledge 'our presence as creatures' is important to Burnside's ecological philosophy. Gaston Bachelard, in *La Flamme d'une Chandelle* (1961) produced a series of 'reveries' on subject-object relationships which tackled this very idea, of humans as 'creatures'. In his 'reveries', Bachelard attempts to deal with the 'convenient passivity' of modern life which sees subject-object relationships in terms of a hierarchy of utility. To reiterate Bachelard's example, a lamp is now operated by the flick of an electric light switch, and the light produced with almost no participation from the person who switches it on, whereas previously the lighting of a candle invited a more creative, meaningful relationship between subject and object. Poetry, Bachelard argues, can 'restore us to the object' and in so doing, it can 'restore to us this sense of ourselves as "creatures", as subjects beyond the conventional limits of subject and object'.[111] Burnside's poems are often wistful meditations on the possibility of such metamorphosis.

> . . . if I could have chosen anything
> but this inevitable self, I'd be the one
> who walks alone and barefoot in the woods
> to stand, amidst a family of deer,
> knowing her kind, and knowing the chasm between
> one presence and the next as nothing more
> than something learned, like memory, or song.[112]

This is strikingly similar to MacDiarmid's wish, on encountering a wild deer, 'not to be ignored but to be accepted'. Burnside's poem, like MacDiarmid's, carries an epigraph from the ecologist, Frank Fraser Darling.[113]

Kathleen Jamie's work also attempts to break down such binary constructions, recognising the need for reverie as a way of examining our relationship with nature. While some of the poems in *The Tree House* can be read as reveries themselves, others comment on the difficulty of reconciling the demands of everyday life, our 'inter-human relationships', with 'our need for reverie'.[114] In 'The Buddleia', for instance, Jamie's attempts to connect with a sense of the 'divine' in her garden are frustrated by thoughts of 'my suddenly | elderly parents, their broken-down | Hoover; or my quarrelling kids'.[115] The poems in *The Tree House* speak of the need to find or construct spaces for reverie as a way of attending to and living with nature. However, for Jamie, these spaces are often 'nothing but an attitude of mind', as in 'The Bower', where she half-sees, half-imagines a 'forest dwelling', an 'anchorage | or musical box', high up in the woodland canopy.[116] This idea again echoes the work of Bachelard, who suggests that spaces, even the physically uninhabitable spaces of a cupboard or a nest, can speak to us as symbols of the primordial dwelling place, containing 'the essence of the notion of home'.[117] *The Tree House* is full of such conceptual dwelling places: a cave on the shoreline, a clearing between trees, a swallow's nest, even the reflective surface of a puddle:

> Flooded fields, all pulling
> the same lustrous trick,
> that flush in the world's light
> as though with sudden love –
> how should we live?[118]

In her earlier work, such questions are often explored in a playful, celebratory way, focused on aspects of gender, as in the figure of 'The Bogie Wife' from *Jizzen* (1999), or 'Bairns of Suzie: a hex' in *The Queen of Sheba* (1994). These poems capitalise on what once were marginalising constructions of feminine identity – the cultural categories of woman/nature/object/other which feminist theorists such as Hélène Cixous have identified.[119] In doing so, they also explore some concepts drawn from 'ecofeminism', a theoretical perspective which posits a continuum between the 'body of nature' and female bodies – similarly 'othered' by Western culture, aligned with the moral ambiguities of nature, wildness, sexuality.[120] For instance, 'Bairns of Suzie' evokes a female kinship with the natural world, opposed to structures of male authority and control:

> Have you not seen us, the Bairns of Suzie
> under the pylons of Ormiston Brae
> running easy
>   with foxes and dogs, high
> on the green hill, high
>   in the luke-warm mother's glance
> of midwinter sun?[121]

Land rights for local people, the freedom to wander at will over the landscape, are guarded by a feminised, pagan genius loci, Suzie 'the witch of this hill', identified with some form of earth mother whose children 'come out to play | on the stone nipple | of the Black Craig'. As borderline creatures, the bairns have hybrid characteristics, part-human, part-woodland, crafting charmed arrows with their 'twig fingers'. With 'dog-rose | tangled | in the hair-nests | of each other's armpits and sex', they are emblems of fecundity, representative of a liberated sexuality which subverts masculine authority, the 'laws and guns' who claim ownership of the land, threatening with their 'courtrooms and gates'. The local people, the 'wifies in scarves' at the corner-shop are complicit in this animistic rebellion against bureaucratic control. Their houses have been constructed from the ruins of abbey and castle, whose grand stones have been reappropriated as 'lintels, thexstanes, hearth', the touchstones of 'home'.

In the work of all three writers, the possibility of breaking down the division between the human and natural worlds is often contemplated in the context of transformative or liminal spaces, particularly water. In the poem, 'The sea-house', Jamie reveals an 'othered' domestic environment, an underwater house where everyday domestic objects and spaces become strange and beautiful: 'the cupboard | under the stair | glimmers with pearl', while billowing through the house are 'laundries of wrack'. This poem brings constructions of home, gender and nature together in surprising ways.

> The sea-house is purdah:
> cormorants' hooked-out wings
> screen every chamber. Inside
> the shifting place, the
> neither-nor[122]

This liminal place is a feminised space, in 'Purdah', it is a house of women, a distorted domestic scene. The 'shifting place, the | neither-nor' reflects a blurring of identity, of self and other.

In Alan Warner's fiction, Morvern's dive 'beneath the nightwater' from the sinking ferry in *These Demented Lands* (1997), a little girl in her arms, performs a similar liminal function. Entry to the cold waters confuses Morvern's senses, the water turning 'the little blonde girl's (girls?) hair jet-black'. Mysterious, confusing, the phosphorescence under the waters of the Sound creates an other-worldly landscape, 'glissanding on the lunar seabeds way below', Morvern sees her own body as strange, her 'black legs slowly kicking so thin in silhouette' against the backdrop of 'a coral reef gone insane in the colours of these killing seas'.[123] Morvern is haunted by a fear of the ocean, telling the Aircrash Investigator of the 'scaredness' she experienced thinking of ships' rudders displayed in a museum, 'held there forever, punished above the cold Atlantic seabeds that were always rolling out below them'. The Aircrash Investigator recognises the fear of the liminal, the 'other', which Morvern experiences:

> You fear underworlds where the seabed is the earth, the unsteady surface a new sky, you hate the Living Things: basking shark or angler fish that might brush against your bare leg and those rudders and propellers . . . their constant immersion, made them thresholds into that underworld.[124]

But both Morvern and the Aircrash Investigator are drawn to these underworlds, the latter obsessed with the wreckage of an aircraft sunken in the bay. This obsession is itself a kind of search for a home, the type of sensation Burnside evokes in 'Ports':

> We notice how dark it is
>   a dwelling place
> for something in ourselves that understands
>
> the beauty of wreckage
>   the beauty
> of things submerged.[125]

The distortions of what might be 'home' are taken literally in Warner's *The Man Who Walks*, haunted by the liminal, ambiguous figure of the Uncle, the Man Who Walks himself, who can be perhaps be read as much a part of the realm of the natural world as human society. His house is no longer a place of normal human habitation, transformed by neglect into something which resembles the 'lair' of some animal. 'The garden was not kept with accuracy. There was no differences [sic] between the scrub around the house and the actual garden when it began, so long since the fence had rotted away'.[126] This blurring of boundaries continues inside the house, where the domestic scene is made even more strange by a 'complex network of papier-mâché tunnels and igloos' which the Uncle has constructed from old newspapers, a labyrinthine 'badger's sett' inside the rooms and corridors.[127] The Uncle's inhabitation of the house renders it uninhabitable by normal human standards, transformed into a sort of 'lair'. This occupancy is punctuated by periods of time spent wandering the hills, living in caves or sleeping rough using a child's Wendy house as a tent.[128]

> It is a fact Man Who Walks once walked across silty beds of New Loch, 'neath the surface, a huge boulder under one arm holding him down, breathing through a giant hogweed stalk; suffering no such side effects as the bends or, unfortunately, drowning.[129]

The crossing of such boundaries, or transformational spaces, provides a context in which to question the relationship between humans and nature, self and other. Physically uninhabitable, they nevertheless constitute conceptual dwelling places. As Warner sets about deconstructing ideas of 'house' and 'home', he also enacts the deconstruction of 'self', showing the body to be literally invaded by external objects, particularly those drawn from the natural world. The Uncle's body is a ruptured construct, his face is in ruins; one of his eyes lost either by violent removal by his Nephew, or his habit of 'breenging around mentally in woodlands . . . licking rare fungus off trees'.[130] His jaw was, he claims, broken when he was 'hit by a ship's anchor' (possibly during one of his underwater excursions?), giving him a gaping, 'twisted smile' from which grows a tomato plant, rooted in a rotten molar which he 'chew[s] . . . once a fortnight to get his greens'.[131] His empty eye socket is used to store objects found on his travels, a 'miniature key-ring torch . . . switched to the ON position' lighting up 'little fragments of red, yellow and green glass, which cluster like large fish eggs in his eye'.[132]

> Face of The Man Who Walks! Baseball cap gone. The hair! Leaves and dead crabs in its grey spiked heights. Constant appearance of shock, dirt in the wrinkles, the haunted, prowling expression, already dark skin, weathered by the endlessness of being forced abroad in all weathers into the wider expanses of the territory.[133]

This fragmentation of the self is accompanied by a conscious rejection of forms of official identification or classification. The Uncle has destroyed the typical markers of identity conferred upon the individual by the state, choosing to be an outsider. At some point in his life, it seems, 'he spun right out of society, burned his treasured wage slips, national insurance number, premium bonds, driving licence and took to scrambling his papier-mâché tunnels in rustling spurts'.[134] This deliberate rejection of settled life, of the ideals of the 'Settled Community' reveals both Uncle and Nephew as practitioners of an existence predicated on survival instinct and local knowledge.

It is striking that the epigraphs to Warner's novel include Walter Benjamin's famous saying, from his *Theses on the Philosophy of*

History, that 'There is no document of civilisation that is not at the same time a document of barbarism'.[135] Warner is clearly playing with traditional associations of the Highlands with barbarism – another epigraph is from a traditional (lowland) satirical portrait of God's creation of a 'Helandman' from a 'horss turd'.[136] 'Barbarism' is of course the proper opposite of 'civilisation', connoting uncivilised ignorance and rudeness, and perhaps cruelty or violence. Significantly, the 'barbaric' is also the foreign, the strange, or the wild – anyone or anything 'other', in fact. Benjamin's assertion conflates these binary opposites, bringing barbarity into the ambit of civilisation, recognising the 'other' as an intrinsic part of one's familiar home ground, even of the self. Georg Simmel's theory of 'the stranger' is perhaps the embodiment of this concept, a figure which encapsulates both proximity and distance, familiarity and otherness, revealing the essential 'unity of nearness and remoteness involved in every human relation'.[137] Encountering a stranger 'throws the doubtful and flickering quality of absence and non-existence back into the faces of those insiders in the local community, throwing into question the sanctity of presence'.[138] The Nephew and his Uncle, the Man Who Walks, are two such strangers, figures who provide an opportunity to assess the interpolation of self and other, the human and the natural world.

This flux of identity is suggested by the violent, Romanticised past of the Highlands. The historical landscape is ever-present to the imagination of the Nephew, Macushlah, for whom traditional tales of local battles, ambushes and escapes are touchstones for his own pursuit of the Man Who Walks across the landscape – a pursuit which echoes 'the problems of the body and the practical intelligence' of highland adventure writing, such as Stevenson's *Kidnapped*.[139] The Highland past is a heritage to which both the Nephew and the Man Who Walks are heirs, but they are also culturally excluded from it by virtue of their liminal gypsy identity, their lack of a settled home. Discarding the familiar Romantic stereotypes surrounding the Highland 'scenery', landscape in *The Man Who Walks* is introduced to us through the eye of the mysterious uncle, revealing an eerie yet thoroughly modern landscape, 'othered' by the strange presence of the 'ghost bags'. These bizarre phenomena, it emerges, are polythene bags loosed from supermarket carparks or land-fill sites, tumbling across the hills during the night to appear 'snared on the top barbed-wire of the roadside fences – vibrating, thrumming wild in prevailing westerlies, non-degradable ends ragged . . . a texture of sickly grey, dead flesh'.[140] The juxtaposition of the historically-inscribed Highland landscape and markers of 'supermodernity' such as the hydro-electric dam also produce an eerie, surreal quality. Lying in his bed at night, the Nephew can hear outside the caravan walls:

> mysterious clicks, the quick bangs of electrics all night long, contacts opening and closing as the electric juice poured down from the hydro's hollow mountain and morning kettles went on in the Settled Community between real walls of bricks and mortar.[141]

There is an irony in this, that the power of the natural world which the Nephew, with his gypsy heritage, knows so well is harnessed to provide domestic comforts for the townsfolk who have rejected him. Clearly, this is a landscape which bears explicit marks of human impact – the environmental and cultural pollution of a homogenising consumer culture, in the form of carrier bags with 'fading blue logos from the multinationals', or the Nephew's borrowed mobile telephone and its 'Rule Britannia' ringtone.[142]

In *Rewriting Scotland*, Christie March has argued that 'In presenting Morvern's Highlands and Islands, Warner illustrates the reach of urban culture and its impact on areas of Scotland long considered reliquaries of traditional Scottish culture. The amalgam . . . represents a hybrid of Scottish culture'.[143] Certainly, Warner (who had been educated at Oban High School by Iain Crichton Smith) recognises the hierarchy often imposed by cultural 'centres' over supposed 'peripheries' such as the Western Isles, perpetuating the perceived dominance of city over countryside, or mainland over island:

> Due to the shrill demands of modern history, the Hebridean world has constantly to justify itself to the dominant culture on the mainland – for no other reason than that the island culture is distinctive and that it exists.[144]

Warner, born and brought up in Oban, although no longer resident in the Highlands, admits to feeling 'protective' of the cultural heritage of the Western Isles; valuing the 'hard, rough activities' of lives lived close to the natural world, 'aris[ing] from a necessary culture and not modern capitalism and its grand plans'.[145] The Hebrides are an example of 'an entire society slipping into invisibility', effaced by the evolution of 'a single, monolithic culture'.[146] In this sense, the Highlands and Islands do indeed constitute the 'reliquary' of tradition which March suggests; as Warner says, 'Some places, by accident of geography, hang on to aspects of the past – some bad aspects, but some good'.[147] March's analysis does, however, miss a crucial point about Warner's writing. What we see in these novels is not simply a transposition of urban subcultures onto a rural backdrop, creating a hybrid in which the urban element is dominant over the 'peripheral' identity of the Highlands, but a more authentic interaction, a correspondence, between the two. The 'traditional distinctions between urban and rural' have, as March says, been blurred, however, Warner's acknowledgement of issues such as consumerism, drugs, sex, or violence, which have in the past largely been limited to narratives of urban places, does not necessarily disrupt or deny the significance of either the landscape or its 'traditional Scottish culture'.[148]

In fact, the rural environment of the Scottish Highlands and Islands has just as active a role to play in defining the oddities and tensions of the 'hybrid' region revealed in Warner's novels as does 'urban culture'. If anything, the excesses of 'urban' culture are well-suited to the traditional identity of the region as a 'barbaric' hinterland – 'demented lands' which might rival the violence and confusion of any urban space. In this respect, Warner's stance might be viewed as a hallucinatory, postmodern version of Iain Crichton Smith's attitude expressed in his essay 'Real People in a Real Place', fighting the stereotypes about the region's cultural identity as a Romantic, escapist idyll by evoking a surrealistic representation of its environment and people. It also draws a link between the Celtic Twilight view of Gaelic temperament – Matthew Arnold's sentimental Celt who is 'always ready to react against the despotism of fact' – and characterisations by Highland and Island writers themselves, as in George Mackay Brown's championing of the 'tinkers . . . [and] surrealist folk' of rural Scotland.[149]

Human and natural histories

Burnside has written of the need for humans to redefine themselves as 'worthy participants in a natural history' – a quest which Jamie also appears to have embarked upon in works such as *Findings*.[150] Contemplating those 'rarities in human history, the places from which we've retreated', which 'suggest the lost past, the lost Eden', Jamie says that places like the ruined settlements on St Kilda or long-abandoned Highland shielings highlight the blurring of distinctions between 'human' and 'natural' landscapes and histories.[151] For Jamie, a description of the Highlands as a wilderness 'seems an affront to those many generations who took their living on that land. Whether their departure was forced or whether that way of life just fell into abeyance, they left such subtle marks. And what's natural?'[152] Recognising the 'domestic normality' of the ancient people who lived at such sites allows the modern human to 'feel both their presence, their day-to-day lives, and their utter absence. It recalibrates your sense of time'.[153] In *The Man Who Walks*, the Nephew recognises the existence of such cultural signifiers embedded in the Highland landscape itself, in a contemplative passage which is reminiscent of Lewis Grassic Gibbon or Neil Gunn:

> The land is here, all round us, but each of us pulls from it or inserts into it what we want, we all see it different, like we could meet the ghosts of other folks' needs and dreams wandering the places at night.[154]

The Tree House also includes a consideration of the changing face of the Scottish landscape, the values and history we inscribe upon it, set against its own 'natural' history; in 'The Reliquary', 'The land we inhabit opens and reveals | event before event', 'but it yields also moment | into moment'.[155] Concurrent to human history, yet also incorporating it, is natural history, where the potential for renewal and rebirth is in itself a sacred artefact – a concept which is picked up in John Burnside's poem, 'Fields', which bears an epigraph from Edvard Munch: 'From my rotting body, flowers shall grow and I am in them and that is eternity'. Here, Burnside meditates on the 'Fife and Angus' agricultural tradition of 'Gude Man's Land', an ancient form of 'Landfill' where 'farmers held | one acre of their land | untilled | unscarred' in an intuitive designation of some places as 'sacred', a place of the dead – or of the devil – which must be left to nature. This gesture of reverence is not, Burnside suggests, the product of any orthodox religious sensibility, but a decision based on the bodily senses, the farmer choosing 'one empty plot | that smelled or tasted right | one house of dreams'.[156]

Such viewpoints contrast the permanence of the natural world with the transitory, shifting histories of humans, and the values or identities they associate with landscape – in a sense, how 'space' is transformed into 'place', or even 'home'. They also demonstrate the extent to which environmental history and human history are intertwined. Simon Schama in *Landscape and Memory* suggests a 'new way of looking', a perception twinned with psychological depth which is akin to a form of archaeology: 'an excavation below our conventional sight-level to recover the veins of myth and memory that lie below the surface'.[157] This might be described as a poetics of archaeology, similar to the philosophical idea of 'unconcealment', the revelation of the truth through a poetic 'making' which Heidegger wrote about. Similar ideas are explored in Burnside's poem, 'Steinar undir Steinahlithum', published alongside his essay 'A Science of Belonging: Poetry and Ecology' in the volume *Contemporary Poetry and Contemporary Science* (2006), produced after a series of meetings with an ecologist specialising in the botany of the Arctic tundra – a topic with which Burnside was already familiar, as a frequent visitor to the northern regions of Scandinavia.[158] This poem, based on the history of an abandoned village sinking into bog-land, speaks of the transitory and difficult nature of establishing a home or settlement in an inhospitable environment – but it also considers the broader philosophical question of whether it is possible to 'dwell' in the world of nature at all, provoked by an epigraph from the religious historian James Carse: 'Nature offers no home'. The land, Burnside muses, 'longs for stories to contain: | households and fiefdoms laid down in the dirt', creating an archaeology or even a text which tells of 'a failure in the science of belonging' – a failure in ecology itself.[159] 'Birth Songs' develops this idea, noting 'how lovingly the earth resumes | possession' of human artefacts, simultaneously erasing the evidence of human presence and preserving it for posterity – a dual action which both alienates and enfolds.[160] Such considerations also echo older traditions in Scottish writing, such as Lewis Grassic Gibbon's *A Scots Quair*, or the poetry of Edwin Muir. All too keenly aware of the difficulty of living close to the land, Muir's farming people are dependent on fields of 'soft and useless dust' where 'things miscarry | Whether we care or do not care enough'. Nevertheless, the farmers and, by extension ourselves, must learn to accept the inherently contradictory aspect of dwelling: 'This is a difficult country, and our home'.[161]

This admission and acceptance of the essential ambivalence in the relationship between humans and the natural world is central to the ecological poetry of contemporary Scottish writers. Jamie's visit to Maes Howe in *Findings* is portrayed as an equivocal experience, a mingled discovery of inauthenticity and unforeseen 'truths'. Expecting to encounter a dark, 'wombish red' chamber in the tomb, Jamie is instead confronted with an interior 'bright as a Tube train', lit by surveyors' lamps which reveal 'every crack, every joint and fissure in the ancient stonework'.[162] However, her encounter with the surveyors and their technical equipment in this ancient space reminds her of the original tomb-builders' craft – an instance of what Heidegger calls *techne* – in which natural phenomena were manipulated in order to create an aesthetic, or dramatic, moment of symbolism. The Maes Howe is, she says, 'a place of artifice, of skill', more like a 'cranium' than a 'womb'. As such, the presence of the surveyors and their light – the metaphor of enlightenment is not lost on Jamie – is entirely appropriate, a modern mirroring of the skilled workmen who built the tomb. But the implications of all this modernity, this scientific technology (as opposed to *techne*) are manifold and possibly disastrous:

> We are doing damage. The surveyors poring over the tomb are working in an anxious age. We look about the world, by the light we have made, and realise it's all vulnerable, and all worth saving, and no one can do it but us.[163]

The dark, which as Jamie notes, has for a long time been appropriated by humans as a cultural metaphor, 'a cover for all that's wicked' rather than 'a natural phenomenon', is representative of the concealed, the hidden 'truth', the mystery of the natural world and of our own natural history.[164] Here, Jamie is striving to rehabilitate the dark as a sacred concept, a new metaphor which is suggestive of life rather than death. All of this points to the development of a poetics which, while valuing the 'light', celebrates and protects the 'dark' – a crucial 'line of defence' which may help to mitigate the environmental and cultural 'damage' Jamie suggests we are capable of causing.

Light and dark are similarly important as phenomenological touchstones in John Burnside's work, in which the transformational aspect of darkness – the encounter with 'its textures and wild intimacy' which Jamie seeks in *Findings* – is central to Burnside's development of an ecological poetics in earlier collections such as *Feast Days*, where darkness suggests the life of animals hidden, out of sight, although the use of light, in Burnside's work, is more conventional than in Jamie's.[165] 'The Light Trap', the title poem of Burnside's 2002 poetry collection, begins with a meditation on catching and identifying moths at night, broadening out into Burnside's habitual philosophical questions of memory, taxonomy and transformation.[166] Here, darkness also connotes mystery and a certain sense of the sacred. The possibility of enlightenment, of knowing both the names of creatures or objects and their essences, seems unpredictable, the 'new moths catch and spark | on nothingness, arriving from the dark | at shapes and names, through light's pure dazzlement'.[167] For Burnside, the attainment of 'enlightenment' is bound up with his interest in the effacement of the 'ego' combined with his appreciation of *techne* rather than technology.

What this means is a poetics of the active body as a way for humans to reconnect with the earth. 'What we need most,' Burnside says in *The Light Trap*, 'we learn from the menial tasks', citing 'the changeling in a folk tale, chopping logs, | poised at the dizzy edge of transformation' or the Buddhist novice, raking leaves:

> finding the body's kinship with the earth
> beneath their feet, the lattice of a world
> where nothing turns or stands outside the whole;
>
> and when the insight comes, they carry on
> with what's at hand . . .[168]

This bodily eco-poetics spills over into Burnside's fiction, as ultimately, the characters in *Living Nowhere* discover a sense of ecological 'belonging' through 'this reconnection with the earth, not in any glamorous or trendy way, but the act of digging . . . hard work . . . getting your hands wet and cold, that's part of the deal'.[169] The novel closes with Francis digging in his father's garden back in Corby, the only certainty in life being the physical engagement with the earth in the present moment; work, forgetting himself; 'a man working in a garden, then a garden and nothing else'.[170]

This, in many ways, is the essence of the ecological vision of modern Scottish writing: an acknowledgement that our relationship with the natural world needs to be physical, as well as contemplative, and above all, that the practice of poetry and prose-writing requires close attention, intuitive observation and a sense of reverence for the 'other': the sacred dark of an Orkney night, a blackbird singing in the garden, or the tug of the wind on a kite.

Notes

1. Kathleen Jamie interviewed by Lilias Fraser, *Scottish Studies Review*, 2.1, Spring 2001, p. 20.
2. John Burnside, interviewed by Louisa Gairn, 31 March 2004 (unpublished transcription) n.p.
3. Jules Smith, 'Critical Perspective on Kathleen Jamie', *Contemporary Writers Website*, http://www.contemporarywriters.com/authors/?p=auth02C5P102112626707. Accessed 12th May 2004.
4. John Burnside, 'Strong Words', in W. N. Herbert and Matthew Hollis (eds), *Strong Words: Modern Poets on Modern Poetry* (Northumberland: Bloodaxe, 2000), p. 259.
5. Burnside, interviewed by Louisa Gairn, 31 March 2004.
6. Daniel O'Rourke (ed.), *Dream State: The New Scottish Poets* (Edinburgh: Polygon, 1994), p. 156; Kathleen Jamie interviewed by Lilias Fraser, p. 17.
7. Kathleen Jamie, 'Author Statement', *Contemporary Writers Website*, http://www.contemporarywriters.com/authors/?p=auth02C5P102112626707. Accessed 12th May 2004.
8. Burnside, interviewed by Louisa Gairn, 31 March 2004.
9. John Burnside and Maurice O'Riordan (eds), *Wild Reckoning: An Anthology Provoked by Rachel Carson's 'Silent Spring'* (London: Calouste Gulbenkian Foundation, 2004), p. 21.
10. John Burnside, 'Bunkered by Mr Big', *The Guardian*, 28th July 2001, and 'Base', *The Guardian*, 22nd March 2001.
11. Ibid.
12. Kathleen Jamie, 'Diary', *London Review of Books*, vol. 24, no. 11 (6th June 2002), p. 39.
13. Kathleen Jamie, *Findings* (London: Sort of Books, 2005), p. 98.
14. Kathleen Jamie, *Jizzen* (London: Picador, 2000), p. 42.
15. Kathleen Jamie, 'Holding Fast – Truth and Change in Poetry' in W. N. Herbert and M. Hollis (eds), *Strong Words: Modern Poets on Modern Poetry* (Northumberland: Bloodaxe, 2000), p. 280.

16. Martin Heidegger, quoted in George Pattison, *The Later Heidegger* (London: Routledge, 2000), p. 51.
17. John Burnside, *The Locust Room* (London: Vintage, 2002), p. 8.
18. John Burnside, *The Asylum Dance* (London: Jonathan Cape, 2000), p. 5.
19. Burnside, *The Locust Room*, p. 175.
20. Jamie, *Findings*, p. 109.
21. Ibid., p. 42.
22. Kathleen Jamie, *The Queen of Sheba* (London: Bloodaxe, 1994), p. 37.
23. Burnside, *The Locust Room*, pp. 175–6.
24. Ibid., p. 28.
25. Kathleen Jamie, 'The Questionnaire', *Poetry Review*, vol. 92, no. 2 (Summer 2002), p. 11.
26. John Burnside, *The Hoop* (Manchester: Carcanet, 1988), p. 48.
27. Burnside, *The Locust Room*, pp. 28–9.
28. Gaston Bachelard. *The Poetics of Space*, trans. Maria Jolas (Boston: Beacon Press, 1994), p. 4.
29. Burnside, interviewed by Louisa Gairn, 31 March 2004.
30. John Burnside, *The Light Trap* (London: Jonathan Cape, 2002), p. 7.
31. Kathleen Jamie, *Among Muslims: Meetings at the Frontiers of Pakistan* (London: Sort of Books, 2002), p. 239.
32. Kirsty Scott, 'In the nature of things', *The Guardian*, 18 June 2005.
33. Jonathan Bate, *The Song of the Earth* (London: Picador, 2000), p. 23.
34. Kathleen Jamie, *The Tree House* (London: Picador, 2004), p. 49.
35. Burnside, *The Locust Room*, p. 174; Hugh MacDiarmid, 'In Talk with Donnchadh Bàn Mac an t'Saoir', in Michael Grieve and W. R. Aitken. (eds), *Complete Poems*, vol. II (London: Martin Brian and O'Keefe, 1978), pp. 1098–102.
36. Quoted in Burnside, *The Light Trap*, p. 1.
37. Burnside, *The Locust Room*, p. 176.
38. Burnside, *The Asylum Dance*, p. 12.
39. Burnside, *The Good Neighbour*, p. 27.
40. John Burnside, *Living Nowhere* (London: Jonathan Cape, 2003), p. 234.
41. Jamie, *The Queen of Sheba*, p. 64.
42. Burnside, *The Locust Room*, p. 28.
43. Burnside, *The Light Trap*, p. 77.
44. Burnside, *Living Nowhere*, p. 234.
45. Burnside, *The Good Neighbour*, pp. 33–5.
46. Burnside, *Living Nowhere*, p. 318.
47. Burnside, *The Light Trap*, p. 77.
48. Edward Said, 'Reflections on Exile', *Reflections on Exile and Other Literary and Cultural Essays* (London: Granta, 2001), p. 454.
49. John Burnside, 'The Invisible Husband', *Burning Elvis* (London: Jonathan Cape, 2000), p. 61.
50. Ibid., p. 63.
51. John Burnside, *The Dumb House* (London: Jonathan Cape, 1997), p. 25.
52. Said, 'Reflections on Exile', p. 183.
53. Burnside, *Living Nowhere*, p. 132.
54. Ibid., p. 236.
55. Theodor Adorno, quoted by Edward Said, *Reflections on Exile*, p. 305.
56. Said, p. 564.

57. Robert Crawford, *Identifying Poets: Self and Territory in Twentieth-Century Poetry* (Edinburgh: Edinburgh University Press, 1993), p. 147; 153.
58. Ibid., p. 147.
59. Epigraph, Burnside, *The Asylum Dance*.
60. Jamie, *The Tree House*, p. 7.
61. Burnside, interviewed by Louisa Gairn, 31 March, 2004.
62. Alan Warner, *The Man Who Walks* (London: Vintage, 2003), p. 105.
63. Ibid., p. 189.
64. Ibid., p. 190.
65. Ibid., p. 189.
66. Ibid., pp. 191–2.
67. Ibid., p. 144.
68. Jamie, *Among Muslims*, p. 210.
69. Ibid., p. 210.
70. Jamie, *The Queen of Sheba*, p. 29.
71. Ibid., p. 30.
72. Burnside, *Living Nowhere*, p. 341.
73. Jamie, *Among Muslims*, p. 227.
74. Kathleen Jamie, 'The Autonomous Region', *Mr and Mrs Scotland Are Dead: Poems, 1980–1994*, selected by Lilias Fraser (Northumberland: Bloodaxe, 2002), p. 86.
75. Ibid., p. 106.
76. Burnside, *The Hoop*, p. 48; 'Haar', *The Good Neighbour*, pp. 18–20.
77. John Burnside, *Common Knowledge*, p. 41.
78. Marc Auge, *Non-places: Introduction to an Anthropology of Supermodernity*, trans. John Howe (London: Verso, 1995), pp. 92–3.
79. Ibid., pp. 96–103.
80. Ibid., p. 103.
81. Burnside, *Common Knowledge*, p. 41.
82. Ibid., p. 42.
83. Bachelard, *The Poetics of Space*, p. 4.
84. Jamie, *The Queen of Sheba*, p. 17.
85. Burnside, *The Light Trap*, p. 42.
86. Burnside, *The Locust Room*, p. 235.
87. Ibid., p. 235.
88. Burnside, *Living Nowhere*, pp. 13–14.
89. Ibid., p. 13.
90. Ibid., p. 13.
91. Ibid., p. 109.
92. Ibid., p. 13.
93. Ibid., p. 39.
94. Ibid., p. 40.
95. Burnside, 'Strong Words', p. 259.
96. Michel Foucault, 'The Order of Things', in Julie Rivkin and Michael Ryan (eds), *Literary Theory: An Anthology* (London: Blackwell, 1998), pp. 377–8.
97. Octavio Paz, quoted in David Halliburton, *Poetic Thinking: An Approach to Heidegger* (Chicago: University of Chicago Press, 1981), p. 20.
98. Ibid., p. 19.

99. Burnside, unpublished interview with Louisa Gairn, 31 March 2004.
100. Victor W. Turner, *The Ritual Process: Structure and Anti-Structure* (London: Routledge and Kegan Paul, 1969), p. 125.
101. Burnside, *Living Nowhere*, p. 57.
102. Burnside, *The Dumb House*, p. 30; Burnside, *The Locust Room*, p. 59.
103. Burnside, *The Light Trap*, p. 26.
104. Burnside, *Feast Days*, p. 34.
105. Burnside, *The Light Trap*, pp. 18–19.
106. Burnside, *The Locust Room*, p. 157.
107. Ibid., p. 107.
108. Ibid., pp. 1–2.
109. John Burnside, *The Myth of the Twin* (London: Cape, 1994), p. 53.
110. Ibid., p. 38.
111. Gaston Bachelard, quoted by Mary McAllester Jones in *Gaston Bahelard, Subversive Humanist: Texts and Readings* (Madison, WI: The University of Wisconsin Press, 1991), p. 157.
112. Burnside, *The Light Trap*, pp. 10–11.
113. See Hugh MacDiarmid, 'In Talk with with Donnchadh Bàn Mac an t'Saoir', in Michael Grieve and W. R. Aitken (eds), *Complete Poems*, vol. 2 (London: Martin, Brian and O'Keefe, 1993), pp. 1098–102.
114. Kathleen Jamie, 'The Tree House', University of St Andrews website, http://www.st-andrews.ac.uk/academic/english/jamie/treehouse.html. Accessed 15 December 2005.
115. Jamie, *The Tree House*, p. 27.
116. Ibid., p. 17.
117. Bachelard, *The Poetics of Space*, p. 4.
118. Jamie, *The Tree House*, p. 48.
119. Hélène Cixous, 'Sorties', in Julie Rivkin and Michael Ryan (eds), *Literary Theory: An Anthology* (Oxford: Blackwell, 1998), pp. 578–84.
120. See Greg Garrard, *Ecocriticsm* (London: Routledge, 2004), pp. 23–7.
121. Jamie, *The Queen of Sheba*, pp. 25–6.
122. Ibid., p. 57.
123. Alan Warner, *These Demented Lands* (London: Vintage, 1998), pp. 5–6.
124. Warner, *These Demented Lands*, p. 85.
125. Burnside, *The Asylum Dance*, p. 2.
126. Warner, *The Man Who Walks*, p. 35.
127. Ibid., p. 37.
128. Ibid., p. 92.
129. Ibid., p. 19.
130. Ibid., p. 210.
131. Ibid., p. 109; p. 103.
132. Ibid., p. 123.
133. Ibid., p. 273.
134. Ibid., p. 237.
135. See Walter Benjamin, 'Theses on the Philosophy of History', in H. Arendt (ed.), trans. *Illuminations*, H. Zorn (London: Pimlico, 1999), p. 248.
136. 'How the First Helandman of God was Maid', wrongly attributed to Alexander Montgomerie by Alan Warner, epigraph, *The Man Who Walks*.

137. Georg Simmel quoted in John Allen, 'On Georg Simmel: Proximity, Distance and Movement', in M. Crang and N. Thrift (eds), *Thinking Space* (London: Routledge, 2000), p. 58.
138. Ibid., p. 58.
139. Robert Louis Stevenson, 'A Gossip on Romance', *Memories and Portraits* (London: Chatto and Windus, 1917), p. 153.
140. Warner, *The Man Who Walks*, p. 1.
141. Ibid., pp. 25–6.
142. Ibid., pp. 2–3.
143. Christie March, *Rewriting Scotland: Welsh, McLean, Warner, Banks, Galloway, and Kennedy* (Manchester: Manchester University Press, 2002), p. 73.
144. Alan Warner, 'Introduction', *Hebridean Light: Photographs by Gus Wylie with an introduction by Alan Warner* (Edinburgh: Birlinn, 2003), p. 6.
145. Ibid., p. 6.
146. Ibid., pp. 6–7.
147. Ibid., p. 7.
148. March, *Rewriting Scotland*, p. 75.
149. George Mackay Brown, Letter to Willa Muir (6 May 1965), Willa Muir Papers, National Library of Scotland. Acc.10557/4.
150. John Burnside, 'A Science of Belonging: Poetry as Ecology', in Robert Crawford (ed.), *Contemporary Poetry and Contemporary Science* (Oxford: Oxford University Press, 2006), p. 92.
151. Jamie, *Findings*, p. 63.
152. Ibid., p. 126.
153. Kathleen Jamie, 'Into The Dark: A Winter Solstice', *London Review of Books*, vol. 25, no. 24, 18 December 2003.
154. Warner, *The Man Who Walks*, p. 67.
155. Quoted in Lilias Fraser, 'Kathleen Jamie Interviewed by Lilias Fraser', p. 18.
156. Burnside, *The Asylum Dance*, p. 36.
157. Simon Schama, *Landscape and Memory* (London: Fontana Press, 1996), p. 14.
158. John Burnside, 'Steinar undir Steinahlithum', *Contemporary Poetry and Contemporary Science*, pp. 107–9.
159. Burnside, *The Good Neighbour*, pp. 74–5.
160. Burnside, *The Light Trap*, p. 50.
161. Edwin Muir, 'The Difficult Land', *Collected Poems* (London: Faber, 1984), pp. 237–8.
162. Jamie, *Findings*, p. 14.
163. Ibid., p. 24.
164. Ibid., p. 3.
165. See Burnside, *Feast Days* (London: Secker and Warburg, 1992), p. 29.
166. Burnside, *The Light Trap*, pp. 23–5.
167. Ibid., p. 25.
168. Burnside, *The Light Trap*, p. 39.
169. Burnside, interviewed by Louisa Gairn, 31 March 2004.
170. Burnside, *Living Nowhere*, pp. 372–3.

Index

Adorno, Theodor, 118, 138, 166
adventure, 2, 11n, 23, 30, 38–41, 57, 60–8, 84, 181; *see also* explorers and exploration
agriculture *see* farming
anarchism, 86, 167
animals
    birds, 28, 51, 58, 67, 95–6, 117–18, 127, 133, 136, 139, 142–3, 160, 162–3, 187
    deer, 129–32, 153n, 162, 164, 173, 176–7
    domesticated, 28–9, 78, 79, 102, 110, 111, 122–3, 175
    horses, 78, 110–11, 117, 121–3, 137–8, 146
    human dependence on, 68, 122–3
    human encounters with, 127, 164, 176
    in human psychology, 15, 60, 121–3, 175
    insects, 121, 126, 186
    wild, 28, 43n, 94–5, 123–4, 125, 127, 128, 130–3, 160, 175, 177
    see also farming; hunting; naturalists and nature observation
animism, 97–104, 135, 175, 178
archaeology, 184–5
Arctic, 23, 184
Arnold, Matthew, 35, 183
    'On the Study of Celtic Literature', 35, 183
atomic age, 110–13, 121, 125
attention, 4, 6, 10, 54–5, 60, 68, 93–5, 124–8, 132–3, 158, 160–3, 170–1, 187

Bachelard, Gaston, 15, 51, 118, 124, 127, 144, 159, 170, 173, 176–7
    La Flamme d'une Chandelle, 176–7
    The Poetics of Space, 15, 51, 118, 124, 144, 170, 173
Bain, Alexander, 11n, 14, 15, 23
    The Senses and the Intellect, 14, 15, 23
Bakhtin, Mikhail, 70, 125, 145–6
    Forms of Time and of the Chronotope in the Novel, 70
    Rabelais and His World, 125, 145–6
ballads, 117
Bate, Jonathan, 4, 7, 8, 10, 48–9, 92, 104, 111, 114, 130, 134, 142, 162, 165
    The Song of the Earth, 4, 8, 48–9, 92, 104, 111, 114, 130, 134, 142, 162, 165
Baudelaire, Charles, 9, 56–7, 59, 60–1, 170
Baudrillard, Jean, 7
Beat poetry, 137, 143
Benjamin, Walter, 56–62, 69–71, 180–1
    The Arcades Project, 59, 60, 70
    Charles Baudelaire: A Lyric Poet in an Era of High Capitalism, 56, 59
    'The Storyteller', 62, 71
    'Theses on the Philosophy of History', 180–1
biodiversity, 1, 148
    as national metaphor, 99
bioregionalism, 49, 60, 92, 97–104; *see also* regionalism
Black, Adam, 25
Blackie, John Stuart, 9, 29–34, 35
    The Scottish Highlanders and the Land Laws, 30–1, 35
    Scottish Song: Its Wealth, Wisdom, and Social Significance, 29
Blake, William, 118
body, 6, 14, 15, 17, 26, 30, 35–6, 37–8, 41, 47, 61, 67, 101, 102, 123, 125, 127, 146, 173, 177, 179, 180, 181, 186; *see also* self and other
boglands, 63, 67, 98–100, 184–5
botany, 14, 24, 25–6, 34, 46, 56, 80, 87, 88, 95, 184; *see also* naturalists and nature observation
Broch, Hermann, 115
brochs, 125, 147
Brown, George Douglas, 8
    The House with the Green Shutters, 8

Brown, George Mackay *see* Mackay Brown, George
Bryce, James, 26–7, 31, 88; *see also* mountains and mountaineering; National Parks
Buddhism *see* Zen philosophy
Burns, Robert, 4, 33, 68
Burnside, John, 1, 2, 5, 8, 10, 114, 148, 156–87
  The Asylum Dance, 159, 163, 166, 179, 184
  Burning Elvis, 165
  Common Knowledge, 166, 169, 170
  Feast Days, 175, 186
  The Good Neighbour, 163–4, 169, 185
  The Hoop, 160, 169
  The Light Trap, 161–4, 171, 175, 176, 185, 186–7
  Living Nowhere, 163–5, 168, 172, 174, 176, 186–7
  The Locust Room, 159–64, 172, 175
  The Myth of the Twin, 176
  'A Science of Belonging', 1, 184–5
  'Steinar undir Steinahlithum', 184–5
  Wild Reckoning, 10, 157
Byron, George Gordon, 21

Carse, James, 185
Carson, Rachel, 7
  Silent Spring, 7
Cartesian thought, 6, 16–17, 30, 52–3, 62–5, 67–8, 127, 129
cartography *see* geography
Celtic Twilight, 78, 147, 183; *see also* Arnold, Matthew; Gaelic poetry and culture
Christianity, 18, 23, 28, 29, 36, 103, 147
childhood and children's relationship with nature, 20, 65, 86, 116–18, 124–5, 141–2
city *see* urban experience
Clearances *see* Highland Clearances
Clough, Arthur Hugh, 26, 33
  The Bothie of Toper-na-fuosich, 26, 33
Coleridge, Samuel Taylor, 17–18, 161
  Biographia Literaria, 17
community, 2, 6, 19, 32–3, 51, 57, 65, 69–70, 77–8, 84, 88, 97, 100, 114, 117–21, 123, 139, 143–8, 164, 167, 172, 181–2; *see also* home; nationalism and national identity
computers, 112–13
conservation, 9, 34, 136–7; *see also* National Parks
consumerism, 10, 110, 113, 156, 182, 183; *see also* mass media; mass production
craft, 51–2, 53, 62, 110–11, 144, 157, 159, 161, 185
  and poetry, 51, 53, 144, 157, 159, 161
  versus mass production, 110–11, 113

Crawford, Robert, 13n, 79, 92, 166, 168
Creeley, Robert, 143
Crichton Smith, Iain, 5, 10, 128, 131–2, 138, 143, 147, 167, 176, 182, 183
  'Deer on the High Hills', 131–2
  'Real People in a Real Place', 143, 183
crofting, 9, 23, 28–34, 69, 94, 98, 100, 102–3, 145–7; *see also* farming; Gaelic poetry and culture; Highland Clearances; land rights and access

Darling, Frank Fraser, 94, 130–1, 177
  A Herd of Red Deer, 130–1
  West Highland Survey, 94
Darwin, Charles, 4, 5, 11n, 14, 18–19, 80, 87, 99
  On the Origin of Species, 11n, 14, 99
Descartes, Rene *see* Cartesian thought
desert, 7, 118
Diffusionism, 104, 122, 151n; *see also* farming and civilisation
doppelgänger, 64, 174–5; *see also* self and other
Dunn, Douglas, 3, 112, 138
duthchas, 30–3
dwelling, theories of, 1, 9, 10, 48–9, 51–3, 57–9, 60–8, 70, 92, 102–3, 114, 119–21, 130, 138, 148, 157, 165–7, 169–73, 175, 177, 179, 180, 185; *see also* home

Earth
  holistic views of, 7, 12n, 80–3, 89–91, 113, 118, 126, 137–8
  as mother or personified, 83, 91, 98–101, 177–8
ecocriticism and ecopoetics, 1–10, 48, 62, 118, 130, 134, 160, 162
ecofeminism, 177; *see also* female identity
ecological science, Scottish approaches to, 2, 6, 7
ecology, definitions of, 1–5, 11n, 118
Eden, 111, 114, 132, 183; *see also* pastoral
Edinburgh, 21, 25, 29, 33, 52, 57–8, 86, 87, 115
education, 10, 60, 86, 94–5, 130
Eliot, T. S., 64, 111, 116, 118, 119, 120
  The Waste Land, 118, 119, 120
Emerson, Ralph Waldo, 18, 20, 119
  Nature, 18, 20
environmental history, 2, 8, 184; *see also* natural history
environmentalism, 2, 5–7, 9–10, 27, 34, 50, 67–8, 84, 113, 133, 136–7, 142, 157
evolution, theory of, 5, 16, 18, 68, 78, 87; *see also* Darwin, Charles
exile, 9, 46–50, 63–5, 112–16, 165–8, 173
Existentialism, 60, 134, 171; *see also* Sartre, Jean-Paul

explorers and exploration, 23–4, 27, 37, 62, 65, 84, 137; *see also* geography; surveys

farming, 16, 24, 28–9l, 40, 46, 69, 78–9, 86, 97–103, 110–12, 115, 120, 122–3, 139, 143, 146, 184–5
  and civilisation, 16–17, 78–80, 87–8, 104, 122, 151n
  ritual and superstition, 122, 146–7, 184
  see also animals; crofting
female identity, 99–101, 157, 168, 177–8; *see also* Earth; ecofeminism
Finlay, Ian Hamilton, 1, 3, 5, 10, 103, 112, 138, 142–5, 147–8
  'Unconnected Sentences on Gardening', 1, 143
Flahault, Charles, 87
flâneur, 24, 41, 47, 56–61, 65, 70, 170
  as 'son of the wilderness', 59–60
  see also urban experience; walking
folk culture, 2, 78, 87–8, 101–4, 115–17, 125, 146–7, 183
forests *see* woodlands
Foucault, Michel, 173
  The Order of Things, 173
Free Church of Scotland, 18, 29
freedom, 27, 24, 26, 27, 32, 49, 50, 55, 66, 69, 147, 163, 165, 178; *see also* stravaiging

Gaelic poetry and culture, 2, 4–5, 9, 24–5, 28–34, 35, 55, 93, 95–6, 99, 128–33, 134–5, 140–1, 183
  natural world, 5, 32, 128–9
  political poetry, 32–3
  praise poems, 55, 128–9
  see also crofting; Highlands and Islands; MacIntyre, Duncan Ban; Maclean, Sorley
gardens, 1, 25, 71, 119, 139, 141, 142–4, 169, 177, 179, 186–7
Geddes, Patrick, 2, 6, 8, 9, 10, 69, 71, 78, 80–1, 84–91, 92, 95, 97, 104, 141
  The Evergreen: A Northern Seasonal, 78, 86
  The Outlook Tower, 86–8
  'Suggested Plan for a National Institute of Geography', 88–91
  'The Valley Plan of Civilisation', 69, 86–8, 141
geography, 6, 23, 69, 71, 80–1, 84–92, 95, 137, 104, 141
  maps and map-making, 23, 71, 84–5, 91, 104
  nature study, 6, 71, 85–6
  see also education; Geddes, Patrick; surveys and surveying
geology, 7, 23, 24, 27, 81, 88, 94, 103, 126
geopoetics, 1–2, 8, 13n, 50, 134; *see also* White, Kenneth

George, Henry, 29–30, 32–3, 38
Gibbon, Lewis Grassic, 2, 9, 19, 71, 78, 84, 88, 92, 93, 97–8, 100–4, 115, 121, 122, 145, 147, 184, 185
  'Clay', 100
  Hanno, or The Future of Exploration, 84
  'The Land', 98, 104
  Nine Against the Unknown, 84
  A Scots Quair, 19, 93, 97, 100–4, 121, 145, 185: *Cloud Howe*, 93, 103; *Grey Granite*, 93, 103; *Sunset Song*, 19, 93, 97, 100–4, 121, 145, 185
  Scottish Scene, 92–3, 94–6, 98, 104
  'Smeddum', 100
  Spartacus, 103
Gifford, Terry, 112, 142
Glasgow, 33, 115–16, 133–6, 138–42
Gray, Alasdair, 138
Green Movement *see* environmentalism
Grieve, C. M. *see* MacDiarmid, Hugh
Gunn, Neil, 5, 9, 78, 88, 94, 100, 123–8, 131, 134–5, 141, 142, 144, 146, 147, 148, 184
  Butcher's Broom, 100
  Highland Pack, 94, 124, 127
  Highland River, 123–5, 141
  Landscape and Light, 127–8
  The Silver Darlings, 123
gypsies and travellers, 86, 117, 167–8, 183; *see also* walking

Haeckel, Ernst, 5, 80, 86
Hardy, Thomas, 48, 49, 80, 141
Hazlitt, William, 49
  'On Going a Journey', 49
Hebrides, 92, 93, 97, 182, 183; *see also* Highlands and Islands
health, 22–3, 27, 34–41, 44n, 49, 58, 65, 69, 93, 118
Heaney, Seamus, 8, 138
  'The Sense of Place', 8, 138
Heidegger, Martin, 48–9, 52–3, 64, 70, 110–11, 114, 117, 119, 120–2, 158–9, 160, 165–6, 184, 185
  'Building, Dwelling, Thinking', 52, 166
  The Question Concerning Technology, 117, 122
Highland Clearances, 22, 28–9, 32, 100, 116; *see also* land rights and access
Highlands and Islands, 2, 4, 19, 20–34, 35, 38, 42n, 47, 55, 63, 93–4, 97, 100–1, 116, 123–7, 128–33, 141, 142, 147, 167, 181–4
  cultural identity, 34–5, 97, 104, 143, 146, 182–3
  Romanticism, 4, 23, 29, 38, 181, 183
  see also Highland Clearances; Gaelic poetry and culture; Orkney Islands; Shetland Isles

Highland Land League, 31; *see also* crofting; Highland Clearances; land rights and access
Hind, Archie, 3, 138–42
  The Dear Green Place, 138–42
Hogg, James, 4, 64, 174
  Memoirs and Confessions of a Justified Sinner, 4, 64, 174
Hölderlin, Friedrich, 160
home
  building, 51, 119
  in ecotheory, 7, 48–9, 51, 114, 135, 166–7
  homelands, 33, 164–9
  homely and unhomely, 48, 64, 83, 114, 119
  and modernity, 57, 113–14, 118–21, 136, 138, 166
  phenomenology of, 46–7, 51, 177
  settlements and pioneers, 58–9, 66–7, 97, 185
  see also community; dwelling; exile; nationalism and national identity
Home Rule for Scotland, 28–9; *see also* nationalism and national identity
Hugo, Victor, 59
hunting, 23–5, 30–1, 39, 43n, 53, 86, 88, 125, 130–1, 175
  deer stalking, 23–5, 28, 31
  see also animals; land rights and access
Hutton, James, 7
Huxley, Aldous, 129
Huxley, Thomas, 80, 85

imagism, 128, 133
imperialism, 23, 25, 35–6, 40, 62–3, 84, 104; *see also* adventure; Cartesian thought
Industrial Revolution, 116
industrialisation *see* technology
Ingold, Tim, 6, 10, 52–3, 71, 84–5, 91
  The Perception of the Environment, 6, 10, 52–3, 71, 84–5, 91
interdisciplinarity, 1, 8, 10, 82, 86, 95
islands, 93–4, 99, 104, 113, 115–16, 138, 142–3, 145–7, 182; *see also* Highlands and Islands

Jamie, Kathleen, 2, 3, 5, 10, 145, 148, 156–87
  Among Muslims, 161–2, 168–9
  Findings, 2, 158, 160, 183, 185–6
  Jizzen, 158, 177
  The Queen of Sheba, 160, 163, 168–9, 171–2, 177–8
  The Tree House, 162, 177, 184
  The Way We Live, 161–2, 168–9
Jamieson, John, 77, 78, 133
  An Etymological Dictionary of the Scottish Language, 77, 78, 133

journalism and newspapers *see* mass media
Joyce, James, 78, 81, 87, 127, 133
Jung, Carl Gustav, 19, 78, 88, 120, 123

Kafka, Franz, 115, 121, 150n
  'Metamorphosis', 121
kailyard, 3, 8, 78, 79, 97, 98, 141
Kant, Emmanuel, 160
Kingsley, Charles, 36
kite-flying, 171, 187
Kropotkin, Pytor, 86

land rights and access, 9, 24–34, 38, 178; *see also* mountains and mountaineering
language, 7, 10, 68, 77–83, 93, 98, 101–2, 114–15, 127–30, 133, 135, 144–5, 161–3
  English, 93, 102, 115
  Gaelic, 93, 129, 133
  Scots, 68, 77–9, 82–3, 102, 114–15, 169
Lawrence, D. H., 129
Le Play, Frederic, 87
Leavis, F. R., and Denys Thomson, 197
  Culture and Environment, 197
Leopold, Aldo, 84
liminality, 59, 130, 164, 170, 174–9
Livingstone, David, 23, 34, 37
Lovelock, James, 7
  Gaia: A New Look at Life on Earth, 7

MacDiarmid, Hugh, 3, 5, 8, 9, 10, 60, 71–104, 117, 119, 122, 129–33, 134, 135, 137, 138, 145, 148, 158, 162, 177, 178
  'Au Clair de la Lune', 80–1
  'The Bonnie Broukit Bairn', 80, 83
  'Country Life', 79
  'The Dead Liebknecht', 79
  'Direadh', 95–6, 98–9, 130
  A Drunk Man Looks at the Thistle, 79
  'The Eemis Stane', 80–1
  'Empty Vessel', 83
  'Farmer's Death', 79
  'Further Talk with Donnchadh Ban Mac an t'Saoir', 129, 131
  'In Talk with Donnchadh Ban Mac an t'Saoir', 129–31
  'The Innumerable Christ', 103
  The Islands of Scotland, 93–4, 99, 104
  Lucky Poet, 79–80, 94–6
  'The Nature of a Bird's World', 133
  'On a Raised Beach', 5, 60, 81, 94, 103, 132–4
  Penny Wheep, 79–83
  'The Praise of Ben Dorain', 131
  Sangschaw, 77, 79–83
  'Science and Poetry', 82
  'Scotland' (from *Lucky Poet*), 94
  'Scotland' (from *Scottish Scene*), 92
  Scottish Scene, 92–6, 104

MacDiarmid, Hugh (*cont.*)
  'Tam o' the Wilds', 94–5, 98
  'Tarras', 98–100
  'The Watergaw', 77
machines *see* technology
MacIntyre, Duncan Ban (Donnchadh Ban Mac an t'Saoir), 4, 5, 28, 32, 128–32, 162, 176
  'The Praise of Ben Dorain', 128–31
Mackay Brown, George, 2, 3, 5, 9, 10, 103, 112–13, 116–17, 134, 138–9, 142–8
  'Brodgar Poems', 113
  'The Broken Heraldry', 116
  The Calendar of Love, 139
  Greenvoe, 145–7
  'Hill Runes', 144
  An Orkney Tapestry, 112–13, 117, 144
Mackenzie, Henry, 14
  The Man of Feeling, 14
Maclean, Sorley (Somhairle MacGill-Eain), 2, 4–5, 32, 99–100, 128–9, 130–5, 153n
  'The Cuillin', 99
  'Hallaig', 135, 153n
  'Màiri Mhór nan Oran', 100, 135
  'On Realism in Gaelic Poetry', 5, 128, 131
  'Poetry of the Clearances', 32
Macpherson, James, 4, 140, 154n
Madox Ford, Ford, 95
Marx, Leo, 139
  The Machine in the Garden, 139
masculinity, 23
mass media, 96, 98, 117, 147, 157
mass production, 110–11, 117
memory, 6, 19, 47–9, 70–1, 78, 83, 85, 88, 102–3, 115, 119–20, 135–6, 184, 186
Merleau-Ponty, Maurice, 14, 15
Modern Scot, The, 79
Modernism, 58–9, 78–9, 82, 87, 88, 92, 104, 118–19
Morgan, Edwin, 1, 3, 84, 111–13, 116, 136–8, 140, 143, 146, 148
  'The Beatnik in the Kailyard', 111
  'The Computer's First Christmas Card', 113
  'Edwin Muir', 112
  'Glasgow Sonnets' (from *From Glasgow to Saturn*), 136–7, 140
  'A Glimpse of Petavius', 136, 137
  The Horseman's Word, 146
  'Memories of Earth' (from *The New Divan*), 137–8
  Nothing Not Giving Messages, 112
  'Roof of Fireflies', 1, 148
  'The Ruin', 138
Morris, William, 172
mountains and mountaineering, 4, 14–16, 19–25, 27–41, 56, 63, 66–7, 84, 88, 95, 99, 100, 124–8, 162
  The Alpine Club, 21–3, 26–7, 31, 37
  The Cairngorm Club, 24, 27
  The Scottish Mountaineering Club, 16, 19–25, 27–8, 36
Muir, Edwin, 9, 10, 96–7, 103, 104, 110–23, 133–4, 137, 139, 142, 143, 146, 147, 148, 150n, 151n, 185
  An Autobiography, 116–18, 120, 122, 142
  'The Combat', 121–2
  'Complaint of the Dying Peasantry', 117
  'The Difficult Land', 120, 185
  The Estate of Poetry, 110
  'The Good Town', 119
  'The Horses', 111–12, 121–3, 137
  'The Myth', 116
  Poor Tom, 113, 139
  'The Refugees', 118–19
  'Scotland, 1941', 118, 120
  Scott and Scotland, 113–14, 115
  Scottish Journey, 96–7, 104, 113
  'The Sufficient Place', 120–1
  We Moderns (Edward Moore), 120
Muir, John, 4, 9, 27, 46–8, 54, 64, 67–8, 71, 124, 125
  'Our National Parks', 67
  The Story of My Boyhood and Youth, 47
  'Thoughts on the Birthday of Robert Burns', 4
  A Thousand Mile Walk to the Gulf, 46–7, 67–8
  The Yosemite, 4
Muir, Willa, 114–18
  Belonging, 114–16
  Living with Ballads, 117
Mumford, Lewis, 86
Murray, Charles, 80
mystery, 1, 160–4, 186

National Parks, 4, 46, 88; *see also* Bryce, James; Muir, John
nationalism and national identity, 79, 104, 134, 156, 167
natural history, 1, 2, 5, 8, 14, 16, 95, 141, 159, 183–4, 186
naturalists and nature observation, 7, 24, 86, 94–5, 128, 160, 176
  influence on literature, 7, 86, 94–5
  see also attention
nature, exploitation of, 6, 17, 51–2, 62–3, 65, 67, 102, 174; *see also* animals; Cartesian thought; Earth; farming
nature poetry, 5, 16–18, 156–7
New Age, The, 79, 120
Nietzsche, Friedrich, 120, 171
non-place, 169–70
nuclear war *see* atomic age

officialdom, defiance of, 26, 31, 125, 142–3, 146, 180; *see also* land rights and access

Orage, A. R., 120
orientalism, 23
Orkney Islands, 92, 97, 111–13, 115–17, 120, 142–6, 185–6; *see also* Highlands and Islands
Orpheus, 162–3
Ossian *see* Macpherson, James
'Other' *see* self and other

pastoral, 19, 26, 112, 116–17, 129, 139–47, 154n
pathetic fallacy, 101, 128, 132
Paz, Octavio, 173–4
perception, 6, 10, 14–15, 17–18, 20, 23, 93–4, 127–8, 130, 159–61, 184
phenomenology, 6, 14–15, 51, 53, 114, 118, 123–8, 144, 159, 161, 170, 186
photography, 23, 159–60
place, sense of, 8, 46–50, 52, 57, 70–1, 83, 87, 93, 96, 114–17, 135–6, 141, 143
poetry, theories of, 1, 15–20, 40, 80–2, 111–12, 128–37, 144, 148, 156–9, 161, 166, 174, 176; *see also* ecocriticism and ecopoetics; phenomenology; science and poetry
pollution, 7, 36, 140–2, 157, 172, 182
Poor. Old. Tired. Horse., 112, 143
postcolonialism, 114, 147, 174

rambling, 24–5; *see also* land rights and access; walking
Reclus, Elisée, 86, 88–91
refugees *see* exile
regionalism, 8, 49, 78, 87–104, 112, 139, 145; *see also* bioregionalism
reverie, 176–7
Rights of Way, 24, 26; *see also* land rights and access
rivers, 51–2, 69, 123–5, 127, 139–42
roads and paths, 25–3, 51–3, 61, 64, 69–70, 102, 117, 120–1, 135, 164
rock climbing *see* mountains and mountaineering
Romanticism, 4–5, 14–15, 17–20, 23, 29, 37–8, 41, 79, 101, 115–16, 118, 124, 126, 128–9, 133
  Gaelic critiques of, 5, 128–9
rural life
  eccentricity, 117, 134, 179–81, 183
  provincialism, 78–9, 92, 104
  psychology of, 77–8, 110–11, 122
  stereotypes, 35, 98, 99, 183
  see also farming; Highlands and Islands; kailyard; pastoral; urban-rural relationship
rural-urban migration, 33–4, 97–8; *see also* farming; urban-rural relationship
Ruskin, John, 37

Said, Edward, 120, 165–6
sanatoria, 38–9
Sartre, Jean-Paul, 60
Schama, Simon, 23, 184
  Landscape and Memory, 23, 184
science
  critiques of, 5–6, 60, 62, 85–6, 113, 125–6
  and poetry, 82, 95, 111–12, 126, 131, 134, 137–8, 157, 161, 163, 184–5
science fiction, 111, 137–8
Scott, Walter, 4, 14, 38, 113–14
  'The Lay of the Last Minstrel', 4
  Waverley, 4, 14, 38
Scottish Renaissance movement, 78–9, 95
self and other, 5–6, 9, 14, 54, 67, 115, 117, 121–2, 126–7, 132, 160–1, 163–5, 170, 173–6, 178, 180–1
Shepard, Paul, 162
Shepherd, Nan, 1, 3, 9, 10, 78, 100–1, 124–6, 130, 135, 136, 148
  The Living Mountain, 1, 10, 124–7, 130
  The Weatherhouse, 101
Shetland Isles, 79, 92, 93–4, 97, 114–15, 135; *see also* Highlands and Islands
Simmel, Georg, 181
Smiles, Samuel, 33–4, 36–7
Smith, Adam, 33–4
Snyder, Gary, 157
socialism, 25, 27, 30, 33, 51
Solnit, Rebecca, 25, 69
  Wanderlust, 25, 69
Stephen, Sir Leslie, 21, 22, 26, 37–8, 39
  'In Praise of Walking', 26, 37–8
  The Playground of Europe, 21, 22
Stevenson, Robert, 51–2
Stevenson, Robert Louis, 2–3, 9, 10, 15–16, 31, 37–41, 47–71, 84, 121, 167, 169, 174, 181
  Across the Plains, 15, 55
  The Amateur Emigrant, 55, 58
  'An Apology for Idlers', 56, 60
  'Edinburgh: Picturesque Notes', 57–8
  The Ebb Tide, 48
  'The Foreigner at Home', 46, 49–50
  'Forest Notes', 37
  'A Gossip on Romance', 38, 61–2
  'Health and Mountains', 38–40
  'Henry David Thoreau', 50, 53, 60, 70–1
  In the South Seas, 60
  Kidnapped, 16, 38, 61, 181
  The Master of Ballantrae, 49, 62–5, 71
  'My Brain Swims Empty and Light', 56–7
  'On the Enjoyment of Unpleasant Places', 48
  Records of a Family of Engineers, 51–2, 58
  'Roads', 52–3, 61, 69
  The Silverado Squatters, 39, 47–8, 53–4, 59, 65–6, 67

Stevenson, Robert Louis (*cont.*)
  'Some Aspects of Robert Burns', 68
  Strange Case of Dr Jekyll and Mr Hyde, 58
  Travels with a Donkey in the Cevennes, 49, 55
  'Walking Tours', 69
  'Walt Whitman', 50, 54–9, 67–70
  'Will o' the Mill', 61–2, 69
stories and storytelling, 47, 53, 62–3, 71, 103, 120, 136, 144, 146, 176
stravaiging, 24, 26, 41, 46, 50, 71; *see also* land rights and access; walking
sublime, the, 4, 14–15, 19, 115, 126
suburbia, 169–70
surveys and surveying, 23, 87–94, 141; *see also* geography

techne, 53, 110, 159, 185; *see also* craft
technology, 48, 51–3, 62, 78, 102–3, 110–17, 121, 138, 146–8, 185–6; *see also* mass production
'thing-in-itself', 6, 8, 131–3, 134, 136, 160, 162, 163
Thomson, James, 48, 59, 64
  The City of Dreadful Night, 64
Thoreau, Henry David, 9, 50–4, 60, 70–1, 97, 115
  On the Duty of Civil Disobedience, 50
  Walden, 50–1, 71
tourism, 24, 55, 168
travel, 37, 46–71, 167–9; *see also* exile; explorers and exploration; walking
Turner, Victor, 174
Twain, Mark, 39
  Roughing It, 39

Upward, Allen, 133
urban experience, 3, 24, 33, 34, 35–6, 48, 56–61, 64, 69, 71, 78–80, 87, 97–8, 103, 112, 122, 136–7, 139–42, 154n, 167, 170, 182–3
urban-rural relationship, 3, 24, 34, 56–61, 79–80, 87–8, 97–8, 112, 122, 138–42, 170, 182–3
utopia, 51, 123, 172

Veitch, John, 9, 15–22, 25, 29, 34–5, 40, 86

The Feeling for Nature in Scottish Poetry, 15–20, 86
History and Poetry of the Scottish Borders, 19, 40

walking, 23–6, 31–2, 34, 46, 49, 56–60, 68–71, 100, 127, 141, 167, 180
war, 33, 62, 65, 84, 86, 102, 103, 110, 111–12, 113, 114–16, 118–19, 121, 124, 145
Warner, Alan, 3, 10, 148, 156, 167–8, 174, 178–83
  The Man Who Walks, 167–8, 179–82
  These Demented Lands, 178–9
wayfinding, 52, 71; *see also* roads and paths; walking
White, Kenneth, 1–2, 5, 8, 10, 50, 71, 80, 112, 128–9, 133–6, 147, 148
  The Bird Path, 134–6
  'Cape Breton Uplight', 135
  On Scottish Ground, 1–2, 80, 112, 128–9, 135–6, 147
  'Ovid's Report', 134–5
  'The Valley of Birches', 135
  The Wanderer and His Charts, 50, 71, 134, 136
  see also geopoetics
Whitman, Walt, 9, 50, 54–9, 67–70, 121
  Leaves of Grass, 54–5, 57–9, 67, 69–70
  'Robert Burns as Poet and Person', 68
wilderness, 2, 4, 15, 48–9, 56–9, 63–7, 125, 139, 183
  North American, 15, 48–9, 63–7, 125, 139
  Scottish, 2, 4, 183
Williams, Raymond, 97–8, 139
  The Country and the City, 97–8, 139
woodlands, 2, 4, 15, 37, 39, 50–1, 54, 58, 59, 64, 65, 67, 102, 115, 125, 135–6, 164, 172, 173, 175, 176, 177, 178, 180
Wordsworth, Dorothy, 126
Wordsworth, William, 4, 7, 14, 17, 20, 37, 40, 104, 119, 128, 161
  'Lines written a few miles above Tintern Abbey', 17
  'The Ruined Cottage', 119

Zen philosophy, 124, 127–9, 131, 135, 186

EU representative:
Easy Access System Europe
Mustamäe tee 50, 10621 Tallinn, Estonia
Gpsr.requests@easproject.com

www.ingramcontent.com/pod-product-compliance
Lightning Source LLC
Chambersburg PA
CBHW071843230426
43671CB00012B/2058